MW00325619

THE MEDAL MAKER

Altamira-Verlag GmbH /
Altamira Creation AG

THE MEDAL MAKER

A BIOGRAPHY OF

VICTOR KOVALENKO

Roger Vaughan

by Roger Vaughan

David —
You will love this man's
energy and philosophy —

Roger.
8/17/18

FOREWORD

Victor Kovalenko is the most successful Olympic sailing coach the world has ever seen. Why is this so? The answer is complex. Much of it is contained within this book.

Victor comes from the Russian school of thinking. He talks about heart, about passion. He is a philosopher, a dreamer. Sailing is Mother Nature's sport at its best, total emersion within the elements of wind and water. Victor is at home in this world.

He had humble beginnings. As a young Ukrainian man working at a Soviet missile base, he had to fight for every step forward during those early days in Russia.

In 2013, he was inducted into the Sport Australia Hall of Fame, a body which represents every sport in Australia including all Olympic disciplines. One can go no higher in sport. His award speech in front of 1000 people, the who's who of Australian sport, was profound. He spoke of the pride and hope he has in young people, the pride he has in Olympic sport: in the Olympic dream of higher, further, faster. He spoke of the passion he has for Australia, his adopted country, and his love for the freedom he now enjoys in an open society. His speech, full of emotion and pride, was one of the most powerful speeches ever heard. Victor was now at home.

After winning three gold and two silver medals at the London Olympic Games, the Australian Olympic Sailing Team became the #1 sailing nation in the world. The Sailing Team also became the #1 ranked sport in the entire Australian Olympic Team. Victor and Peter Conde, head of High Performance Sailing, addressed the sports world at the final press conference. Afterwards, Victor said to Peter, "We have done well today." "Why," Peter asked. "Because," Victor said, "we have spoken a lot but have told them nothing!"

It has been difficult for Victor to have revealed his story in this book, because for Victor, prevailing in Olympic sport is the ultimate goal. To keep his 'system' secret is part of this difficult, all-encompassing journey. One Olympiad moves into the next and possibly the next. The bar is always getting higher. The level of competition advances significantly at each consecutive Olympics. That is the nature of elite international sport.

I first met Victor when I was a mentor to the entire Australian Olympic Team for the 2000 Sydney Olympics. I asked Victor about his philosophy.

He said it is simple. Year one is to excite the imagination of his athletes, inspire them to explore the possibilities of 'what if'; to unshackle their minds, their imaginations; to contemplate the potential of pure boat speed; to be at one with the wind and the water. Year two is to get them race-hardened in international fleet and match racing. "To do that," he said, "we must compete in the World championships, the European championships, the US National championships, and all the top world class regattas. Year three is to dominate the world."

How good is that? When young people hear that, they ask, how can I be involved? How exciting to have this man ready to share his knowledge, his wisdom, his passion, with our athletes.

Victor has brought a bright light to the sport of sailing in Australia, and indeed, around the world. He is the greatest Olympic sailing coach the world has ever seen. To understand more, read on.

John Bertrand AO
Winner of the America's Cup.
Legend of the Sport Australia Hall of Fame.

INTRODUCTION

Born in Ukraine in 1950, Victor Kovalenko was raised under the Communist system. He discovered a love of sailing early, with home-built models that often sank. He succeeded as a competitive sailor, earning the rewards bestowed upon outstanding athletes by the Soviet system.

His insistence on a college degree, politics (the boycott of the 1984 Games), and an injury combined to dash Victor's own Olympic dreams, and reinforce his early interest in coaching. When the USSR collapsed in 1991, against all odds he coached 470 dinghy teams to the Ukraine's first ever gold and bronze medals in sailing (Atlanta, 1996).

Political jealously interfered. The post-Soviet Ukrainian System wasn't working for a man of Victor's evolved sensibilities and global curiosity. When Victor was invited to coach in Australia, he jumped at the chance. The decision meant leaving his family in Ukraine, and taking on an Australian team with only three years to prepare.

Those who thought it was mission impossible underestimated the strength of Victor's philosophical approach. At the Sydney Olympics in 2000, both his men's and women's 470 teams won gold medals. His family joined him in Australia. That was when Victor Kovalenko was dubbed, "The Medal Maker." The moniker is well-deserved. To date, in eight Olympic Games, Victor's teams have amassed ten medals, six of them gold.

For Kippy

CONTENTS

AUTHOR'S THANK YOU

Heartfelt thanks and deep appreciation go to Victor, for opening his life to me. Also many thanks to Victor's friends, acquaintances, and sailors who took the time and made the effort to talk to me about their experiences. They span the globe.

Thanks to Anna Maria Gregorini for conceiving this book.

Thanks to Daniel Forster for his support.

And thank you to Olga Hoffman for translating Russian to English.

CHAPTER 1

January, 2014

The plan was to meet Victor Kovalenko, head coach of the Australian Olympic sailing team and men's 470 coach, at the U.S. Sailing Center on busy Bayshore Drive in Coconut Grove, Florida. For sailors, the Sailing Center is a formidable place. Over the main entrance is written, "A U.S. Olympic Training Site." Walking through that portal onto a couple acres of grass crammed with a variety of sparkling Olympic class sailboats with all their gear strewn about is as intimidating as walking into a professional sports locker room, pre-game. The collected commitment of the hundred or so athletes in their prime working on their boats was palpable. In such a gathering, sailors of average competence tread softly.

Victor was expecting me. We had exchanged emails. But I had no idea how to recognize him, or to know where he would be in the crowd of Olympic hopefuls from twenty or more countries who had come for an International Sailing Federation (ISAF – the name was changed to World Sailing in 2016) World Cup event, one of five such regattas that help determine the world rankings in the eight Olympic classes. No worries. Everyone at the Center knew Victor. When you have coached your sailing teams to six gold medals in the course of the last seven Olympic Games, won an additional three Olympic medals as a coach, when two of your athletes have been named ISAF Rolex World Sailor of the Year, when your teams have won 17 world championships and hundreds of less important trophies, sailors know where you are.

I was sent toward a group of three 470 dinghies on trailers near the water. Two sailors were working on each boat. An older man was sitting nearby on an empty box of gear studying a small piece of paper. One of the sailors confirmed this was Victor. He got up, we shook hands, his eyes steady on mine. He is a spare man, rawboned, a fit 64 years old, standing at around 5'10", 160 pounds. In black jeans and a polo shirt, he wore a straw hat with a flat brim and chin strap, and a pair of dark Maui Jim glasses against the Florida sun. He spoke so softly, and with a Ukrainian accent, it took concentration to understand him, but I gathered there was no wind yet, and if I came back at 11:30 they would probably be going out to practice. I asked if I might go on his coach boat. He paused, looked at me hard, said he rarely took anyone on his coach boat. Come back at 11:30. He would think about it. With that, Victor turned away and gathered his six sailors for a quiet conversation.

At 11:30 I found Victor on his boat, a narrow, 18-foot RIB (rubber inflatable boat), organizing gear that included a couple large yellow buoys in need of air. I may as well not have been there. He kept working, bent to his tasks. The hat, the glasses, and the accent created an impenetrable shield. I sat on the dock and waited. After many minutes he said I could come with him, making sure I knew how unusual that was, naming a couple impressive VIPs whose requests he had rejected, then indicating I should come aboard. He put me to work holding the hose end into the fittings while he pumped air into the buoys and wrap-around rubber bumpers that give the boat its classification. He coiled lines, stowed gear, checked the fuel. I did what I could to help and stay out of his way at the same time. This was obviously a very set piece, a one-man operation. Meanwhile his teams were launching the three 470s. We cast off. He told the sailors he'd catch up after he got fuel.

At the fuel dock I asked if he wanted any food. He shook his head. I was already hungry, and did the best I could at the vending machines while he filled the tank. I offered him his choice of the "goodies." He shook his head, put on his foul weather gear. I did the same. Off we went.

The seat in this chase boat is a motorcycle-style saddle running fore and aft. A passenger sits behind Victor, who drives like James Bond being chased by hoodlums armed with machine guns. We caught up with his team, and soon he instigated "full motion" training, first with a jibing drill: all three boats jibing 30-40 times in a row, the sails barely filling before they were jibed again. After that he started a roll-tacking drill upwind, same frequency, the boats seeming to be constantly on the verge of capsizing. I was watching a ballet. The boats seemed extensions of the sailors' bodies. Victor used the throttle aggressively, jerking it back and forth in a neck-wrenching manner to zoom to within inches of the boats, studying the details of every jibe, every tack. Then he set a starting line and a windward mark, and conducted 15 or so short races. "No bumping!" he would admonish, as his teams battled in close combat for position. Next was an upwind speed drill. He drove in close, suggested that one sailor trim his jib half a centimeter.

By 3pm the junk from the vending machine was tasting pretty good. Victor ate an apple. An hour later the wind had retreated. Victor took the three boats under tow at planing speed. At the dock, I asked him about tomorrow. He said okay, 10 o'clock.

The next day, Victor was more relaxed, more talkative, even accepting my help with the marks and lines. I brought along some decent food to share, and Victor had two apples, one for me. By the third day, he was friendly, conversational, and seemed comfortable in my company. The previous evening I'd had dinner with Victor and his two star sailors: skipper Mat Belcher and his crew since 2012, Will Ryan. The two were on an unbelievable winning streak (18 straight regattas). Most of the conversation had been among Mat, Will, and myself. This evening Victor suggested we again meet for dinner, but it was just he who showed up.

We went to a little French place, where he suggested we share everything. He had a brief but serious discussion with the waiter about the wine. His English is passable, with only a few curve balls that have to be fielded on the run. Victor says "here" for "her"; "young kids" is "jan keets"; "cups" are "caps." Since the Russian language omits articles, they are mostly missing in Victor's English. But he wades into our language with admirable vigor, making up in dramatic presentation what he lacks in vocabulary and pronunciation, an approach that makes him an enjoyable conversationalist.

Because he frequently produces gems, one makes extra effort to listen when Victor speaks, a situation he understands and uses to advantage. Always learning, he will not hesitate to ask about a word he is unsure of. He enjoys picking up a new slang expression (I contributed "dodging a bullet"), and his sense of humor is keen, always lurking just below the surface. He is quick to share a laugh even at his own expense. He is not the least bit shy about relating his accomplishments, but the stories are more entertaining than self-serving. He shared inside facts about the last America's Cup; gave me his picks ("black belts") of the top four sailors in the world; spoke about his involvement in Australia's America's Cup bid (he would be coach and Mat would soon be announced as skipper); and carried on with good nature about the proper way to enjoy wine : "You need to roll it in your mouth for a moment," he said with professorial flourish, expansive gestures, and a smile, "then swallow it slowly. A good wine will give you two or three wonderful waves of flavor, a great wine will give you as many as five."

Lots of people pontificate about the virtues of wine, vineyards, years, and grapes, and most of them are quite boring. Victor had made an engaging routine out of it with a big smile and twinkling eyes. But his strong feeling about those waves of flavor was obviously heartfelt, a discovery he wanted to share. It wasn't until several months and several bottles of wine later I realized that every time I had drunk a glass of wine since my dinner with Victor, I had thought about those waves of flavor with a smile of my own. It was then I realized I had been coached.

I was leaving in the morning. In the parking lot, Victor shook my hand warmly and called me a great new friend. His goodbyes were prolonged, and somewhat formal.

The 470

Of the four 470s I had watched at practice with Victor, one stood out for the seemingly effortless way it was handled; for the perfection and efficiency of its maneuvers; for how regularly it won the starts and short course races; and for the impossible quickness of its spinnaker sets, jibes, and takedowns. This was sail number 470/AUS 11. The 470 is in gold letters designating the current (and fifth straight) world champion, Mathew Belcher – 470 gold medalist at the London Olympic Games in 2012; ISAF Rolex World Sailor of the Year in 2013 – and his crew, Will Ryan. In competitive sailing, it doesn't get any better than that list of credentials. Words like "domination" and "unbeatable" come to mind. And yet, there Mat was, on the water every day, practicing basic maneuvers with Will, his relatively new teammate. Mat's ambitious goal: winning a second gold medal at the 2016 Games in Brazil.

Sailing is one of those deceptively difficult sports. It's easy to learn to sail. Wind flows across sails, boats move. It requires the logical comprehension that boats cannot sail straight into the wind, that they must fill the sail on one side or the other of where the wind is coming from, and "tack" through the wind onto the other side when shallow water, obstructions, or other boats with the right of way interfere with their progress. Elementary aerodynamics explains why boats can sail a zig-zag course "upwind." Sailing off the wind is as easy as floating a walnut shell with a sail on a matchstick in a puddle. Many people learn the few basic maneuvers of sailing, pick up some boat handling, learn the essential right-of-way rules, then spend their leisure time plopping around the local pond having fun on the water. It's like flying kites: simple unless you want to become a master at it. Then a lifetime is not enough to explore all the intricacies of sailing.

Australian Olympic gold medalist Tom King (470, Sydney 2000), one of Victor's sailors, says that of all sports, sailing is the one that demands the broadest range of skills: "Physical, technical, and mental. It's a hugely challenging sport," King says, "a decision-making sport at a high level. At low level it's about basic sailing skills. At a moderate level it's about boat speed and racing skills. But when you get to the world championship and Olympic level, the top people are pretty evenly matched physically and technically and it becomes a decision-making game; chess on a moving playing field."

The 470 centerboard dinghy is one of the more difficult boats to sail to its full potential. Those who race the 470 are called "professors," because of the intellectual as well as the physical challenges it presents. At 4.7 meters (15.42 feet) overall, it has a fascinating hull shape starting with a rounded stem that flares stylishly into a maximum beam of 1.68 meters (5.50 feet) amidships, then flattens out into a classic planing underbody that carries to the stern. It has little freeboard, with a gentle taper in profile from bow to stern. The deck line is virtually straight bow to stern, and there's just a bit of rocker (curve) to the bottom along the same line. It displaces 269 pounds. The slender mast is 22.7 feet off the deck. Designed by André Cornu in 1963, the 470 looks like a knife in the water. It has been a men's Olympic class since 1976, and for women since 1988. Sailors in more than 60 countries race 470s.

To a novice coming upon a 470 sitting on a trailer ready for launching, what stands out is the mass of lines that lie coiled here and there like so much spaghetti. The biggest line is 3/8ths, but many of them are ¼ inch or less. The lines provide a clue to the intellectual aspect of the boat: there's virtually no part on the boat that can't be tweaked (adjusted) while sailing. There's also a single trapeze: a wire on each side attached high on the mast, ending at an adjustable ring into which the 470 crew clips his or her harness. This enables the crew to plant both feet on the rail and to suspend him- or herself over the water in order to keep the boat flat when the wind is trying to knock it down – because dinghies are fastest when sailed flat.

As with all the Olympic classes, body types are important on the 470. Skippers tend to be on the compact side, and must weigh close to 61 kilos (135 pounds). Crews should be six feet tall or more, and weigh 70 kilos (155 pounds). There is little room for variation, meaning that dieting can be as important to a 470 team as it is to wrestlers or jockeys trying to make weight.

Just assembling the boat is an exercise in science-based creativity. There are no designated lengths for the rigging. The spreaders are adjustable, and the rules allow for variation in mast, appendage (rudder, centerboard), and sail design. Each sail is a full-on project in itself. Mainsails and jibs undergo thousands of hours of study through computer programs and full-size testing, with shape changes often measuring in a few millimeters.

Mainsail shape and weight of cloth must be fully compatible with stiffness of the mast. Mainsail and mast must function as one. There is a different spinnaker shape for every five-degree change in downwind sailing angle. The rigging can be adjusted while on the water, but not during a race. And mainsheet, traveler, vang, Cunningham, jib leads, centerboard, and rig tension all can be adjusted while racing. The object is to find the "package" – the combination of a hundred or more elements – that is faster than what the other crews have put together. Achieving that package is a constant struggle. Just when you think you've got it, you get passed.

There's much more. Kinetics describes the movements of skipper and crew in the boat. Around 2004, infamous Racing Rule of Sailing 42 *("Except when permitted in rule 42.3 or 45, a boat shall compete by using only the wind and water to increase, maintain or decrease her speed. Her crew may adjust the trim of sails and hull, and perform other acts of seamanship, but shall not otherwise move their bodies to propel the boat")* was waived by the 470 class when the wind reached a speed of 12 knots. Four years later, wind speed was reduced to eight knots. At that point, the race committee raises an "O" flag, and suddenly the 470 fleet becomes very animated, as crews begin "pumping" the sails by body movement, a technique made famous by board sailors. The legalization of pumping created an entirely different and very athletic approach to sailing the 470. After 12 years of experimentation, techniques for pumping are still being refined. Breakthroughs and innovations are carefully guarded secrets. The physical demands pumping exerts on the crew are extreme given the fact that there is never a moment when the playing surface (water) and propulsion system (wind) are not changing. Most often there is little harmony between the two. Both sailors are doing their best to react to the changes by trimming and using kinetics as quickly and efficaciously as possible.

The crew is usually in charge of boat speed. In mid-race, when the "O" flag is flying, a 470 crew's heart rate is pounding at around 170-180 beats per minute, or the same as a bicycle racer climbing the Col de Tourmalet in the Tour de France. Add staying on top of race strategy and tactics to all this, and a 470 crew has a very full plate.

Belcher

Mathew Belcher, from Gold Coast, Queensland, Australia, had won the 420 world championship with his brother crewing for him in 2000, when he was 17 years old. The 420 is a slightly smaller (4.2 meters), less sophisticated version of the 470 that is often used by college sailing teams. It's viewed as a trainer for the 470. Belcher had moved directly from Sabots, 8-foot, blunt nosed dinghies sailed by youths ages 8 to 16 in many parts of the world, to the 420s. His last year in the Sabots, he had placed 5th in the national championships. Belcher confesses to having had Olympic dreams since he was 15. His success in the 420 led to serious thoughts about the 470, and began turning those dreams into possibilities.

Belcher had long admired Tom King, who had been sailing 470s for ten years and was at the top of his game when Belcher met his hero at the 1999, 470 world championships in Melbourne, a regatta King won. A year later, Belcher met King's coach, Victor Kovalenko, at Kiel Week, one of the largest sailing events in the world held annually in June in Kiel, Germany. After the Olympics, the two met again.

Mathew Belcher is the essence of calm. He has little affect, not the least bit of swagger or heroic posture one might expect from an athlete of his abilities and outstanding accomplishments. One would not pick him out a lineup as a winner. His movements are efficient, purposeful.

Otherwise he is still. He's not a big talker, but ask him a question and his response is complete, on point, and could even include thoughts he is considering. His sense of humor is keen, his smile is quick.

"Victor was looking to the future," Belcher says of their meeting. "He came to Brisbane, invited me into the 470 squad." Belcher was in university at the time, studying law and business. He never imagined sailing would be his career. He figured: do the Olympics then go into business. But in February, 2001, Belcher was offered a national team scholarship by the Australian Yachting Federation. "That was Victor's first move," Belcher says with a grin.

"I went to my parents. I had just turned 18. I told them I got this scholarship and had to go to Europe. They asked when I had to leave. I said next week. Victor talked a lot with my parents, helped encourage them. They said okay, but you have to finish university. I said okay, but didn't give a time frame. I went to my professors, said I had to have my exams. I stayed one week, passed four subjects and went to Europe. That's how it started."

Victor had spotted talent, and had moved quickly. Mat Belcher was an unusual 17-year-old. At age 12 he had earned a black belt in Tae Kwon Do, the youngest Australian ever to achieve that level. His golf handicap was under 10. He played ice hockey and soccer. He was smart as a whip. And he was a very good sailor with Olympic dreams.

CHAPTER 2

Love

Victor Kovalenko remembers his first sail in a 470 as if it were yesterday. He was 24 years old, a student at University Nikolaev in Ukraine when he saw a 470 and asked if he might sail it. For five years he had been a member of the Soviet national team, sailing Flying Dutchmen and Dragons. He and his skipper had won the Flying Dutchman national championship in 1974. Victor always sailed as a crew, the job he preferred for its athletic challenge, and because the crew got to handle the spinnaker. He also had the right build. When he saw the 470, it was love at first sight, an affection that has lasted 40 years. Ask Victor today what boat he would sail if he had it to do over, and without hesitation he names the 470.

"It was blowing 30 knots, maybe more," Victor recalls, his eyes widening at the memory. "My skipper was older, but with good technical skills. I had a good ability on the trapeze. My shoulders were phenomenal. I was in good shape from the Flying Dutchman. Maybe I was a little light for upwind work, but for downwind I was just right. It was incredible. We were flying over the water, planing. On the FD the genoa sheet had ratchet blocks. On the 470 it was pull in and jam in the cleat. The 470 spinnaker is small, I could hold it easily. I said wow ! I was enjoying controlling the boat. It was an amazing, fast ride in a very lively boat. In a 470 you get used to being on the edge a lot of the time in strong winds."

Pioneer

Some people are born with a strong, inexplicable affinity for a natural element: earth, air, water, fire. For Victor Kovalenko, it is the sea. We all have salt in our veins. Victor just has more than his share. That he was born in the city of Dnepropetrovsk, on the Dnieper River (Ukraine's largest) had no bearing on his predilection for navigable water, but it did make it easier for him to get his feet wet. He did that in a notable way when he was eight years old. His father had a small outboard motor boat that was moored in the river, close by the shore. One of Victor's chores was to bring the boat to the beach every week and clean it. One day when he arrived at the boat, on a whim he fixed an oar upright and tied a beach towel to it. That playful act changed his life. "It was as if time stopped," Victor says, the memory sharp as a photograph. "I felt the wind in my hands, the quietness interrupted only by the whispering of the water on the bow of the boat, lapping, burbling…it opened my senses. I could smell the water and the smoke from the land. It opened my heart. I never in my life wanted to be without that feeling."

Victor was one of those ever curious, innovative kids driven to fully explore whatever engaged him. Soon he and his friends were cutting up old bed sheets and any material they could find into triangular shapes for sails for the motor boat. They made a jib, then fastened crude leeboards to the boat to keep it from slipping sideways. In colder weather they made models out of available scrap and tried to sail them when they didn't sink right away. The hook of sailing had been set. It was just a matter of time before Victor would find sailboats big enough to hold him. That happened quicker than might have been expected.

In 1950, when Victor was born, it had only been 5 years since the Germans had been driven out of the Soviet Union. The devastation the German troops left behind them with their Eastern Bloc offensive defies comprehension. Hitler's Einsatzgruppen, paramilitary death squads of the Schutzstaffel (SS), followed the advancing German troops into Russia for the purpose of committing mass murder. In addition to eleven million

Soviet troops, seven million civilians were killed (1.5 million of them in Ukraine). Twenty-eight thousand Soviet villages and more than 700 cities and towns were destroyed. Nineteen million Soviets were left homeless. There was no food, no fuel for stoves against the brutal Russian winters. Cannibalism was said to be practiced on the black market. Furniture and books were burned to keep those left barely alive from freezing.

Victor's family was lucky. Both of his parents survived. His father had served in a tank battalion. "He was burned out a few times," Victor says matter of factly. "He had a few bullets in him." By the time Victor came into the world, his father was driving a truck for the Yuzhmash missile plant in Dnepropetrovsk, an enormous operation, a "secret city" covering thousands of acres with over 100 buildings and a hundred thousand employees. It was surrounded by a double fence, guarded by armed men in towers. The missile plant had its own bus transportation system. To the outside world it was such a well-kept secret it did not appear on any maps. In the early 1970s, the factory began building the Satan, considered the most powerful of the ICBMs, capable of carrying 10 nuclear warheads a distance of 10,000 miles.

Like everyone else in their situation, the Kovalenkos lived in state-provided housing. A two-room, cold water, fourth floor walkup was home to Victor's parents, his younger sister and himself, and his grandfather. The adults slept in one of the small rooms. The children slept on couches in the equally small "living room." There was a tiny kitchen and bathroom the Kovelankos shared with other tenants on their floor. Water for bathing had to be heated in pots on the stove. One of Victor's jobs when he was six years old was to take a cart (a sled in winter), pull it more than a mile to a sunflower oil factory, and load it with husks to burn in the cook stove. He did this twice or three times a day.

"Soup was for dinner almost every night," Victor says. "Pasta sometimes, or potato. There was no salad in winter. Maybe some apples. But food was very scarce. Summer you could buy fruits at the market, and from 1959 when Cuba became part of the Soviet system we got some bananas. The first time I had a banana was in 1961 when I was 11. We drank tea, or water, had some bread with butter." Victor says it was common for his mother to borrow a few rubles from neighbors (or vice versa) for food at the end of each month.

At age 6, Victor and his friends had adventures in the city. In summer, dressed only in underpants and sandals, they would jump on the back of the tram that went across the river to the beach. "There was a hard, slow turn as the bridge ended," Victor says. "If you jumped out there it saved a 15 minute walk. It was dangerous, because trams were coming the other way. Now it could not happen, no no no you cannot do this! Now in Australia you have a kids' chair in the car until you are 12, and a baby sitter until you are 14. Can you imagine what we were doing at 5 and 6 years old, jumping from the tram in our underpants? Until I was 6, I was barefoot. We went to the beach and taught ourselves to swim. I mimicked the tadpole. One day I saw my neighbor. I thought maybe she saw me, so I ran all the way home to beat the tram she would take. When she arrived, I was sitting there, innocent. But she said she saw me. My parents touched my undies and they were dry. But the elastic waist band was still wet. I was caught. A double penalty for also lying. They took the belt and hit me, whack, whack."

There was no telephone in the apartment — as late as the 1990s, Ukrainians waited as much as 30 years in the cue to get a telephone — and no car outside. Victor's father and all the other workers walked to their jobs. There was radio through a loud speaker affixed to the wall that carried the one, state-run station broadcasting music and propaganda, and announcing when it was time for exercises. It was more public address system than radio. Victor's neighbors had a television, and sometimes he had permission to watch bits of the one or two hours of programming broadcast every day. In 1960 his family got a small television of its own. But the best fun was when they hung a bed sheet on the wall of the building and watched slides in the back yard. "There was a great comradery of people," Victor says, "thirty or forty kids and their parents from the building, with one parent showing slides. We watched Pinocchio, things like that. In a few years my parents bought me my own projector and slides. The kids shared and traded their slides."

The high degree of comradery was an offshoot of common plight. "Everyone was at the same level," Victor explains. "There were no rich people at that time. There were no special kids, no special schools. We knew some people who were high up in the city, like the district secretary of the Communist Party, but their kids were the same as us. Now there are rich people who have body guards and a special school for their kids, but not back then."

Kids are natural scavengers, and what Victor and his friends dredged up were frequently weapons that had been left behind by retreating German troops. There was a sign on Victor's building indicating it had been swept free of mines, but handguns, rifles, ammunition, knives, and various other paraphernalia of war turned up in the strangest places. Many boys had a prized cache of military items they kept hidden. One day when he was quite young, Victor was on the street in front of his building playing with a hand grenade. A stranger seized the grenade and demanded Victor lead him to his mother. The man scolded Mrs. Kovalenko for letting her son play with such a thing. Victor says his mother wasn't concerned – all the kids played with weapons – until the man told her the grenade in Victor's possession was live.

School started at age seven. That would have been 1957 for Victor, the year the Soviet Union startled the world by taking the lead in space exploration with the launch of Sputnik, the first artificial Earth satellite. Victor liked school. It made it even more enjoyable when the authorities had come to his classroom asking the children what sport or other activity they would like to sign up for. The missile plant had a strong social system. In addition to study rooms and libraries, it had facilities for almost any sport one could name. In 1966, the Yuzhmash missile plant had built The Meteor Club sports complex at huge expense. The Club boasted four separate, attractive facilities that include a 25,000-seat stadium for football; an Olympic swimming pool; tennis, badminton, and basketball courts; rooms for fencing, wrestling, archery, and gymnastics. One facility on the river was dedicated to rowing and sailing. All this was organized through a large social club they called The Palace of Culture. Young people could go there and learn to be dancers, potters, model makers, craftsman… and none of it cost a penny.

Meteor Club operation was partly funded by Yuzhmash; by federal funds from Moscow; and by the Trade Union, part of the state-run athletic system. The sailing club's operating budget was in direct proportion to how well its sailing teams performed against its rivals (primarily the Navy and Police teams). As a result, the recruitment and development of athletes thought to have potential was a priority. Promising young sailors were given extra food, and coupons as incentives to perform well. Excellence was rewarded up and down the line. The skills one learned at The Palace of Culture could lead to a job as an apprentice in a factory. Or if one excelled in studies, and passed exams, students could obtain scholarships to university, and money to buy food and books.

Like the great majority of the kids, Victor had become a Pioneer when he turned nine. The Pioneers was a youth indoctrination organization of the Communist Party. He wore his red bandana around his neck every day at school. "I felt patriotic," Victor recalls, "proud to be in the Communist Union. There weren't many rebellious kids. Maybe there were in Moscow and the bigger cities. But Dnepropetrovsk was a blue collar city. My family was working class. We were loyal to the system. And of course that is what we knew."

Victor remembers Yuri Gagarin, the first human into outer space, with great clarity. "April 12, 1961," he says. "They wrote it on the blackboard at school: we are into space! I remember watching Gagarin on TV, a real national hero. He flew to Moscow when he returned, stood next to Khrushchev. We listened to the beeps from Sputnik on the radio."

The contrast between Victor's upbringing and what was going on in other, first- world countries at the time is stark. But from a kid's point of view, there was a prevailing anxiety that has a familiar ring. In the late 1950s and 1960s, school children in the USA and Europe were taught about the Russian aggressors, and regularly went through nuclear bomb drills by hiding under their desks and covering themselves with newspapers. The Russian kids were equally on edge. "We worried about the United States," Victor says. "We had training alarms when the city went dark and we had to put blankets on the windows. We had gas alarms when we put on our masks. I had nuclear war dreams with planes in the air and war all around and I thought oh my life is so short and I will be dead. My nightmares were about when war started."

In summer, buses queued up in front of the Palace of Culture where a band was playing and refreshments were being served to many hundreds of kids. Then they trooped onto the buses that took them into the countryside for two weeks of camp. Victor remembers it fondly, with canoeing and sailing on a lake, woodsman activities, hikes, all sorts of games, and cookouts aplenty.

Sport

Victor began sailing at the Yuzhmash facilities when he was 12, first crewing on 25-foot M-class sloops. He found that the real thing exceeded all expectations. Sailing quickly took over Victor's life. His natural affinity for the water made play out of the dedicated application required to become outstanding. His abilities and his focused approach to sailing made him a stand out. Soon Victor's vision was to become an athlete in the Soviet system. He knew how it worked. "Athlete" was as legitimate a profession in the USSR as teacher or doctor. Athletes were employed by the military, a trade union, or the police, and while they were required to fulfill certain duties (training, drills, etc.), their main job was to practice and compete on the playing fields of their particular sport. Their rank, pay grade, and privileges advanced according to how well they performed in competition. There were official titles: Third- (city), Second- (state) and First Class (regional) Sportsmen; Candidate for Master of Sport in USSR (a nationally ranked player); Master of Sport in USSR (a national champion); Master of Sport USSR International Class (a world champion); and Honored Master of Sport USSR (a world champion who has made special contributions to the sport). Every category was reinforced with medals, varying degrees of celebrity status, and access to better food, cars, telephones, and more desirable living quarters.

"There were only two times the Soviet flag was raised on foreign soil," Victor says. "One was when our president made a visit. The other was when Soviet athletes won in major competitions. That was the athletes' goal: to raise the Soviet flag on foreign soil."

James Riordan's scholarly study, *Sport in Soviet Society*, reveals that the value of sport (physical exercise) in the Soviet Union dates back to the 1800s. Riordan credits the biologist/anatomist Pyotr Lesgaft with being the founder of the new discipline of physical education in tsarist Russia. Lesgaft felt that physical education instructors should have knowledge of chemistry and physics, particularly the general laws of mechanics, "so as to be able to apply them to the human mechanism."

The Russian physiologist Ivan Schyonov did extensive studies of muscular activities, concluding that (as Riordan summarizes) "physical education should be an integral part of all-round education as a means of strengthening the material foundation of consciousness." And Ivan Pavlov, the physiologist known for his conditioned reflex studies with dogs and other animals, avowed that exercise was highly salutary for the central nervous system : "hence the need for regular sporting activity by all citizens, for the good of society as well as of the individual." (The quote is Riordan's.)

Karl Marx was also writing about the value of sport in the 1800s. Marx said that in liberal capitalist societies, sport was seen as the concern of the individual, unconnected with classes and social values, or with economics and society's mode of production. He felt that the nature of sport could be expected to alter with any change to a new, socio-economic philosophy. Marx was right about that.

Playwright Anton Chekhov was a founder of the Russian Gymnastics Society, and a firm believer in the value of sport. In 1898, he told the Society's members, "(You) are the people of the morrow, the time when everyone will be as strong and skillful. Therein lies the nation's hopes for its future and its happiness." Speaking of liberal capitalist societies, it's fascinating to note than less than a year later, U.S. President Theodore Roosevelt was expressing a similar view about the value of physical exertion. Roosevelt had boxed as a student, hiked, swum regularly in the Potomac River, and played polo and tennis in spite of a heart condition he was warned about. While he didn't advocate sports per se, he admonished Americans to embrace a "strenuous life." "I wish to preach," Roosevelt said, "that the highest form of success comes to the man who does not shrink from danger, from hardship, or from bitter toil….it is only through strife, through hard and dangerous endeavor that we shall win the goal of true national greatness."

Vladimir Lenin echoed Roosevelt's goal of national greatness through physicality, but coming from Lenin, and expressed within Russia's authoritarian political philosophy, it had a more ominous ring. As a young politician, Lenin had been asked how young people should spend their spare time. His light-hearted answer : "Wrestling, work, study, sport, making merry, singing, dreaming – these are things young people should make the most of." But at the Third All-Russia Congress of the Russian Young Communist League (October 1920), the more radical Lenin's view of sport had changed from physical enjoyment and self-betterment to a means of developing the ideal, all-round member of Communist society. "Today," he told that Congress, "physical education has direct practical aims : (1) Preparing young people for work; and (2) preparing them for military defense of Soviet power." Lenin's strong statement left no doubt as to the role of sport in the Soviet system.

Temptations

As a young teenager and enthusiastic Pioneer, Victor hadn't given any thought to the larger, political implications of becoming a professional athlete in the Soviet Union. All he knew was that sailing had a tenacious hold on him, an affinity he used to help him through more immediate problems. "It was a really good and interesting time in my life until I was around 15 years old," Victor says. "Then there were lots of temptations. Drugs came into our neighborhood. Three or five people in each of our classes were dealing marijuana and other drugs, and were getting involved in crime. And of course there was liquor. Many times I was very close to trouble. Many of my friends went into the trap easily. Some lost their health. I tried marijuana and I said to myself I am in sport and I cannot do this, I am a sailor, I have to be strong. I chose sport. My family supported me, my school supported me. And my love of sailing saved me, gave me the power to resist the temptations."

Message

By the time he was 17, Victor Kovalenko had become an accomplished sailor. He was so enamored with sailing, so convinced he could make a career of it, that he refused an opportunity to attend a military school that had been arranged by a family friend. "Even then I felt it was a great position in life to be a sailor," Victor says. "I always had feelings of being part of a special world, a special community." Sailing was such a priority for him that Victor didn't even consider the offer. "I said I love sailing, I love freedom, why would I want to be an officer?" That had left him only one alternative: going to work at the Yuzhmash missile plant.

He started as a lathe operator. After being injured by a piece of metal that flew into his eye, he transferred to working as a mason. "That was the same every day," Victor says, "but it was a better job because it was outside. There was less security, and it was more physical. When you lay bricks, every day is something different – wind, rain, snow – and you are around lovely people. It was a real nice job. I enjoyed it." He also worked at the Palace of Culture swimming pool part time as a lifeguard. But mainly he was able to sail every day when he got off work.

At the Meteor Yacht Club, Victor had soon graduated to the Flying Dutchman, a 20-foot, two-person dinghy that was an Olympic class at the time. He did well, winning his share of regattas. He says he was good – "not super good" – but good enough to attract the attention of the Chairman of the Meteor Club, Anatoli Gajduk.

Like all boys who turned 18, Victor was required to register for military service. A year later he had still not been called for active duty, but every recruit had to take pre-enlistment training of some sort. For Victor, it was typing school two or three evenings a week. There he met a fellow his age named Alex Belopolski. The two boys were free spirits enjoying life's simple pleasures: wine, cigarettes, and the pursuit of girls. They became friends. Victor would often stop by Alex's apartment to pick him up on the way to typing class.

One such evening would change his life. He arrived at the apartment, but Alex was not there. His mother, Maria Belopolski, welcomed Victor, said Alex would be back shortly. The apartment was very similar to Victor's, two rooms with shared kitchen and bathroom. The furnishings were rudimentary, as simple as possible. "If you wanted a large comfortable chair in those days, even if you had the money you could not buy it," Victor says. "But Mrs. Belopolski kept everything meticulously clean."

She poured tea for them. Victor had gotten to know Alex's mother in the course of many visits. She was a single mother in her late 40s who worked hard as a cleaner at the missile plant to provide for her son. "She was a tough lady," Victor recalls, "short, very reserved. She was not smiling by nature." The two chatted over tea. Victor can't recall what in their exchange led to Maria Belopolski's sudden admonition. But he says when her dark eyes fixed on his, it was as if time had stopped. He remembers her words with eternal clarity: "She said, Victor, if you want to be successful in this life, you must take care of yourself because no one else will carry you or care for you. You must open doors for yourself. If you don't do it, no one else will. You must know what you want and fight for it, fight for yourself, achieve what you want by all of your actions, all of your heart."

Victor admits being stunned by the power of Maria Belopolski's words. Alex had arrived shortly thereafter, and off the boys went to their typing class. Victor did not share with Alex what his mother had told him, and nothing in Victor's behavior that evening prompted Alex to ask what was on Victor's mind. But Victor's ears were ringing. As we will see, as a coach, Victor Kovalenko has made a life-long study of when and how to send messages to his sailors. That study began in Maria Belopolski's apartment when he was 19 years old. His friend's mother had touched his core by seizing the moment when his mind was open and available, ready to embrace the information – a rare moment when one is 19. Mrs. Belopolski had seen or felt something in Victor that evening, some sign that this was a moment to be seized, and in her wisdom she had made her move, delivered her message. "I think she realized I was a special friend," Victor says, "and wanted to help me, guide me. Maybe she realized I had a chance in this life, and she said her piece. We are all messengers, and she made the effort."

It would not be long before Victor acted on Maria Belopolski's admonition.

Moscow

Victor entered the Soviet Army in 1969. He was sent to a base in the middle of Russia for basic training, and to go through the regimens of fitness, running, marching, and general harassment common to all military establishments. He learned that some of his unit were to be sent on to other assignments after training, and some were to be kept to learn Morse Code and train as radio men. Victor was not on the list to be kept. Without hesitation, he went to his commanding officer and protested, said he would like to stay and become a radio man. The officer told him he already had a military specialty, typing, that he could operate a telegraph machine.

"I said to him, what is wrong if I get another specialty?" Victor recalls. "It will make me even more valuable for the Army. I told him for you it is good because I am very motivated, I want to learn Morse Code. You don't need to force or encourage me to do it because I really want to learn this. This will give me a bonus. I will be more valuable. And my commanding officer said okay, you are right, I will leave you in school to learn Morse Code. Soon I became one of the best students. There were two of us who were really good, we practiced all the time, we had the highest speed. We became top experts."

Victor had consciously tested Maria Belopolski's theory of standing up for oneself, and it had worked. His next move followed quickly, and was a big risk given the formidable nature of the military chain of command in the strictly regulated Soviet system. He wrote a letter to the Minister of Defense requesting a transfer to the Navy, or more specifically the Navy Sailing Team, part of the Navy Central Sport Club located in Moscow. Such inter-service transfers were not unheard of in those days, but they were rare. "I wrote to the Minister saying I was a good sailor, spoke of events I had won, listed some references, and said I would like to keep sailing with the Navy team."

The plot thickened when Victor received an offer from the head of the Morse Code school to be an instructor. It was not considered very healthy (patriotic?) for a lowly private to reject such an offer, but having made his play with the letter, Victor thought it was necessary. "If I stayed and became a teacher," Victor says, "there was little chance they would let me go when the Navy exchange came in. They would have a grip on me. So I elected to stay in the regular Army while waiting to hear about my transfer."

If there were odds makers in Victor's barracks, chances are they were not taking many bets on a letter from the ranks making an impression on a Minister. For a while, it looked as if they were right. Victor was being given extra duties for his failure to embrace the system, and found himself belittled by his fellow soldiers. "It didn't matter," Victor says, "because I was following my dream."

His proficiency with Morse Code could not be ignored by his superiors, and caused Victor to be transferred to the headquarters of a big missile defense division. It was an important central control hub dedicated to "Sky Protection," and Victor loved it. There were no computer systems at the time, but Victor was assigned to a large room filled with clear plastic panels on which the position, course, and speed of every airplane entering Soviet air space was written by hand in grease pencil, and frequently updated.

"First I was working getting the signals and information and giving that to the people updating the maps. They decoded it, and made their entries. Then, because I was fast, they put me in a special room where there was a link between the Headquarters of the Soviet Army and our division. It was all high speed, typing and then getting Morse signals. I was first to hear what was happening. If a special signal came in, I had to open a hatch, remove a seal, and press a red button. That was real. I was excited by this. It was interesting work. There were a lot of politics at that level, and some of that was terrible because different people were playing politics, fighting for control of us. But it was a good life school. I was moving forward with my skills."

In the midst of the excitement, it occurred to Victor that his letter to the Minister of Defense had gone unanswered. So he wrote again (!), asking why he had not heard from him. This time he got a reply. The Minister's office said they had been in touch with his superiors who had reported that Kovalenko had broken his arm, and could not play sports. "I responded right away," Victor says, "told them it was not true, that I was in good shape, that all was okay. They wanted to keep me because I was good !

"There came a serious signal from the Headquarters of the Red Army to send me to Moscow, to the Navy. The signal said I had to be there in 24 hours or they were in trouble because they had lied."

To a Westerner's cliché-ridden sensibilities, what could be viewed as Victor's impertinent short cut through the Red Army's chain of command sounded like a one-way ticket to the frozen wilds of Siberia might be the upshot. Westerners are under the impression that individual initiative was not rewarded under the Communist system. One can only admire Victor's courage. He doesn't see it that way : "My commanding officer was upset, of course, but this was my life at stake, my destiny, I had to be pushing it to protect my destiny. So they bought a ticket and sent me to Moscow !" Victor Kovalenko had been in the Army less than a year.

CHAPTER 3

Mankin

In Moscow, Victor was given a blue Navy uniform and a bunk in a floating barracks built on a barge that accommodated 120 men. Both the Army and the Navy had their big sport clubs in Moscow. The Army focused on track and field, soccer, volleyball and basketball, fencing, wrestling, boxing – all the dry land sports. The Navy Club included all the water sports, including sailing, rowing, water polo, swimming, kayaking, and water skiing. In Moscow, Victor had a clear window into the system. He didn't, however, encounter any of the top athletes – Olympic, world, and national champions – because they were all living at home, in attractive quarters their accomplishments had earned them from the State. But they were still considered regular Navy troops, required to be at the Club within 30 minutes when an alarm sounded.

Victor got off to a good start in Moscow, sailing with one of Russia's outstanding Flying Dutchman sailors, Alexander Shelkovnikov. Shelkovnikov had finished 6th in the 1960 Olympics in Rome-Naples, and was leading the Tokyo Olympics in 1964 until his rudder snapped (he finished 5th). He'd also sailed in the Mexico Games in 1968.

But the man who would have the biggest effect on his sailing, and coaching, was Valentin Mankin, the legendary Soviet sailor who died in 2014 at the age of 75. Despite the 20-hour drive, the Navy sailing team often went to Sevastapol, then a strategic Russian Naval port on the Crimean peninsula, on the Black Sea, to practice in open water conditions. Sevastapol was where Mankin had established his headquarters after winning his first Olympic gold medal in the Finn Class at the 1968 Olympic Games in Mexico. He would win two more gold medals, in the Tempest

(Munich, 1972), and in the Star (Moscow, 1980). He also won a silver medal in the Tempest at the 1976 Games in Montreal. Mankin's record stands alone atop the ranks of Russian sailors.

"He was amazing," Victor says of Mankin, "a role model not just for Soviet sailors, but for all sailors. His dedication and commitment to the job were incredible. His headquarters in Sevastopol was like a fortress where he lived with his many books and all his equipment. In summer he would start training at 5am. He'd come in, have breakfast, and rest before he went out again. He would sail again in the evening."

In deference to his gold medal in 1972, the commander of the Sevastopol base asked Mankin what he wanted above all else: a car, more luxurious lodging, access to better food? All he had to do was name it. Mankin replied that he would like to be able to go sailing in the Black Sea whenever he wanted. True to his word, the commander gave Mankin the power to have the security nets at the harbor entrance opened whenever he wished to go sailing.

Victor got to know Mankin better in 1973, after he became a member of the Soviet National Sailing Team, of which Mankin was the leader. A friendship between the two sailors grew out of the obsessive way each of them approached his sport. "We were the transition generation," Victor says. "Before, sailors raced, then had parties with much drinking and some smoking. There were even some Olympic champions smoking. In 1972-74, a new generation of sailors arrived with an emphasis on fitness, running, chin ups, sit ups…many physical activities. No smoking or drinking. And all our money was spent on sailing."

Even at that early stage, one of Victor's canons about racing sailboats was well developed: *you can race for fun, which takes little money and little time; you can race for results, which takes a lot of time and much money; or you can fight for glory, which takes all your time, all your money, and requires the best possible support systems.* "Glory," Victor is fond of saying, always with a smile, "is a capricious lady." Then Victor ran into Mankin, who fought for glory at an extreme even Victor had not imagined. "He was completely focused on sailing," Victor says. "It was his reason for existing on the Earth. That's why he was successful. He thought about nothing but sailing 100% of the time, 24 hours a day. He was really insane."

When asked, Victor says he thinks about sailing 90% of the time. One American coach who knows Victor laughed when he heard that.

"After one world championship, the next day everyone was relaxed, partying," Victor says. "Not Mankin. He had finished second. He said that was not good enough. While the others partied, he was out sailing. Everyone noticed.

"He was always first on the water. You would go to the club early to launch, and he was gone. It was the same at a regatta. If the start was at noon, he was launching at 9am. Once when sailing Tempests, one competitor came early, launched at 8:45. The next day Mankin was there at 8:30. That was Mankin. Always sailing, always dreaming, always competing."

It appears that Mankin saw in Victor a younger version of his highly-committed self. When preparing for the Olympic Games in Montreal (the sailing was held in Kingston, Ontario), Mankin insisted Victor share a room with his new Tempest crew, a man named Vadim. "He thought I would be a good role model for his crew," Victor says, "because I was in really good shape, and I ate a lot. His crew needed to eat a lot to put on weight." Previously, during a week at the Russian Olympic training center in Sochi, Mankin had been impressed by Victor's prowess at arm wrestling. Mankin watched Victor win several matches, then suggested he take on Vadim who outweighed Victor by 14 kilos. "I took him, *boom*!" Victor says. "Then Mankin says to his coach, 'Constantine, can you try with Victor,' and for me it was easy, *boom*!

"He had a mobile van when he was sailing the Tempest. Everything was in there, tools, gear, sails…the Tempest was on a trailer behind. At one regatta we worked long after sailing, so instead of driving to the hotel we slept in the van. We got to bed at 11.30pm. At 4am Mankin arrives, wakes us up, says he has an idea about recutting the sails. So we get up, start working on the sails."

One of Victor's treasures is a dog-eared copy of *White Triangle*, a book Mankin wrote in 1976. Victor says he must have read *White Triangle* 20 times. "It is a spiritual book focused on Mankin's life, his dedication," Victor says. The book is a fascinating mix of advice and philosophy mixed with questions and some doubts that plagued the great sailor. As these excerpts suggest, it is a book that any coach who deals with top level athletes would find intriguing.

– *Every start is the part of life you remember because it made you more mature and wiser.*

– *I work on my starts always. Starts are the hardest. It is hard to catch up later. Who wins the start is half way to victory as a rule.*

– *Sailing is pursued by multi-century romantics.*

– *(My dad) was teaching me how to take a boxing stance and telling me that is how you should stand strong in life, not running from hits, but accepting them wisely and responding, hitting back in time.*

– *I thank my coach who strengthened my love for sailing, who taught me to work and believe that only hard labor achieves anything. Yes, sailing was the purpose of my life, the point of my life.*

– *Inevitably the day comes when students exceed the teacher's results.*

But the teacher has always to be superior on the level of tactical thinking and theoretical preparedness. That's why the teacher must be a life student.

– *In sailing, I like to fight with the elements. Racing in strong wind arouses feelings in me that once on a wonderful day, the yacht will come off the sea surface and fly above the waves.*

– *I came up with my first device when I sailed in the Olympics. It was difficult to keep my legs in the right position. I decided to make special loops I could shove my legs in without help from my hands.*

– *Now I always win all regattas in my country. Maybe I will have to taste defeat, but who said the taste of defeat will kill the desire of learning, or the struggle ? Who said that mastery is not growing through hard wrestling ?*

– *Desire to practice was constant. It is like insatiable hunger. Besides, I was successful.*

– *In many cases I did not know how to maneuver in comparison with my competitor. I scored myself on the start, tacking, rounding the mark, the whole course. Then I break it down into smaller pieces. But I have no clue how my competitor does it. There is no time to look around while sailing.*

– *Victory, that's it. Is that how victory feels ? Is it really how most cherished dreams come true ? Everyone from the shore ran up to me with congratulations, but I didn't even feel the joy. My rival came up to me and said "It was a pleasure competing with you." Was ? It means it is all over.*

Victor says he was lucky to become a good friend of Mankin's. "We had many dinners, talked sailing, exchanged ideas about big strategies and how to prepare. But mostly he was my role model."

Books

White Triangle wasn't the only memorable book Victor was exposed to in Moscow. The best thing about the otherwise barren barracks floating on the Moskva River that twists through the heart of the city, was the well-appointed library that shared the first floor of the barge with the mess hall. It was here Victor was exposed to the Great Dane Paul Elvström's book, *Paul Elvström Speaks on Yacht Racing*, first published in 1969. For many sailors, Victor among them, this 55 year-old book remains "the" bible of the sport. "I look at it often," Victor says. "There is wonderful advice on every page. You can read it five times and still miss something."

Elvström was a precursor of the transition generation. As early as 1948, at age 20, when he was preparing for the Olympic selection trials in Denmark, Elvström admits that his full-focus approach to sailing was contrary to the prevailing attitude about the sport. "People would laugh at you at that time if you would prepare in a way so that you had a better chance to win," he writes in *Elvström Speaks*. "In those days, practicing for something just wasn't thought to be the right thing to do."

He would win his first of four consecutive gold medals in 1948. The first was in the Firefly class. The other three were in the Finn. Elvström would also win eleven world championships in 8 different boats. Only one other sailor, Great Britain's Ben Ainslie, has equaled Elvström's accomplishment of winning four consecutive gold medals. As Victor has said, Elvström's book is a treasure trove of advice that still applies on any race course in the world:

- *In a shifty wind you must only sail to follow the wind and not cover the others.*
- *The evening before the last race I was concentrating on everything that might happen and that's really, I should say, a disadvantage.*

– *(Helmar Petersen and I) were sailing for one month every day for 5-8 hours – I could play with that Finn under all conditions.*

– *I could not see how I could lose. They must have thought I was very big-headed, but I was not really. I was so well prepared I felt there wasn't anyone who could beat me. And I think when you have no inferiority complex that helps you along.*

– *On the two reaching legs I gained at least 12 boats because they all sailed a circle instead of going straight to the mark – skippers don't realize that to look straight ahead of a boat you have to look a long way to windward of where you think you are.*

– *My advice is that you have got to spend all your time at it if you want to have a chance to win.*

The library had a rich mix of international literature, including a complete Shakespeare, and all of Jack London's work. One book Victor found of particular interest was *How to Win Friends and Influence People*, Dale Carnegie's best seller. The first of the self-help genre that was published in 1937, *How to Win Friends* has sold over 15 million copies. One copy, in Russian, resides in a small book case next to Victor's desk in his Sydney apartment. One quote from the book was very much to Victor's liking, and can be found scribbled in his personal notebook: "Always start a conversation in such a way that the response will be positive." One would have to search long and hard to find a more positive person than Victor Kovalenko, to find someone who conducts more of a constant war against negativity in all forms. He does not, for instance, tolerate cursing on a race boat because he feels it creates a negative atmosphere. Several crewmen who could not curb their tongues have found themselves off the boat Victor was directing.

Certain books were not found in the library on the barge: books that had been banned by the Soviet Union. Smuggled copies were circulated at considerable risk among a small group of confidants that included Victor. "It was very dangerous," Victor says today, "but we were very careful." Among them were the novels of Aleksandr Solzhenitsyn that exposed the gulag, and the Soviet's forced labor camp system. Solzhenitsyn was awarded the Nobel Prize in 1970 for his work. He was expelled from the Soviet Union in 1974. He returned in 1994, three years after the Union was dissolved. Victor says he started to read *Gulag Archipelago*. "It was too much for me. It was too depressing. At the time – even today – I was trying to avoid negative things. I was not watching movies about killing because I was working in an environment where I had to be supportive to my sailors, positive."

One of the banned books Victor did read and puzzle over was *The Heart of a Dog*, by Mikhail Bulgakov and Mirra Ginsberg. The book is a viciously anti-Soviet work that is rife with dark humor and sarcasm. It's about a professor who adopts a beat up mongrel dog that has had a hard life on the street. The professor feeds the dog well, and cares for him. Then the professor's hidden agenda takes over. He operates on the dog, giving him a portion of a human brain. The resulting creation goes very badly, chasing cats and women and drinking to excess. The dog/human demands to be given human papers. The authorities comply, and he gets a job as a purge director, in charge of eliminating counter-revolutionary cats from Communist society.

"I could not understand it back then," Victor says, "but now I understand how it reflects the philosophy of the Russian system. It is still the same. Leaders accept power, and can be corrupted because they have power. But as soon as they lose power they will be punished. In the book is the idea of how all money should be confiscated and then shared equally among the population. But the leaders use this idea to grab the wealth of the nation and hold it in their private areas."

Life's other side

By 1972, Victor had advanced to the National Sailing Team, racing in both Dragons and Flying Dutchmen. The team's program included training 20 days a month at the national training center in Sochi, 1000 miles from Moscow, on the east coast of the Black Sea. "My job was to be a sailor," Victor says. "I was paid to do my job, sailing. Every day the coaches would ask who is absent. No one, unless someone was sick. We sailed two times a day. There were only a few reasons accepted for not sailing. One was a storm. Not a strong wind, but a storm, an official storm warning from the Navy. Or if it were below zero degrees (32f). We trained in January and February. If it was not zero, no problem. First we took snow from the boats. Then we got buckets of hot water to unfreeze the ropes. Then we sailed."

Within a country the size of USSR, traveling for racing in various locations consumed a huge amount of time. The sailors were always dreaming up ways to make it easier. Victor and another crewman had what they thought was a great idea for making the 600 mile trip to Riga (Latvia), on the Baltic Sea, from Moscow, for a regatta. They would ride in the Dragon that was to be towed behind a truck full of gear, sails, and supplies. The idea made terrific sense to the young sailors because getting a train ticket to Riga in high season (August) was virtually impossible. The two young sailors gathered their supplies – mattresses, blankets, food, water – and were very pleased at their creative plan. "We would have an amazing trip," Victor recalls, "we would see the country."

The truck was to depart at 4am. At three, the young men were making their final preparations when their coach, Alexander Sovolev, arrived. He asked them what was going on. "We said we didn't have tickets," Victor says, "so we would ride in the boat. Getting tickets during the holidays was 100% impossible. You had to either know someone, or have huge money to get tickets."

Alexander shook his head. Bad idea. The boys argued, and Alexander finally had to issue an order: absolutely not. If they disobeyed, they would be off the team. "We were upset," Victor says. "It was not logical. But we respected Alexander very much. We took our stuff off the Dragon." Their next problem was how to get to Riga.

Victor says making instant friends of strangers in those days in the Soviet Union was easy. Because everyone lived the same hand-to-mouth existence, a willingness to help one another prevailed. When Victor and his friend wandered into the city in search of a solution to their problem, it was not a far-fetched approach. Indeed, before long they came upon a crew of alpinists who were painting high, steeply pitched roofs of houses. "We got to know them," Victor says, "told them our problem, and had a few drinks with them. They said okay, if we helped them the next day with labor, they would help us with tickets."

The next day at lunch, one of the roofers called a friend, who called a friend (etc.) and before long Victor and his pal had train tickets to Riga in the lowest class car. It turned out to be an uncomfortable trip. "We could not breathe," Victor says, "it was so crowded, so hot. There was no oxygen. It was a nightmare. We feared something would be stolen. Crooks were known to gas a car, jam the doors shut, and steal what they wanted after the people passed out."

As bad as it was on the train, riding in the boat would have been a lot worse. They spent two days in Riga waiting for the truck. Then they got the news. The driver had fallen asleep at the wheel, swerved into the oncoming lane and hit a car. The collision jarred him awake and he swerved back. But now the trailer and boat broke loose and rolled over. The three-ton trailer ended up on top of the crushed Dragon. Two people died in the car hit by the truck. The Dragon and all gear were completely destroyed.

"If we had been in that boat we would have been dead," Victor says. "One hundred percent dead! If Alexander had not come early that morning and forbid us to ride in the boat...! This was a very special case in my life. Alexander saved our lives. He was a normally friendly, easy guy, but he was tough in that situation as he should have been. His strict order saved us.

"It made me realize sometimes to save lives you don't have to risk your own life and be a hero. It's those two letters: N-O. If you said no, you saved your life. If people are following you and you say no, people say okay. That's how Alex saved our lives. Once in university I was at a skiing camp. Two guys were on top late in the day ready to ski down a steep trail. The teacher said no, take off skis and walk down. They argued. The teacher said no, walk. One did. The other skied down, lost control, hit a tree and was killed."

Traveling outside the country ran contrary to the Soviet Union's isolationist policy for its people, but if the Soviet flag were to be raised on foreign soil, it was necessary for its athletes to compete on foreign waters, in the case of sailing. Victor's first trip "outside" was to Estonia on the Baltic Sea. "It was still part of the Soviet Union," Victor says, "but we considered it overseas because their culture was different. They spoke their own language, their broadcasts were in Estonian. The Estonian people were more educated and polite. They didn't like Russians or Ukrainians because they thought we were rude, and lacked respect. But if you were polite, respectful, they accepted you."

Bulgaria on the Black Sea – bordering Greece to the south – was Victor's first trip to the West. The trip was two months in the making. That's how long it took for every sailor to collect at least a dozen signatures of his superiors up the chain of command. The signatures were assurance that the sailors would return to the Soviet Union. If they did not, the twelve men who signed off on their sporting venture (and their families) would be in serious peril.

Once in Bulgaria there were strict rules enforced by several "minders," KGB security personnel who accompanied the team. The KGB affiliation of the minders was supposed to be a secret, but the sailors knew. The sailors could not leave their quarters and wander around the city unless there were at least three of them in a group, because (they were warned) anything could happen. Victor and his group ate in a restaurant. "We were completely shocked," he says. "You could buy salami in the restaurant, wow! You could go there and eat it every day. In the Soviet Union at that time – this was 1973 – normal people could not buy salami. If you were a top athlete or a special person you might have access to salami twice a year, May 1 and New Year's Eve. You could go to a special shop with permission to buy 1 kilo of salami. But in Bulgaria they ate it every day. And beer. German beer. We had beer in the Soviet Union but it was different.

"I collected a little salami to bring home to my family, and a bottle of beer for my father. And a can of Coke. And a bottle of Classic Coke. Coke was like a symbol of capitalist life. Unbelievable. I also bought chewing gum. My family was amazed."

On subsequent trips to the West, the Soviet sailors were better prepared. They packed all sorts of canned meats, pickles, pasta, salt, butter and bread in the buses that were transporting boats and gear, using their daily food allowance (the equivalent of $15-$20 a day) to buy goods they couldn't get at home. "People had two different approaches," Victor says. "Some bought things they could sell back home for big money, like clothes, artificial hair, or radios, tape cassette players. A video cassette player could be swapped for a car, or sometimes for an apartment. The rest of us bought presents, and also stuff for ourselves, like jeans and boots. The others thought we were stupid not to buy stuff we could sell. I didn't care, it was for me. I ate ice cream because you have to be normal if you want to be a winner — you have to spoil yourself by having rewards. Winners are not thinking about how to make money. They are thinking about how to build character, about how to build an attitude about life and sport that makes you stronger every day. If I say I cannot eat ice cream because I have to save money to buy sails, that is understandable. But not to eat ice cream to make money is not good.

"Those with a material mentality bought things to sell. Our group of close friends brought back a new vision of life, a new approach to lots of things. In France some years later I bought a skateboard. The Italian sailors were teaching me how to use it. Our minder warned me, said I was talking too much to capitalist people. I said they teach me to skateboard! He said my morals were not the community morals, there was too much communication.

"The skateboard helped my coordination. The price was high. I could have bought a music system and sold it for big money. But the skateboard was me, my life."

CHAPTER 4

Disabled

The Soviet Navy discharged Victor because of an injury he received while sailing. He had his finger all but cut off on a flush cleat, a mushroom-shaped, stainless steel towing bit Dragons used to have up forward that retracted into the deck when not in use. To be flush with the deck, the overhanging rim of the top of the towing bit was finished quite fine. After a light air race in large waves, Victor's Dragon was being taken in tow by a chase boat. He was attaching the tow line to the bit when the chase boat accelerated prematurely. The index finger of his right hand was forced against the sharp rim of the bit by the tow line, and was cut deeply at the metacarpophalangeal joint where the finger joins the hand. "There was just a bit of skin, maybe 5 millimeters, holding the finger to my hand," Victor says. He carefully held the finger in place while he was taken to the medical center.

"I thought it was very important to keep the finger in position. The body is not only sending blood and electrical impulses to the finger, it considers the finger part of the body. If you take it away, the body says okay, the finger is lost, and it will stop sending signals. I was sending a message to the body that the finger was not lost, and that I would fight to maintain it as part of the body."

The finger was reattached, but it was unresponsive. The medical verdict was that the finger would never move again.

As far as the Navy was concerned, Victor was now disabled, unable to continue competing for the national team. He was also nearing the end of his tour of duty, so he was summarily discharged. Feeling mistreated, he returned to Dnepropetrovsk and moved back in with his parents, his sister (now 17), and his grandfather, all of whom were squeezed into the same tiny, one bedroom apartment. Victor says he often slept on the floor. He returned to the Meteor Club and rejoined the Trade Union sailing team. Meteor Club chairman Anatoli Gajduk was not only pleased to have Victor back, he was delighted to add a member of the Russian national sailing team to his club. Competition for good athletes remained intense among the military, the police, and the trade union. Victor was also glad to be back. Not one to spend more than a fleeting moment on the negative side of any situation, Victor began rebuilding an old Flying Dutchman while he worked at bringing his dormant finger back to life.

He began with daily visits to a clinic for paraffin therapy. He would insert his hand into a pot of melted wax. After the hand was sufficiently warm, a therapist would begin slowly and repeatedly bending the finger. "They would bend it, one-two, one-two," Victor recalls. "I started doing that at home, but the finger was too cold and I damaged it." He gave up the paraffin treatments and began running, whipping his right arm in circles as he ran to force blood into the extremities. "After a while I felt this sensation in my finger, like *Biing*!, and I thought this had to be good, that a new blood channel had opened up." Victor kept at it day after day, running and running, whipping his arm in circles as he ran to make the blood flow, and he kept feeling the sensation – *Biing*! – that had to mean more channels were developing.

"After a lot of exercise, massage, and trying to bend the finger carefully, it moved. I kept at it because I know you can never give up, and then I was using a little piece of shock cord to give it resistance, and then a small rubber ball." In one year the power began to come back.

Victor says he had been sailing the whole time he was bringing his finger back to life. He claims the inert finger did not interfere with his work on the trapeze and with the spinnaker. In any event, he began sailing with Valerij Maydan. They clicked as a team. In 1973 they finished well in a regatta in Bulgaria. In 1974, the two won the national Flying Dutchman championship, beating Victor's former Navy team. For Victor, it was a satisfying moment. "I put the medal on my injured finger and held it up for the Navy to see," he says with a smile.

At age 24, Victor Kovalenko had become a Master of Sport of the USSR. His timing could not have been better. The Olympic Games were first politicized by Adolf Hitler in 1936, and the political aspect had only accelerated over the next twenty years. Socialist countries had seized upon sport as a popular way to prove their global superiority. Leonid Brezhnev, who became General Secretary of the Community Party in 1964, said he considered Russia's top athletes to be front line fighters on the ideological front.

Scholar

With a national championship under his belt, Victor's thoughts returned to his education that he had suspended in order to sail. Most men his age had finished university and were embarked on a career. He decided he should begin further studies before he got any older. And if one had a university degree, he would be at a different level of society. He would major in sport because he was, after all, an athlete.

He went to the University at Nikolaev (Nikolaev State Pedagogical Institute), a huge shipbuilding center on the Black Sea, and took the entrance exams. He passed, and was accepted. The trouble started when he went to Anatoli Gajduk with his plan. As a student at the University in Nikolaev, he would keep sailing, and the results he got would belong to the Nikolaev Trade Union, not the Dnepropetrovsk Trade Union. Gajduk was loathe to lose one of his top sailors, telling Victor the trade union could arrange for him to study if that's what he wanted. Victor was set on Nikolaev because for one year at the Meteor Club his skipper had been a Nikolaev graduate. From him he had learned of the university's high academic standards, and about Nikolaev's fleet of the best boats and equipment made possible by donations from the nearby shipbuilding company.

A battle ensued. There was pressure at all levels. The Meteor Club suggested they should receive half of any points Victor accumulated while racing. Nikolaev said if Kovalenko sails for us, the points he collects will be ours since he is using our boats and equipment. Nikolaev recruited Victor aggressively, telling him if they found someone with equal skills he would lose his opportunity to have a higher education that was totally underwritten. Gajduk had to approve Victor's plan because an official transfer was involved, but he refused. Victor insisted it was his life, his decision, but Gajduk would not budge.

Determined to take his case to court, Victor went in search of a lawyer and came up empty. Gajduk was very influential within the system in Dnepropetrovsk. He knew all the officials, all the lawyers and the judges. The lawyers he consulted told Victor that Gajduk was right, and they could not help him. They said maybe he could make a case, but he would lose. Victor spent months exploring the possibilities, and finally had to admit he was not making progress. "I said if I cannot beat him, I have to go to him because it was a battle of principles. I was 24, he was twice my age, more experienced, a wise man. He was very good at running the Meteor Club, a good diplomat, very close to the Yuzhmash officials, very powerful in the trade union organizations. I respected him a lot. I went to him and I said you are the winner. I apologize for taking your time and energy, but I was trying to do the best for me. I was trying to fight you, but I lost because you have more power.

"Anatoli stood up and shook my hand and said, `Victor, you are a wise man. We will give you permission to go to Nikolaev. But don't forget we are your native club, you are our athlete. After you finish your studies come back home and we will do our best to support you in this life.' It was unbelievable."

The Meteor Club's loss was Nikolaev's gain. Having a national champion arrive on their campus was a happy day for the University officials. They told Victor he would be treated well because he would bring credit to the institute as Master of Sport, and that his "studies" would be a formality. "I said no, this is a new challenge for me," Victor says, "new knowledge, an interesting world. I want to be better in sport, and I will use this opportunity as a platform toward that goal. I intended to study hard.

"The students were six years younger than me, but unlike most of them, I was eager for these studies. It was cold, with snow on the ground. Some students were sleepy, late for their classes. I would wake up at 6, go running, eat a good breakfast, do my exercises, and would arrive at classes fresh. I became more and more ambitious, driving ahead."

The curriculum was both difficult and comprehensive. The study of sport at the university level was initiated in the Soviet Union after the revolution in 1917, and it grew to be as challenging as any other academic major by the mid-1970s. Courses included anatomy, chemistry, biology, physiology, history of sport, history of the Communist Party, politics of sport, Marxism, Leninism, methodology of sport, and the development of sport. Students had to learn basic techniques and physical requirements for many games, from basketball and soccer to rowing, tennis, and skiing. "We learned all the muscles and bones, the blood system, the bowels and kidneys, and how the demands on the body varied with different sports," Victor says. "We also studied effective medicines and treatments for athletic injuries."

His age and his aggressive approach to his studies made Victor stand out in the classroom. He recalls once having to present an answer to a professor's question in front of his anatomy class. The professor said his answer did not pass. The class stirred, expressing their disagreement with the professor. "The professor said they did not understand," Victor says. "He said I had a lot of character, that I was ambitious and always trying my best. But if he gave me a 5, the highest score, it would not serve me well because he thought I could do better. So he would suspend my score and ask me to answer that question one more time in a few days and be more ready. After this I was studying even more seriously. I went to all the lectures and sat in the front row because in the back they talked about girls. In the front you could focus on what the professor was saying."

In those days, the demand for beds in the USSR – from hotels to university dormitories – exceeded their availability. Solo travelers got used to the idea that the other bed in their hotel room would usually be occupied by a stranger. Victor says he met some interesting people that way, including a visiting professor of bio chemistry of sport, who was his roommate for a period at Nikolaev. The professor had written the text book Victor's class was using, and was working on a new book about blood systems. "In our room I talked with him about his work," Victor says, "so when they asked me in class to talk about oxygen transfer in the blood and the energy of the heart, I spoke about what I had learned from the professor. They said wow! this is something new. And I said yes, from the professor who is writing the book."

Victor looks back on his days at Nikolaev with satisfaction. He says it was a time of revolutionary developments in sport, with memorable professors in a variety of fields. "I feel I was in the front line of sports science," Victor says. "I learned a lot, got the highest marks, and a red diploma" (the equivalent of summa cum laude in the United States).

He kept sailing at Nikolaev, switching to 470s in 1977, but perhaps for the first and only time in his life, sailing was not Victor's primary focus. He attended a 20-day training camp each summer, and raced in many regattas, but while his younger classmates went to parties, evenings would find Victor focused on his books. Looking back, he thinks he was subconsciously preparing to be a coach during this phase of his life. "To understand what I needed to be successful in sport," he says, "I built a very good foundation of sport from all aspects. That helped me be a better athlete, and for sure prepared me to be a coach."

In his third year at the university, Victor concentrated on racing the 470 full time. At the European Championships that year, a regatta generally thought to be right behind the World Championships in importance, his team did poorly. He knew why: he and his skipper lacked experience in international competition. The Soviet system for sailing was comprehensive, run by two giants, the Navy and the trade union organizations. Both oversaw many different "minor league" sailing clubs of students and service people that were supported by industrial and military budgets. All of them competed against one another, which aligned nicely with the Soviet isolationist policy. But there is no substitute for international competition, which provides a close look at techniques and innovations other nationalities have developed.

Victor wasted little time bemoaning his performance at the European Championships. As usual, he focused on the why of it, and on the positive aspects of losing. "When you are sailing," he says, "and hopelessly behind, it gives you a great opportunity to practice, to create enthusiasm and spirit for racing. You cannot achieve those things when you are in front. It is all about the sword and the shield. When you win, you are sharpening your sword. When you are losing, you are working with your shield because you know why you lost and you will not repeat that in the future. The shield of young sailors is not strong because they don't have enough experience."

Later, when he first began coaching with the National Sailing Team, he would develop that concept into one of his guiding principles: the essential need for his athletes to change themselves for the better. "Nothing happens in this world without reason," Victor says. "Every setback is either a test, a warning, or a penalty. Every problem or bit of trouble we encounter can make us stronger, smarter, wiser. It's an important part of evolution, learning from setbacks, and from our adversaries. If you cannot understand it, if you ask `why me?' then your perception is wrong. But even if you pass one test, do not expect the next one to be easier. The next one will be harder, but it will be within your abilities. The Universe does not often test you above your abilities. When it does, you have to find a different way to manage it. Maybe it is a lesson for you to be tolerant, or it gives you the wisdom to accept what you cannot change."

An associated principle of Victor's is what he calls, with some amusement, the "Shit Index," a way of describing one's reaction to adversity. It comes under the general heading of *the art of communication with yourself under pressure*. "Something bad happens and people say `shit, aw fuck, I'm an idiot, it's happened again, oh no!' and they pound the counter, or their boat. When something difficult happens, you have to realize it is always good," Victor says. "It's one more test, one more opportunity to improve yourself. You can't improve your abilities when you are leading. There is pressure when you lead, but it is glory pressure and that's different. You can only improve yourself when something difficult happens, and your first reaction is very important."

From a practical standpoint, having a low Shit Index threshold is costly. Aside from the spike in blood pressure and loss of focus it causes, stopping to curse and carry on costs precious seconds of inactivity on the race course. "I think people in the American White House have the highest Shit Index threshold," Victor says. "Obama for sure. He is not emotional. He is balanced, judicious. He would say okay, this happened, let's make a decision how to deal with the situation. This is good because it will happen again and again and again. You are at the back of the fleet and instead of saying`aw shit! you gain one boat and you say beautiful, and you gain another boat and now you are 28th and you have to say "cool, I have a situation to test myself again, let's see who I am", and that's the point. If they understand this process, athletes are growing up as sailors and people – not only in sailing but in business, politics, everywhere. But you need a coach who reminds you. If something happens and you say 'shit,' I say 'no, no.' Psychology is the most interesting part of sailing."

Victor tells the story of Australian Nathan Wilmot, whom he ranks in the top 5% of sailors who have come to him with a huge amount of raw talent. Wilmot was also rebellious and hard-headed. In 2007 Wilmot had a large lead in the final race of the European Championships. But at the last mark, the wind first dropped to nothing then changed direction radically several times, leaving Wilmot at the back of the fleet. That race cost him the podium.

At the awards ceremony, Wilmot's Shit Index was red-lined. Victor found Wilmot drinking and complaining about his cruel fate on the race course. "I told him there are two approaches. One was to drink plenty of beer and tell everyone how you got screwed, how upset and frustrated you are. The other was to show strong character. Because the key to success in any sport, in any activity in this life, is strong character.

"In a tough situation you have to say, this will harden me. If you pass the test with pride, honor, and grace then you will become stronger. If you collapse, then what will happen if you meet the same situation again ? You will say bloody hell it's happened again and you will collapse again."

Victor suggested to Wilmot that instead of staying at the bar he had to say yes, it was a test, and he had to go home, listen to some music, have a good sleep and focus on the next event. Wilmot said okay, and went back to his hotel.

CHAPTER 5

Love

In 1978, after graduation from university, Victor hitch-hiked back to Dnepropetrovsk and rejoined the Trade Union team at the Meteor Club as he and Anatoli Gajduk had agreed. He was sailing for the team and also doing some coaching. He was living with his family in the same cramped apartment. Despite the good facilities of the Meteor Club, Victor found the sailing situation wanting. "For a coach boat, I found an old aluminum boat with a 10 hp engine. The sailboats were a disaster. They had to be brought up to speed. The sailors were loyal and hardworking, but there was no opportunity to move forward because of the equipment. They asked what they had to do. I told them set the bar high, study English because that is the gate to the new world."

Victor saw the woman he knew would be his wife on the trolley bus one day not long after he returned to Dnepropetrovsk. He says it was one of those moments when the world stops. He had had many girlfriends, had thought he had been in love with one or two of them, but when he saw Tatiana Savenkova, he knew he had found his mate. It was, truly, love at first sight. She was 18, fit and gorgeous, an athletic girl with wistful, wide-set green eyes over a model's high cheekbones. She was a track athlete who ran the 400 meters, Victor would later discover. And she could whistle through her teeth. Her beauty was striking, but Victor says he felt something deeper. She was struggling with a heavy bag, so Victor got off at her stop and offered to carry the bag for her.

Iryna Dvoskina, a celebrated track coach of Paralympic athletes in Ukraine, has been close with Tatiana since the two girls were in elementary school together. They were best friends when Tatiana met the man on the bus. "Tatiana said 'Can you imagine,' " Iryna recalls, "'one guy asks me if he could help carry my bags to my house. Then he asked to meet me again. I said no.' She was really young, 18 at the time. Victor was 28. She said she wouldn't meet him. Then a few days later she said, 'Can you imagine, he came and knocked on my door !' She was pretending she was not at home, not opening the door. But Victor is a pushy guy. I know him. He is pushy with everything. But I like high achievers, and that's Victor."

Thirty-seven years later, Tatiana still looks as if she could run a creditable 400. At their home in Sydney, she recalls her initial meeting with Victor. "He said, you need help and I said oh yes, please. I was visiting my mom and my grandmother had given me a lot of food. The bag was heavy. He found my house the next day. I knew he was a sportsman. I had seen his picture at the Sports Commission. I didn't imagine I would meet him. He starts smiling. I said uh oh. But my mom said he is an old man for you. I had plenty of boyfriends."

Victor was puttering in the kitchen as Tatiana reminisced. "Not boyfriends," he interjected. "Friends."

In 1978, Victor's persistence won him a date with Tatiana. She had agreed to meet him at a monument in a park. "She was one hour late," Victor recalls. "But I waited. I was a national champion with a choice of many girls, but I waited 15 minutes, then 30 minutes, an hour, an hour and five minutes. She arrived one hour seven minutes late. She thought she was seven minutes late, a confusion. I knew nothing except her first name. She told me she studied at the Institute of Sport in Dnepropetrovsk. We became friends."

"Tatiana's mother was very concerned about Victor being 10 years older," Iryna Dvoskina says. "In Ukraine, people married early in those days. A man who did not marry until he was 30 was very unusual. All of us

01 | Victor skiing as a child

Привет из
Днепропетровск
1953 г.

02 | Age three

03 | Family dinner

04 | Early sailing

05 | The M Class

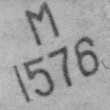

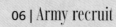
06 | Army recruit

07 |
Flying Dutchman crew

09 | Victor sailing 470 as a crew

10 | Wedding day

11 | Victor with medals, and Tatiana

12 | Newlyweds

13 | First car – a Lada

01 | Victor skiing as a child – At age two, Victor is introduced to skiing.

02 | Age three – Victor, age three, dressed for summer in the city.

03 | Family dinner – Victor, third from left (seated) at a family dinner in 1956.

04 | Early sailing – Jury-rigged bed sheets drove the first real boat Victor sailed.

05 | The M Class – Victor skippered a 25-foot M class dinghy when he was 14.

06 | Army recruit – Victor as a Soviet Army recruit in 1969, age 19.

07 | Flying Dutchman crew – In 1973, the Flying Dutchman trapeze harness was a work in progress.

08 | Regatta in Bulgaria – Kovalenko and other sailors from Ukraine, Russia, and Bulgaria at the Burgas Cup in Bulgaria. This was Victor's first trip to the West, in 1973.

09 | Victor sailing 470 as a crew – Working on his first 470 boat (Jeanneau Marine) in 1977, Sevastopol.

10 | Wedding day – Tatiana Savenkova and Victor on their wedding day in 1980.

11 | Victor with medals, and Tatiana – In 1981, Victor with Tatiana and his medals won as an athlete.

12 | Newlyweds – Mr. and Mrs. Victor Kovalenko, newlyweds in 1980.

13 | First car – a Lada – Victor with his first car, a Lada.

were questioning why he was not married. All my friends married before they finished university. But I played a big role in convincing Tatiana to marry Victor. Her dad had died of cancer when she was 16. And Victor was well-grounded in life. I could see he would be good for her future. But it was hard to convince her mom."

Victor helped with that problem. He got to know Tatiana's track coach, who gave a glowing report to Tatiana's mother about him. "My coach told her," Tatiana says, "he was the right man for me. But my mother kept worrying about his age." Finally, Mother agreed, with one stipulation: Tatiana would not marry until her 20th birthday.

It was a two year courtship, but with Tatiana studying and running track, and Victor constantly away training and sailing, they had precious little time together. Staying in touch by phone was difficult. Tatiana would have to go to Iryna's, where there was a telephone, and hope Victor could get a call through from the telecom station or post office where he was located. He'd have to wait in the queue for an hour to talk for three minutes, a conversation that was often cut short by interference.

Victor arrived back in Dnepropetrovsk one day before his wedding in 1980. There were 150 guests, sailors from all over the USSR, and school friends. The party went on for two days, after which the bride and groom went off on a friend's boat for a brief cruise. "We were married," Victor says with a big laugh, "one day after Tatiana turned 20."

Coaching

In 1979, Anatoli Gajduk had arranged a studio apartment for Victor, a momentous event. It made an excellent home for the newlyweds. Tatiana was studying for a second degree in teaching, an interest that had overcome track as a career. Victor's hard work in sailing – the constant traveling – paid off with a national championship in the 470 (with Michael Kudrjautsev) in 1981. After that, he was rewarded with a luxurious, three-bedroom apartment – free – from the government. He also bought his first car, a Lada, a boxy Russian-made sedan that has been the butt of jokes for 40 years: the difference between a Lada and a golf ball? You can drive a golf ball 250 yards. Why does the Lada have a heated rear window? So you can warm your hands while pushing it. But it was a car, a cherished object well beyond the grasp of most Russian citizens in 1981. The apartment and the car were timely. On November 24, 1981, Tatiana delivered a baby boy. They named him Vladimir.

Victor continued to be displeased with the equipment provided by the Meteor Club. Anatoli Gajduk had died of a stroke in 1983, and the boats and gear had been neglected after that. They were in serious need of upgrading. "We were sailing old boats, and the sails were so old they were yellow," Victor recalls, "but my skipper Michael Krudrjautsev's abilities were incredible." Victor and Michael won a lot in '81 and '82, and were on track to peak at the '84 Olympic Games in Los Angeles until the Russian boycott dashed their plans. The United States (and 59 other countries) had boycotted the Moscow Games in 1980 in response to the Soviet Union's invasion of Afghanistan in 1979. The boycott of the 1984 Games involving 14 Eastern Bloc countries, was widely considered to be retaliation for the 1980 boycott.

Victor and Michael decided to split in 1983, because they wanted to prep for the national games – the Spartakiada Narodov SSSR – a big competition between Soviet republics held every four years, and the two were from different republics. Victor found himself a Ukrainian skipper, and Michael engaged a Russian crew. Victor competed in Spartakiada, but was not up to speed with his new skipper. They did not compete in the 1984

Friendship Games, held in Russia at the same time as the Olympic Games in Los Angeles.

Victor's racing career had ended prematurely, and the situation at the Meteor Club was not improving. He was enjoying his first real coaching job, but felt that his hands were tied by the Soviet's isolationist policies. "I needed access to equipment not made in the Soviet Union," he says, "and access to more information, better training camps, international regattas... we needed boats and masts from France and Germany, and North Sails."

Victor again took pen in hand. This time he wrote a treatise on coaching, a lengthy document that critiqued what was commonly being practiced, and advanced his ideas toward what needed to be done. One might ask how someone with Victor's limited hands-on coaching experience would have the temerity to produce such a document, but Victor was 34 at the time, an athlete of Grand Master ranking (having won two national championships), and with the equivalent of a summa cum laude university degree in sport behind him. He'd been involved in coaching since his university days, and if Victor is involved in something, he is fully involved. As Iryna Dvoskina has observed, he was a pushy guy, a high achiever with a head full of ideas.

"I wrote about the structure of the coaching system," Victor says. "The methodical sense of coaching at that time was all about modeling situations. Back then everything focused on the amount of time spent in the boat. Everyone thought more and more hours in the boat would make you a champion. I said that more time was needed for fitness programs, and tactics and strategy sessions that should be learned ashore in classrooms. Many situations could be modeled in the classroom, then executed on the water. And lots more psychology should be included."

The document has been lost, one of the very few papers or photographs Victor has not carefully filed over the years. The lineup of bulging, three-ring binders on his book shelves contain notes and hand-drawn graphs from training and coaching sessions dating from the 1980s that meticulously document attendees, wind speed and direction, the nature of the current, numbers indicating how sailors were feeling (along with their weights), results, and a raft of other pertinent data (some of which is still confidential). But alas, the treatise on coaching is not among the other papers. "It's too bad it is lost," Victor says. "I'd like to read it again myself."

Victor sent the document to the national team, and to his trade union team. The trade union's response was measured. They liked the ideas, saw the potential, said that maybe something could be developed along the lines Victor suggested, and if so, he would be involved in helping prepare the trade union team. The response of the national team, which was run and coached by the Navy, was more direct. "They said come work for the Navy in the Central Navy Club in Moscow," Victor recalls. "I waited to see if something more would come from the trade union, because I had been sailing for them a long time, from 1973 to 1983 in Flying Dutchman and the 470, and I was loyal to them. But they said wait until the next training camp and we will see. The Navy said come to us now. I said okay to the Navy because time was factor number one.

"The Navy was a monster. To fight them would be difficult. The Navy was consistent. They always sent the same two teams to international regattas, and those guys kept improving because they were getting experience, being exposed to modern trends and ideas, information, equipment. Even if the trade union had strong teams they sent them here and there without a plan. If you go once or twice to international regattas and you are there for a short time, can you improve? Yes, but not enough."

Big Time

Victor returned to the Central Navy Club in Moscow where he had finished his military service, but this time as a civilian employee. He was working as a junior coach. In appreciation of Victor's age and maturity, in addition to his expertise and his balanced, philosophical approach to competition, his superiors would often send him to regattas as mentor/ crew for younger skippers. His salary was a pittance, 110 Rubles a month (about $50 USD), so small that Tatiana wondered how they would make ends meet. He had been paid more working at the Meteor Club. Victor asked for help, and was told that the scale had been approved by the Minister of Defense and could not be changed. He was told if he wanted more money, they could put him in the Navy and give him some rank, make him a senior sailor and he would get three times the salary. Or they could put him in one of the fleets, maybe on a submarine where he would make five times as much.

"I said no," Victor recalls. "I had to be independent. If I were a senior sailor, the fleet would dictate to me, force me to promote their sailors, select them for the national team. If I didn't agree to do that, they would keep me away from competitions, confine me to the vessel. They would have control. So I remained a civilian and took less money."

He was not living in Moscow. The training system for sailors was decentralized. There were training camps in Sochi, Sevastopol, Tallinn, and other centers on the Black and Baltic Seas. He traveled constantly. The typical monthly schedule involved working 20 days at one of the training centers, and having ten days at home.

Citing a good team atmosphere, Victor says his treatise on coaching did not antagonize the Central Navy Club coaching staff. But Oleg Ilyin, who is currently the General Secretary of the Russian Sailing Federation, paints a slightly different picture. Ilyin was a leading coach of the Navy team when Victor arrived on the scene. "He was young, just the beginner of a coach," Ilyin writes of Victor. "Add to this the typical suspicions of the older coaches, veterans of the National Soviet Team who were not wishing to move aside to give up space for any novice."

Victor remembers Ilyin fondly. "Oleg was one of the first who saw my potential to be a coach," Victor says. "He was a good psychologist who had a big impact on my development. Oleg put a coaching virus in my blood."

He worked with the junior sailors for a year or so. He says if he brought anything different to the job, it was stressing the regularity and consistency – the necessity – of sailing under all conditions. This gave him a reputation as a tough coach in the eyes of the sailors. Even if a bad storm was forecast, Victor would move ahead with the scheduled plan to sail. "When it started to blow, my sailors would ask what to do, and I would say rig the boats, we will sail. I did not say sailing was canceled, or we could sail but it would be dangerous. They would come to the launching ramp with the boats rigged, and if the weather had gotten bad I would find a reason not to sail, like the motor boat was broken. But it was important they were ready to sail no matter the conditions. They got up for it: the wind is strong, it could be dangerous, but we can do it. They were ready, mentally. That's probably what was different."

The M.O.

Beginning in 1983, the National Sailing Team was collecting women sailors from all over the USSR to begin training for the Olympic Games in Korea in 1988. That year it had been announced that women would be invited to sail in the Olympics for the first time. The 470 was one of the classes designated for women's teams. This pleased Victor, but it would not have a direct impact on him until 1985, when the national team was selected. Coaching positions were also assigned at that time. Victor thought he was in line for head 470 women's coach, but lost the job to a former Flying Dutchman coach. It was a political choice. "They told me I did not have enough experience," Victor says.

Victor was given a women's team to coach. "They said okay, we give you a chance to do some coaching," he says. "There were many women from Moscow, and only one from Dnepropetrovsk. That's who they gave me to keep me busy." Her name is Larisa Moskalenko, and while she was an excellent athlete, she had little competitive sailing experience. Victor had watched her compete in her specialty, the sea pentathlon, a grueling, para-military event that included distance swimming, an on-the-water obstacle course, shooting, and rowing. He was impressed by how furiously Larisa worked to win.

Oleg Ilyin remembers her well. "Don't forget she was only 17," he writes. "She was as beautiful as a young pretty girl can be, a girl but with all the women's `instruments,' also in full consciousness of how attractive she was, and looking upon the world with widely opened, ambitious, vivid eyes."

"She was so determined," Victor says of Larisa. "When she was older, she once entered a rowing race after not competing for many years, maybe on a bet, I don't know. But she won it, and after the finish I thought she might expire, she had worked so hard. She was white as a sheet, hardly able to stand up."

Larisa arrived with a crew, Iryna Chunykhovska, who was light for the 470, and also too short by 470 standards. "Iryna also competed in sea pentathlon," Victor says, "and she was very dynamic. I thought okay, we will find another crew, but temporarily, Larisa will sail with Iryna."

Perhaps it was the near Mission Impossible of bringing two rank amateur sailors to Olympic level competitors in three years that caused Victor to formulate what has become his modus operandi. Time (and timing) has always been of primary importance to him. Victor says there are three factors in any endeavor : "Time, System, and Money. The system has to do with experience, coaches and managers, sailmakers, etc. Money is only a tool to reach your goal — if money is your goal you are wasting your time — but Time is number one, because time is always limited, and can never be altered."

From the outset, Victor's approach has been grounded in simplicity. "My job is to supply people with basic, structured messages," he says. "Because the decisions they make on the water have to be absolutely fast, even in advance of the moment. A half second can be too early or too late. Superfast is sometimes not fast enough. So I have a lot of tricks, models and matrixes in the system — many graphs and drawings — to help sailors make decisions and operate successfully. The key to our training is what to do, where to do it, and when to do it."

Strength of character has been the foundation of Victor's coaching philosophy from the beginning. But of course that presumes the participant is well-trained, technically and physically, one of the very best at his game. To accomplish that, when he first started coaching sailing, Victor brought what he'd learned from other sports to the table. "Tennis, badminton, volleyball, "he says, "they are the same as sailing. They require fast reactions, and you have to be smart with strategies and tactics. Tennis is more a head game. In tennis you have maybe two times more time to think about a shot than in badminton. In light wind, sailing is more like tennis. In stronger winds, it is more like badminton. It requires lightning reflexes. I learned a lot from badminton. I was playing myself, and watching the best people. They would take one element, one stroke or shot, and would do it many times, over and over. They divided the game into small elements, and practiced those elements. So I broke down sailing the same way."

There's little doubt that the necessity of making Larisa and Iryna into top 470 sailors in barely three years was the mother of the coaching fundamentals Victor would develop for the rest of his career. Over lunch one day, I asked him about how he approached the enormous task of teaching the two women the complicated basics of racing a high performance dinghy like the 470 in world class competition. Victor took my pen and sketched this Magic Box on a napkin.

Basics	Boat Speed	Starts	Tactics	Strategy
Fitness	Boat handling technique	Vision of line	Weather mark	Wind strategy
Intelligence	Tuning	Positioning	Leeward mark	Fleet strategy
Psychology	Selection of equipment	Acceleration	Open water	Regatta strategy

Then he explained it. Across the top are the major categories involved in racing a boat: Basics, Boat Speed, Starts, Tactics, and Strategy. Under each of those headings are listed the essentials of each category. Looking at it, my eyes started doing circles as I thought about my own sailing career that began at age 9. Over the years I had worked on many items on the chart, but I had never thought to organize them in a way that made any sense. I was a weekend sailor, never a top of the fleet regular, but even so I applied myself. I read books, I observed, I practiced, had some good days. Even though I consider myself a quick study, it was slow going. What a difference it would have made if I had woken up one morning and found Victor's concise little chart under my pillow; how many years of trial and error it would have saved me! Because in very little space and with few words this Magic Box is all any sailor needs to understand what's required to be competitive. It is deceptively simple, like flying Indian fighter kites or printing black and white photographs. Most anyone can achieve what it calls for on a rudimentary level. But mastery takes tens of thousands of hours; even more to attain Olympic potential. But as a comprehensive, easy reference guide of what is required, the Magic Box is as good as it gets. It's something sailors need when they begin racing, and it will be just as valuable if they are going for a second Olympic Gold Medal.

"Under *Basics*," Victor says, "we have sailing intelligence, your level of education in aerodynamics, weather, hydrodynamics, the rules, how sails work, all this theory. The psychology of sailing has to do with your attitude when you get in the boat – your approach, your degree of confidence, your mental readiness.

"Under *Boat Speed* are techniques, or boat handling…" (practice 20-30 hours a week for a couple years, come back, and then we'll move on). "Tunings are the scores of things on the boat that can be adjusted individually and in combination, like sail trim and shroud tension; then selection of materials or just materials, what to buy – this boat, that mast, this sail…. When you are at the *top* top, it becomes 'development of materials' because you can't buy them, you have to develop them.

"Under *Starts* you begin with vision of the starting line. Then it is the positioning game where you select where you want to be on the line and obtain it or protect it. And then acceleration. Maybe you can see the line and you have a good position but if you accelerate one second too late you are dead. One second means everything in some situations. One second too early and you are dead as well because you are OCS (over the line early: "On the Course Side").

"*Tactics* are easy, they only apply when boats meet. Tactics are actions taken to obtain or maintain an advantage. Tactics take place in three places — at the upwind mark, the downwind mark, and in open water. You use tactics to execute strategy.

"*Strategy* begins with wind strategy: where is the wind from and what is it doing, trending to the right or left, increasing or decreasing? Before each race question number one is always wind strategy, how to approach the race given the wind conditions. There are many sources of information: the internet reports, a coach who can mislead you, flags, local knowledge, history, smoke, other boats, wind patterns on water... Also conditions, waves and wind together. Light wind calls for different strategy than strong wind. If the wind is strong and that's your strength and it is club racing, your strategy is to have fun because you know you will kill all of them.

"Then there is fleet strategy. Maybe you only have to beat one boat, so never mind the wind. You have to cross him and stay ahead. Race and regatta strategy depends on the format: how many races, how many discards? If there is only one race, to win you have to maximize risk. If there are 20 races, a marathon, minimize risk because if you are conservative you will be the winner if you have good speed. Next look at the competitors: who is your main competition and what are their strengths and weaknesses?"

The discussions stimulated by the Magic Box will last a lifetime. Its genius is that every element of sailing is contained within it.

Victor's four-year plan for Olympic readiness compliments the Magic Box by establishing how the various essentials will be approached if he is your coach.

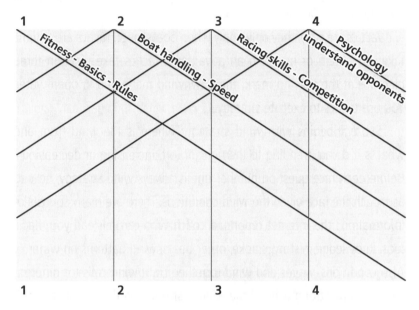

The first year the emphasis is on fitness (basics from the Magic Box). Year two, boat speed and boat handling (starts, tactics). Year three, racing skills and a large volume of competition. Year four, psychology: understanding your opponent(s) and the effect of conditions on the race course (strategy). And now the work on character becomes primary. It's all accumulative, with the emphasis from years one, two, and three being sustained throughout the four-year program as each new element is added.

With those two little illustrations tucked in a jacket pocket, it's quite easy for even novice sailors like Larisa and Iryna to understand the job at hand. Any questions? Okay, let's get to work.

The elements of the Magic Box and the 4-year plan took shape in the very private, small, 3-ring notebook Victor has been keeping since the

1970s. He has three copies, so concerned is he about losing it. He always has one on the motor boat with him, another copy where he is staying when on the road, and a third copy at home. All are updated regularly. The notebook is written in hand, in English for every day entries; in Russian for important entries; using an English/Cyrillic hybrid for very important things; and in number code known only to Victor for extremely sensitive material. He says he reads through it a couple times every week – "or why bother keeping it?"

Oleg Ilyan was impressed by Victor's approach. "I looked after Victor and what he was doing," Ilyan writes. "We talked a lot, and I could see how hungry he was for every bit of fresh knowledge, how he tried to use in his practical work all the achievements of the Soviet Sport Training System which was based on strong scientific background. This was the reason he grew so rapidly as a coach. He showed himself as a coach of completely new formation: intellectual, full of modern knowledge, with the ability to employ his knowledge in line with sailing. He also was, and of course is, extremely consistent, self-disciplined, and with clear vision of the goals of the training."

Victor says when he was a young coach, his product was *results*. But as he gained experience his vision kept changing. *Sailors* took over from results, because it's the sailors who produce the results. Then the *system* replaced sailors, because the system is what produces the good sailors. After a few more years, *principles* and *truths* prevailed. Principles are what has been discovered: how sails work, or tactical principles like staying between your opponent and the mark once you are ahead of him, or making the first tack after the start the longest. "It's the same as chess that has been developing for hundreds of years," Victor says. "Now everyone knows the various options available for specific situations.

Sailing is the same. We know what happens when we pull tension on the boom vang. Fifty years ago there was no vang. Then someone said we have to control the leech tension of the sail, so the boom vang got invented. The vang also controls mast bend. Step by step we learn how to do it. Principles in tuning, tactics, race strategy, wind analysis develop quickly.

"There are principles of psychology. For example, you cannot say to sailors, `Don't do this.' That is a principle. Because if you say `don't do this,' they will definitely do it. You will give them a magnet if you say, `Don't start at the pin end of the line !,' because they will start at the pin end every time. In their heads there will only be one word : pin pin pin pin. You have to say 'start in the middle, or start at the committee boat,' and they might do it."

Victor laughs. "If God told a group of ten sailors how they could win a race — tell them where to start, tell them how many tacks left and right and the duration of each tack so they would be first at the weather mark, first at the finish — only one of the ten would do it. The others would say `oh but we were getting a nice lift on the left,' or `there was more wind pressure on the right.'

"Being positive is another principle. Lots of coaches are negative, screaming at their athletes and abusing them. This is not right. As soon as you don't follow principles you will be penalized."

Victor says the concept of truth is more about life, a vision of the big picture. "Principles apply to the technology of preparation, the technology of performance," he says. "The rest is about life because athletes are not only racing, they are living. They have a life. In that area truth is working : friendships, love, success. Here is a truth : I say to sailors trust yourself and follow your dreams."

Back in 1984, with Larisa and Iryna, it was about results. The women brought the essential commitment to the boat, essential because even in those early days unless his sailors were ready to be on time every day and put full effort into the program, Victor was not interested in working with them. As Australian sailing journalist Di Pearson has observed, "Victor puts in 120%, and asks 110%." By all accounts, Victor was a very hard man in those days. His tolerance for lateness, for less than 100% commitment, was non-existent. As he likes to repeat, sailing for fun costs little in time or money, and doesn't require a system. Sailing for results requires much time, much money, and a good system. Sailing for glory – world class and Olympic medals – requires all your time, all your money, and a superb system. When he says glory needs it all, that she is a capricious girl, he means it. Show up a few minutes late on the race course for practice, and Victor will have motored on. Be late more than once and it could be weeks before he will even acknowledge your presence.

Taking advantage of both women's superior athletic abilities – Larisa's manic intensity, and Iryna's unbridled enthusiasm, Victor drilled them unmercifully on the water, performing "from the ground up" modeling for these two. They tacked and jibed, hoisted, set, jibed and doused spinnakers many thousands of times until they could go through the maneuvers while semi-conscious. "Sail trim is a feeling you get from time in the boat," Victor says. "It has to do with how the boat is balanced. After a while you can feel leech tension in your shoulders."

Victor tested the women's fitness every month. "One of the keys to their success was fitness," Victor says. "Iryna could do 15 chin-ups. Larisa could do ten because she was heavier. They could run all day. Their endurance was high. They did not tire as much as the other teams. And if they capsized, they could right the boat easily because they could do chin-ups. If other women's teams capsized, they were finished because they could not right the boat."

As for teaching the women tactics and race strategy, Victor was doing his homework by having a bi-lingual friend translate articles in American sailing magazines like *Sailing World*, and *Sail*. "I read interviews with top American sailors," Victor says. "I remember one very interesting piece by Dave Ullman about how to race in big fleets. He said you can be more conservative with 100 boats on the starting line. In small fleets, you have to take more risks. But in a big fleet, you can win without ever finishing a race in the top 3. Consistency is what counts most. I shared all that with Larisa and Iryna, we talked about it. The fundamentals for tactics are based on the rules, and they knew the rules very well, word for word. We had tests on the rules all the time.

"Debriefs were another key. After every training session, after every race, we would have a debrief session, talk about what was right, what was wrong, how to improve, why this or that had happened, what was the key. Weather was a factor of course, but we were not big experts in weather back then. There were no global forecasts like we have now. We could only apply what we knew at the time."

As for the psychological aspect of bringing Larisa and Iryna to a top competitive level, Victor says both women arrived with strong, winning characters. "My approach was to give them racing experience," Victor says, "talk to them about racing psychology. They not only needed to be eager to win, but they had to learn how to manage risk, make good decisions under pressure, and control themselves. Wanting to win isn't enough. It was a big test for them, and a big test for me because at the time I was not very experienced in international competitive racing.

We were in the same situation. We had pressure from all sides. It was a tough time, different from now."

Different, Victor explains, in several ways. The equipment available to him and his team was a far cry from what is currently available. "Now we use a new jib and spinnaker for every regatta," he says. "Back then we had one spinnaker and maybe two jibs to use for one year. And the boats were copies of American Vanguard boats that were made in the USSR. A few times I went to the factory and was building boats myself, using fiberglass, involved in the process. Only in that way could I customize the boats a little, make them stiffer by building up certain areas, or flexible by removing material."

All this was happening during the transition between the old Communist system that had been in place for many years versus the new changes President Gorbachev was trying to bring about. "Gorbachev made everything open, understandable," Victor says. "He imagined a new life for everyone, said we have to move in new ways to keep up with the world, not like the restrictive policies of Stalin or Brezhnev. And of course sport, which had long been a tool to promote socialism over capitalism, was caught in the middle. To live in a transition time is always difficult."

Victor says Larisa was stable and smart, while Iryna was more emotional. "But that they were different was a good thing. If both were the same, they would not make a good team. Crew personalities must complement each other, work together like a mast and a sail."

A big deterrent to coaching for Larisa and Iryna was the travel restriction imposed by the Soviet Union. Until 1985, all their training and development — and Victor's growth as a coach — had to take place exclusively in the USSR. Despite that obstacle, the Soviet 470 men's teams had done well. Using Vanguard boats built in the U.S.A. by the Harken brothers, North sails and Russian gear, the men had curried favor with the Soviet sailing authority by winning the European Championships in 1977 and 1978. Otherwise they were competing only against other Russian sailors, an unthinkable situation for today's athletes with Olympic dreams.

Breakthrough

Then, in 1985, a breakthrough : the women were allowed to represent their country at the 470 World Championships in Marina de Cararre, Italy. Victor did not accompany them. He had been assigned as their personal coach, not made a national coach. The women did not do well in Italy, but at home they were emerging as a dominant team, winning the 470 national championship in 1986. Later in 1986, racing in a strong fleet at the Goodwill Games, they won a bronze medal behind the Johnson sisters from Canada (gold), and Americans JJ Isler and Pam Healy (silver). The next year they went to regattas in France and East Germany, finishing poorly, but again won the Soviet national championship.

Victor repeatedly petitioned the authority for new boats, sails, and equipment, but was told there was no money. In 1986, Vanguard had been sold. "Suddenly the authorities decided let's try because the sailors are good, they've had good results in homemade equipment, but they have lacked consistency," Victor says. "So they bought good boats for us – Ziegelmayer's from Germany – and new sails, and we were on fire."

The Federation would not commit to sending the women to the Olympics. Instead, they allowed them to participate in Garda Week (now Garda-Trentino Olympic Week), a big international regatta in Italy. Victor was told if the women did well there, the authorities would consider sending them to the Olympics at Pusan, Korea in 1988.

Victor has good memories of Garda Week for two reasons. It was the first time he met the Australians and their legendary coach, Mike Fletcher, who held the record (at the time) for producing the most Olympic and World Championship winning performances. And Larisa and Iryna would register their first international success, a silver medal. Only Australia beat them. And it had blown hard all week, not ideal conditions for the light-weight Iryna on the wire. Victor was impressed. So was the sailing federation. "They said okay," Victor says, "send the women's 470 team to the Games. We had a good Soling team, a good catamaran team, and a very strong Finn sailor. They felt the 470 women had no chance, but their attitude was to build for the future."

Pusan was expected to offer light conditions. But when Victor took his team there for a test event in 1987, the first thing they noticed was that all the trees were supported with wire stays attached to stakes hammered deep into the ground. Then they saw the sea conditions: "Huge big waves and very strong wind. When the current was against the wind, conditions were very difficult. We had to get training in strong wind. We had to replace Iryna. But then we said no, we can't get a better crew than her. Her techniques were very good, and she worked very hard. She had become a top crew."

Training in Vladivostok was the solution. Vladivostok was a high-security naval base in those days, a 10-hour flight to the east. The harbor there is on Ussuri Bay with the Sea of Japan beyond, open to the south and the strong prevailing winds. All went well in Vladivostok until the last day when it was blowing 25 knots with higher gusts. "I said to myself I am crazy to send them out in these conditions," Victor recalls. "They could be injured, or break equipment, and I am saying why did I do this ? But they sailed well, never capsized, and had great downwind speed. I said they are in really good shape, ready for the Games."

Victor was right. They were ready for the wild conditions thrown at them in Pusan. Larisa and Iryna won a bronze medal, behind the USA (Gold) and Sweden (Silver). For the first time ever, the Soviet women beat the vaunted East German team. The 470 sailors won the only Soviet sailing medals at the 1988 Olympic Games. The highlight for Victor was Larisa and Iryna's victory in Race 4. "When they won that race" Victor says, "I knew I had not lived my life for nothing."

CHAPTER 6

Teams

Larisa Moskalenko acquired a new crew. The question of Iryna Chunykhovska's physical self being below standard (too short, too light) for the 470 had been an underlying issue from the outset. Iryna's outstanding athletic ability and excellent dynamics in the boat had made her a top crew, as Victor has acknowledged. He says she was the best he has coached on the difficult downwind legs, when catching waves for planing runs is so dependent on the constant, athletic dance of the crew shifting weight and applying pressure to the boat at precise moments. But Victor admits the strain on her was telling. "We always spoke of her being too light, too short, and were always testing crews of a more suitable size. She was working very hard to prove to us she was a good sailor." Iyrna never stopped being apprehensive about being replaced, and after sailing four years with Larisa, that pressure served to undermine the women's relationship.

For sheer intensity, the skipper/crew relationship in a two-person Olympic-quality sailing team ranks with that of figure skating pairs. Imagine spending a thousand hours a year training hard on an unstable, uncomfortable, wet and often cold 16-foot platform where every movement – every thought ! – must be coordinated with your partner. "Team," as in two-person sailing team, takes on very special emphasis. On boats like the Star and most of the dinghies that are sailed by two people, the names of both sailors are always mentioned because both are equally responsible for results. A unique combination of personalities is required to prevent the team from coming apart at the seams; to prevent blame, ego, or frustration from creating disarray.

An Olympic campaign lasts at least 4 years. Most teams need two or even three campaigns before they either win a medal, or decide to call it quits. Marital relationships seem simple and easy by comparison. Keeping a dinghy team's relationship healthy and smooth is every coaches' daunting challenge.

With Victor's teams, it has always been a tight, three-way collaboration. He may as well be the third person in the boat. Communication is constant, personal, and in today's world, also by telephone, email, Skype, and Face Time. With all three people eating, living, and breathing sailing nearly 100% of the time, ideas about everything from how a sail might be redesigned to concepts of centerboard flexibility to another half inch of mast bend flow like a river. Notepads are kept on bedside tables for recording midnight inspirations.

Victor makes sure his teams are apart when not actually training. As he says, athletes also need to live, and he makes sure they have that opportunity. His current 470 team, Mathew Belcher and Will Ryan, is a prime example of how well it can work. Belcher is a six-time 470 World Champion, an Olympic gold medalist (London, 2012). By the time Rio rolls around in 2016 Mathew will have been with Victor for 16 years, "half my life," he often says. Their communication is often telepathic. "I will motor toward their boat during practice to suggest a bit more cunningham tension," Victor says, "and as I approach Mat will pull more cunningham. He called me once to tell me something important. I said Rike (his wife) is pregnant. He said, `How did you know?!'"

Ryan has been Belcher's crew since just after London. Together, in 2013-15, they ran up an extraordinary string of 18 straight regatta victories including the World and European Championships. As of August, 2015, they were ranked #1 in the world in the 470. If there were a ranking for compatibility, they would no doubt top that list too. Two more balanced, calm, intelligent, and also interesting and likable athletes would be hard to find. Their personalities would seem to be more similar than Victor considers ideal, but the two work together like toast and jam.

"Will is amazing, extremely talented," Victor says. "It's difficult for him. He is often caught in the middle when Mathew and I have different opinions. He must keep a good relationship with Mathew, so his position is not easy. He is diplomatic, but accurate. And if he understands something will impact the team's performance, he has enough guts to know it is not time for diplomacy. He can tell it to me straight – or to Mathew. Mathew listens to him. Will is often the swing vote."

Larisa and Iryna were friends before Victor began coaching them, so his job of integrating himself as the "third person" was even more difficult. Their bronze medal at Pusan was testament to how well the trio succeeded. But in the end, Larisa couldn't help obsessing about a taller, heavier crew, and Iryna was replaced.

Larisa's new crew was Olena Pakholchik, a tall girl originally from Belarus who had given up basketball for sailing. Olena's husband is Ukrainian sailing coach Dimitri Tsalik, a former 470 sailor on the Soviet national team who was also coached by Victor. Dimitri says that when the Olympic Committee opened up sailing for women, several athletes interrupted their sport of choice to try this new game. In 1985, Olena was invited to observe a sailing regatta. She liked it, and began sailing with a former tennis player who had taken the helm of a 470. "Olena was not really tall enough for basketball," Dimitri says, "but for the 470 she was just right." Olena and her tennis player skipper sailed together two years. Victor first met Olena at a national regatta. Olena says she started working with Victor six months before the 1988 Olympic Games in Pusan.

"She was tall, a fast runner," Victor says of Olena, "but in the boat she was inexperienced, slow. In the first world championship, Larisa and Olena finished 10th. Larisa said maybe she should go back to Iryna, but I said no. Let's do one more year. Iryna was outstanding, but we will make Olena outstanding as well."

Father and Son

There was another sailor Victor had been working with in his spare time, his son, Vladimir. Victor rues the fact that because his job has always required so much travel it has drastically reduced the time he could have spent with his son. "I have spent more time with the sailors I coach than with my son," he will often say. His dream, he says, is to fly a kite with his son. "I bought the kite years ago," he says. "It is still in the garage."

But Vladimir, a tall, confident young man who is the Operational Manager for Australian National Car Parks Pty Ltd in Sydney, doesn't seem to carry any resentment. "I remember great time we spent together," he says. "His mind was always trying to be with me, but I know it was back in the coach boat or thinking about sailing. But when he was home, he put effort into it, compensating for being away. We played hide and seek in the house. He taught me swimming at age four or five by throwing me off the front of the motor boat and making me swim to the back. I flew to Sochi with him to training camp. He let me drive the motor boat, and put me in an Opti, showed me how to control it."

Victor also taught Vladimir, who was too tall to skipper, how to crew in a 470, a job he knew well. "He never tried to train me," Valdimir says, "he just exposed me to the ways you can appreciate something. I was a kid, just sailing and fooling around, pulling the spinnaker lines and collapsing the sail just for the fun of it. He came up in the motor boat and said, Jean Claude Van Damme would never let the sail do that. Van Damme, the martial artist, was a big hero of mine at the time. Victor always knew what to say. All the way back to the sailing club the spinnaker never collapsed once. He showed me how to do it, but if I failed he didn't start yelling at me. He kept it simple.

"He showed us secrets about how to train. He drew a picture on how to turn a mark. Then he said go out and do circles around the mark, tack jibe tack jibe nonstop for fifteen minutes. He saw me looking for lines on the boat during maneuvers and said no no, you don't look for them, you have to know where they are. He said the skipper doesn't need to tell the crew when to jibe or tack because the crew should feel it. So I asked the skipper to stop telling me, I wanted to feel it. I made a few mistakes, then I started to feel it. We talked about other things in the boat, but not tacks and jibes."

Valdimir and his skipper would win the junior 470 nationals in 1996. Vladimir was 15 years old. "He helped us get there," Vladimir says, "with a few small secrets and a couple training sessions. He's a great coach."

Land boat

Working with Olena caused Victor to come up with the land boat. Like so many good ideas, it was simple. In winter, Victor wheeled a 470 lashed on a trailer into a gymnasium. He raised the mast, attached the boom, hoisted sails, and attached the boom vang. Then he put Olena in the boat in her crew position, clipped to the trapeze wire with her feet on the rail. It was a new and very efficient way to break down the crew's job into elements that could be endlessly repeated. On the land boat, Olena would go through the routine of tacking, over and over, a procedure that often seems impossible to manage with only two hands. Olena would bend her knees to get back in the boat while disconnecting from the trapeze wire; duck under the boom while avoiding the vang and grabbing the new jib sheet; snapping the old jib sheet out of the jam cleat as she grasped the new trapeze wire and clipped in while trimming the new sheet as she planted her feet on the rail and straightened her legs. Elapsed time for a good tack in medium strength wind: three and a half to four seconds from helm down to acceleration on the new tack.

Olena would be doing as many as 400 tacks a day on the land boat. Very quick tacks in succession, and then extra slow motion tacks that would be called for in light wind, which are very physical and demanding. And 200 jibes every day, spinnaker jibes disconnecting and reattaching the pole, and takedowns, getting the spinnaker stowed quickly and the jib drawing before rounding a mark and coming into the wind. To make it even more challenging, Victor hung bells on the mast that would ring if Olena's movements were not smooth enough.

The land boat training paid off. In 1991, Larisa and Olena won the women's 470 world championships in Long Beach, California (Americans JJ Isler and Pam Healy were third). "They were excellent with all maneuvers," Victor says proudly. "They were a racing machine. At the medal ceremony, an American couple was standing next to me. The guy said to his wife he never thought it would happen in his life he would stand for the raising of the Soviet flag on American soil."

Confusion

That was very possibly the last time the Soviet flag would be raised on American soil, or anywhere else. Back home, events of the past three years – starting with the Geneva Accords in 1988, a conciliatory gesture to the West that included Soviet withdrawal from Afghanistan – were eating away at the very foundation of the Soviet system. The precise, militaristic chain of command under which the Soviets regulated all aspects of the country was in a shambles. President Mikhail Gorbachev's domestic reforms (Perestroika) had caused an economic tail spin. His struggle against the old imperial Communist elite (and the military-industrial complex) had culminated in a coup in August, 1991. The coup failed, but still undermined Gorbachev's power. Soviet Republics began contemplating sovereignty. Victor's home republic of Ukraine was among them.

But for Victor and his team, 1991 had been a good year. After receiving an invitation from the Spanish to come sail with them, Victor went in search of a sponsor. The invitation was too good to refuse, and it was a long trip: 2200 miles from Moscow to Barcelona. Through a string of connections he had established – Victor rarely forgets a name or a contact – he approached the Osama Company in Italy, makers of writing instruments. They were interested. Victor asked if they could help with transportation. "I went to Milan," Victor says, "spoke with their president. He said the best they could do was a Fiat Panda."

The 1991 Fiat Panda is a small, boxy car powered by a 34-horsepower engine that delivers 40 miles per gallon. Top speed, as listed by the factory, is 78 miles an hour. With the boat lashed on top, overhanging the car on each end and both sides, with the 22 foot mast somehow strapped alongside the boat on the roof, and with three people and all their gear crammed inside, the Ukranian women's 470 team was a sight when it pulled into the parking lot where a regatta was being held. Victor says he, Larisa, and Olena drove 21,000 kilometers in the

Panda that year, from the Ukraine into Spain, France, Holland, Germany, Norway; round trips all.

"Once, in Italy between Genova and San Remo on the coast road, the cops stopped us and said we had to take the mast off the car," Victor says. "I said no, we can't move it. They said we had to pay $100 fine. I nearly cried, told them that was almost one year of my salary! They let us go."

In Spain they drafted behind buses in order to go fast. But they were overloaded. One night Victor smelled fuel, so they stopped. "I saw the fuel line had been worn through by the tire rubbing it. I duct-taped the fuel line. The car started running badly because the glue from the duct tape got into the fuel. We went past a scrap place full of cars. I jumped over the fence with my tools, found a wrecked Panda, took off the carburetor and put it on our car."

It was a successful, year-long road trip, highlighted by Larisa and Olena's 1st place finish at Kiel Week, and their silver medal in the European Championships at Bergen, Norway. But the news from home was unsettling. Victor checked in with his head coach, Stanislov Oreshkin, who was extremely nervous. "He said, 'where are Larisa and Olena?' I said they are training, racing. He said his superiors in the system were very nervous. They had told him if the women didn't return to the Soviet Union he would be sent to prison. Having them outside the country was a big risk. He had told his bosses that he trusted the women, that having them sailing at international regattas was good for business. He had a new vision, a new understanding of the demands of the sport. But it was very dangerous then, with the system failing and many people trying to take advantage of the confusion. Stanislov was a brave man. He trusted us. He was a hero, and he did not end up in prison."

The Soviets sent Victor's team to Brisbane, Australia, in December 1991 for the women's 470 World Championships. It was Victor's first visit to Australia, and he fell in love with the climate, the steady winds, and the people. Brisbane is a lovely, subtropical city a few hundred miles up the east coast from Sydney, providing a contrast with conditions in the Soviet Union that was extreme for Victor and his team. "Brisbane was very warm," Victor recalls. "We were staying in a good hotel with a swimming pool. Back home it was cold. In the shops, the shelves were bare. There was nothing besides bread and milk. In the petrol stations, there was no fuel. In Brisbane, after a long day on the water, we relaxed in the pool eating mangos and other fresh fruits and we were saying wow, life is good."

The racing was also good. Larisa and Olena had the lead at one point, but they ended up second, edged out for gold in the last race by the American team of JJ Isler and Pam Healy, who had become their arch rivals. Isler and Healy took advantage of a shift that occurred three minutes before the start, port tacked the fleet, got away clean and could not be caught. That was on December 21, 1991. Four days later, on Christmas Day, the Soviet flag was lowered from atop the Kremlin for the last time. A week earlier, representatives of 11 Soviet Republics (Ukraine included) had met to declare their independence from the once formidable USSR, an act that probably would have gotten them all incarcerated during a more stable time. But on Christmas Day, the well-intentioned President Gorbachev resigned, admitting (among other things) that the old controlled economy had collapsed before his "perestroika" (private initiative) had time to begin working.

Victor says it was a shock. There was no forewarning, no hint that the end was near. "There had been a lot of big shocks," Victor says, "including the coup that summer. There were a lot of new politics, a new time was promised, then the coup came with lots of conservative people behind the idea of returning to the old system with more iron curtains. We were advanced in our understanding of democracy and revolutionary changes. The coup was an absolutely scary moment because if it had succeeded, all that progress would be finished and the country would be brought to a bad place, bad for morale, bad for relationships – back to an old regime when people were slaves and could not talk about their feelings. Fortunately, the coup was finished in a few days."

For a population long used to a fearsome degree of governmental control, the period of Glasnost ("openness" of social and political discussion) that had been instituted by Gorbachev in the late 1900s created confusion. Many were eager to explore the new freedoms that were implicit, but having been both restrained and isolated for so long, they were ill-prepared to understand the ways of the world outside Soviet borders.

"Today," Victor says, "you hear the Russian language everywhere. Russians are all over the world showing big money and big ambitions. But back then the iron curtains shut the borders. Less than 1% of the people traveled to other countries. Can you imagine? Athletes were not abroad for very long, just a week or ten days for a competition. It was really tough."

It was also very dangerous because defections did result from those travels. To mention just a few, in 1989, hockey players Petr Nedved and Alexander Mogilny defected to the United States, as did gymnast Nadia Comaneci. In 1990, hockey player Sergei Federov defected, as did ice dancer Gorsha Sur.

"People understood that another world was existing where people had cars, where you could buy salami every day in the shops, where there was Coca Cola and German beer," Victor says. "The first priority was to get recognition so you would have access to that life. As a top athlete on good salary you could feed your family, and also the level of recognition was high, you had all social benefits, and carpet for your home, furniture made in Romania. That `CCCP' on your chest was really special. If you were an Olympic or world champion you were not only a hero, but an idol. That's why our sailors worked really hard, trained 20 hours a day, slept on the floor, sacrificed anything to move to the top level, and were willing to drive thousands of kilometers without sleep to be able to cross the border, touch that magic world, to sail and race.

"It was not the same in the west. In many countries sailors ask why they have to give everything. They don't realize it is to make their life special. That's why I say we are not normal, we are a little bit crazy. But if you give them a dream, this dream can become their goal and they will see new horizons, and see how interesting is the way to their goal, how many changes they must go through to reach this goal. They become more interesting even to themselves, with their new personalities they are discovering. This is the process.

"I remember at one regatta one of our women sailors who had no English spent more than two hours talking with the outstanding American athlete, Betsy Allison, who had no Russian. They just opened their hearts and somehow talked with each other."

Learning to deal with that other world would take some time. Vlad Murnikov, designer of *Fasizi*, an 84-foot Russian yacht that competed in the 1989-90 Whitbread Round the World Race, told of calling North Sails Germany and asking if they could help him with sails for the boat.

They said yes, of course. The sails arrived, with an invoice. "They said they could help us," a flustered Murnikov said, "then they send us a bill!"

Victor and his women's sailing team encountered confusion of another extreme. It had to do with shipping their 470 to Cadiz, Spain, for the next world championships in 1992. Victor told Stanislov, his head coach, that the Italian team had offered to share its container with the Ukrainians. All they had to do was get the boat to Milan and it would be sent to Cadiz (1300 miles) for only $500 USD, a bargain. Stanislov checked with his superiors, who had a much better idea. The boat could be sent to Vladivostok, 6,000 miles to the east, by ship. From there it would be put on a train to Moscow, retracing its track 5,600 miles back to the west. From Moscow it would be put on a train to Cadiz, another 3,000 miles. Most important, it would cost nothing. As Victor says, "Every dollar was very tough during this time of crisis."

And so the mad, 15,000 mile trek of the Ziegelmayer 470 began. Weeks passed. When it was time, Victor and his team went to Cadiz to get the boat. They were on fire after a successful year, looking forward to another good Olympic Games (1992 in Barcelona). Then the boat arrived. The hull was bare, empty. Everything that could have been removed – every block, every line, every piece of gear including cleats, rudder, tiller, centerboard – had been stolen while the boat was on the train. "We started to re-rig it," Victor says, "pulling gear together from here and there, and had many troubles. We did not sail well. We were not among the medalists. It was quite bad."

The next regatta was the European Championships in Belgium, but Victor was told to bring his team home and compete in the national trials at the Sochi training center in the USSR. That was harsh, a step backwards for a team that had won the previous world championships and had been ranked #1 in the world. Victor protested, but was rebuffed. He was told if Larisa and Olena were successful at the trials, and at Kiel Week, they would be sent to the Games. He went to Moscow and negotiated. The team director agreed to send the team to a regatta in Holland. If they did well, he would agree to the European Championships. In Holland they finished second, thanks to a penalty caused by their use of a borrowed boom on which the clew of the sail was one millimeter off the black measurement mark. Second wasn't good enough. They were ordered to come home and sail in the trials at Sochi. Victor resisted, suggesting once again they go to the European Championships – only 250 miles from Holland – instead of Sochi, nearly 4000 miles from Holland. He offered a deal. "I told him if we medal at the Europeans," Victor says, "he will send us to the Olympics. If we don't medal, no Olympics. He said okay, deal."

The women raced well in Belgium, but continued to be plagued with the hand-me-down gear they had begged and borrowed. At the end they slipped to 4th place. It was their good luck that Americans JJ Isler and Pam Healy finished third. For perhaps the first and only time Larisa and Olena were happy to be beaten by the Americans, because only teams east of the Atlantic Ocean counted in the final scoring. The Americans took third, but the Ukrainians got the bronze medal, ensuring their trip to the '92 Games in Barcelona.

Helping hands

In Belgium, Victor lent a hand to the US 470 team of Morgan Reeser and Kevin Burnham. They had first met at the Goodwill Games in Estonia in 1986. "We went out of our way to chit-chat with the Soviets," Reeser says. "It was a dangerous time for them, but it was hard for us to believe any of that. We saw them as sailors. Victor didn't talk much about what was going on. He was a passionate coach. I remember we got a lecture from Estonian harbor security about where in the harbor was off limits. A guy on the breakwater counted every boat and crew going out and coming back. Against orders, once we sailed over toward three cruisers at anchor, with Kevin pretending to take photos. You could see they had binoculars trained on us."

At the Europeans in Belgium, Reeser and Burnham broke a shroud during a race and bent their mast. "It was a Gold Spar," Victor says, "a great mast. Only Norway and the USA had one, and both teams were very fast. They threw it on the grass at the boat park. I said to them let's try and bend it back. They said it was rubbish, I could have it."

"Most capitalists would have tossed the mast and purchased a new one," Reeser says, "but Victor, being from the equipment-challenged society he was in, made the best use of everything."

Victor made a special rig, protected the mast with old tires, and began bending it straight a millimeter at a time. It took more than three hours, but eventually they succeeded. "It was absolutely perfect," Victor says. "Reeser and Burnham went to the Barcelona Olympics with this mast and got a silver medal. I understand we are opponents, but we are one family. We fight on the water, but ashore we are friends."

At Kiel Week, Larisa and Olena broke their mainsheet block, another piece of borrowed hardware, and never recovered. And in Barcelona, it was another near miss. Once again, equipment played a role. Victor had been after his head coach to buy Larisa and Olena a new spinnaker for the Games. US sailmaker Dave Ullman had given the women a set of sails for the 470 World Championships in Long Beach in '91, where they had won. And they had won silver with those sails in Brisbane.

"After six regattas," Victor says, "we had a dead spinnaker. Now we use a spinnaker for only one regatta. I asked the coach every day. He said no money. He had to buy things for the Fying Dutchman class. I invited him to go with me on my motorboat. He sees Larisa arrive first at the weather mark, then watches boats passing her downwind. He asked me why I did not force him to buy a spinnaker for her."

The centerboard Larisa had been using for four years broke. Victor went to see "Mr. Fix It," the late Carl Eichenlaub, the beloved San Diego boat builder who spent eight Olympic Games working as Boatwright for the USA team and whomever else needed something fixed. "I asked Carl if he could give me a little epoxy," Victor says. "He had his cigar. He looked at the centerboard and said don't worry, come back in the morning and it will be ready. I reported to our head coach and he said I had made a big mistake. He said they are our opponents – Isler and Healy – the Americans will not fix it. At that time we were in a medal position. I said this is a different world. Carl is a great man. But I admit I was a little worried. I went to Carl in the morning and he said all fixed, and gave me the board."

Once again, the bronze medal came down to the last race between the Americans and the Ukrainians. On the windward leg, Larisa protested Isler for tacking too close. "The Americans were very smart," Victor says. "They went to the media office and got tape shot from the balloon above." Isler says Larisa had asked Valentin Mankin, then coach of the Italian team, to write up the protest for her. Mankin had seen the tape of the incident which he gave to his friend, Carl Eichenlaub who handed it to Isler before she went into the protest room. "It was a very good picture," Victor says. "It was clear on video that when JJ tacked she was extremely close, definitely an infringement of the rules. But Larisa's biggest mistake was she did not alter course to avoid collision. And there was no collision, but maybe there was 10 centimeters (4 inches) between the boats. Larisa didn't alter course because she was trying to catch JJ. If she had changed course even a little, she would have been finished. It was a special moment. The decision was fair. JJ and Pam won the medal. Larisa and Olena were fourth."

CHAPTER 7

Ruslana

About a year before the Olympic Games in Barcelona, a new female sailor appeared on Ukrainian waters. Today, in her 40s, Ruslana Taran is a compact 5'4". A coach, she moves with the focus of a Border Collie herding sheep and talks a blue streak when she gets going. One can only imagine her energy at age 15, when she first met Victor Kovalenko. Before sailing, she had tried gymnastics, fencing, ballet, and basketball. "I remember the gym teacher gathering us basketball players together," Ruslana says, "and saying to this really tall girl you are good in basketball but Ruslana will play and you will never play because Ruslana is aggressive and determined to win. So I had potential, but running was too hard and I loved sailing because of the freedom we had in the boats. It was fun."

Ruslana's mother had identified Victor as the coach she wanted for her daughter, and had approached him. While winning her share of races, Ruslana hadn't exactly set the world on fire as a youth sailor, but Victor saw the same qualities that had impressed her gym teacher, and took her on as #2 behind Larisa and Olena. Her crew was Iryna Chunykhovska, the dynamic girl who had sailed so well with Larisa. They immediately got into the training routine of 20 days in camp, and 10 days at home. Because Ruslana had begun working with Victor the summer after the breakup of the Soviet Union, training camp schedules were more flexible. Victor and his teams practiced where opportunities presented themselves, sometimes in the Crimea where Ruslana lived, sometimes in Dnepropetrovsk, or Cyprus, but most often in Europe.

"We traveled a lot," Ruslana says. "We lived together like a family. We traveled and slept in one car or tent, ate together. Everything Victor taught us was mental. He could feel my mind. And it was non-stop. He knew just the right time to ask about results, the second race, the second upwind leg, why I didn't tack sooner. There was always conversation. We talked so much about sailing, and I never realized we were talking about sailing. It was a normal life, like living with your parents. Only my family was where I could go and hear from them they love me no matter the results. Because Victor and I were born in the Soviet Union maybe we had a different connection. He was like an uncle. I trusted him more than family. If Victor said I could do it, I was ready to kill everybody."

Victor's coaching priority had advanced from focusing on results to focusing on sailors. His summation of the tools a sailor needed to be a winner — the body, fit for speed; the mind, sharp for making quick decisions; and strength of character for the courage to execute those decisions — was two-thirds psychological. He reminded his sailors how easy it is to negotiate with themselves, and worked on improving "the art of conversation with one's self," especially during competition.

Ruslana took that to heart. "I explained to Victor how when I am racing I have a monologue with myself, but I am talking to him. I say 'Victor I know you want me to tack right now but I will go a little bit further to the right first, sorry Victor.' I was always talking to him, thinking about what my coach said, like he was the 3rd person in the boat."

"Ruslana has a lot of character," Victor says. "She has good judgement of situations. She was very good at having conversations with herself. And she has great intuition. All women have fantastic intuition. If a man says he feels he should go left, don't trust him. If a woman says she feels she should go left, it will be much more reliable."

During those long car rides around Europe Victor had plenty to say to his team. His conversation was based on a growing list of coaching principles that were slowly earning their way into his three-ring notebook (there were 22 of them as of August, 2015), principles like *be unique, different, but not complicated; it's easy to be kind to athletes, but you betray them if you do; avoid saying what is wrong because it destroys confidence – say what is right; the earlier you can make a decision, the higher will be the quality of resolution; avoid judgement, leave that to the athletes; the battle for the stability of the mind is based on one's ambitions and goals, with the object of destroying your opponent's mental stability.* But as Ruslana has said, the conversation was never about sailing per se. It was always couched as general observations about life. Victor is very fond of stories and analogies, and uses them all the time because of the way they stick in one's memory. How to handle having the lead in a race, for instance, is about a bird: "When you have a bird in hand," Victor says, "hold it firmly but gently. Don't squeeze it, don't kill it. Feel the heart of the bird." Victor tells his sailors if others are leading, do not worry. "They know they have a small chance because having the lead is a kind of pressure they are not ready for."

As for the battle for mental stability, Victor has a story about Valentin Mankin stalking a competitor for an entire morning before the last race of a regatta, even into the toilet. When the other sailor realized what was happening, and became angry, Mankin told him he was following him because to win the regatta he had to be right behind him at the finish.

Another principle that belongs near the top of the list is risk management: *You need courage to take risk, wisdom to know when to stop.* On a sailing race course populated by accomplished athletes, managing risk is perhaps the primary key to success. Risk taking is available everywhere: at the start, at every tactical move, and when planning and executing strategy. Victor says one must know when he *cannot* take a risk; when he *can* take a risk; and when he *must* take a risk. His risk management drawing is telling.

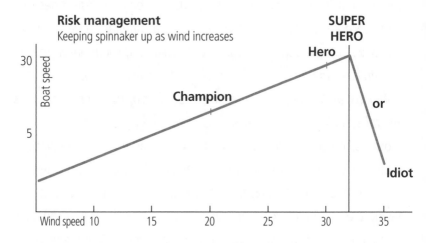

The illustration addresses the risk of flying the big spinnaker as the wind increases. Along the bottom line is wind speed. The ascending risk line approaches "hero" status between 15 and 20 knots. At 25 knots, "super hero" status is reached. At 30 knots, one becomes "champion," or wait…possibly "idiot" as the spinnaker maybe splits in half or capsizes the boat in a fashion dramatic enough to get a million internet hits. "But if you don't take some risk," Victor says, "you are no one, a gray mouse.

"A coach's job," Victor says, "is three-fold. One, be able to read athletes. Two, be able to see the future. Three, be the first to get there." Victor compares coaching with sculpting. With young sailors the coach must work in clay, adding material all the time. With more experienced sailors, the coach works in marble, carefully removing excessive material to create the essential athlete. "When sculptors work in marble," Victor says, "they have to think a lot before they delete some piece. Then they decide alright, delete it, shape it, polish, and they can say that's what I mean. They can transfer their meaning through hundreds of subsequent years and touch people who also feel their effort, their meaning, their love. Athletes are marble come alive."

Victor also likes the sword analogy, how the concept of super-heating a prime piece of steel, beating it into shape with a hammer, then plunging it into cold water and repeating the process over and over with ever smaller hammers applies to the development of a sailor. "Do that and you will have a sword you love," Victor says, "sharp and strong but also flexible, because the process changes the structure of the metal. It is the same with athletes. You have to heat them to a high temperature, then cool them off. They have to pass through all this to be tough, in good shape, both flexible and sharp. If they are not flexible they will break under pressure."

Behind all of these analogies is Victor's immutable conviction that to be an Olympic champion, a person must change, just as the structure of the metal is changed in forging a sword. "All of us change ourselves all the time," Victor says. "If people set serious goals, if they have a mission, they have to change. If your life is tough and demanding, you have to be disciplined, stay in good shape, keep your mind in good shape, follow certain routines. Because your ultimate goal is to bring something to the world, like a painter who has a vision. You do that not only for people to say 'Wow!' but to change yourself — to grow, broaden, expand yourself. Everything we experience or touch changes us.

"Each success gives us more confidence and understanding of basics and principles, confirmation of ideas, and it widens our horizons as well. It's a developing process. I'm always thinking I don't know enough, but always on an absolutely different level."

Victor says recognition by others also changes you. He likes to tell his sailors that if they win a European Championship they will be famous for half a day. If they win a World Championship, they will be famous for 2 days. If they win gold at the Olympics, they will be famous for four days, until the world is overcome by another crisis. He also tells them the satisfaction of all accomplishments will last a lifetime. But at a regatta in Shishido, Japan, in 1989, Victor saw how recognition can also change one's priorities, one's vision, one's approach to goals. The twelve women (including Larisa and Iryna) who were invited to the regatta were all Olympic medalists. They were picked up by limousine at the airport and taken to the best hotels. Prominent citizens of Shishido were guests at gourmet dinners held every evening. The racing was well-organized, and televised from helicopters on the race course. "This attention to the details of honoring the sailors and the event was how the Japanese built their future," Victor says. "They developed the women's 470 class significantly after that. They were 5th in Barcelona ('92); silver medalists in Atlanta ('96)."

Ruslana remembers a day that changed her. Ruslana's crew, Iryna, had become more and more convinced that in order for them to realize their potential as a team they had to find a different coach. She argued that if they stayed with Victor, they would always be playing second fiddle to Larisa and Olena. Resistant at first, Ruslana came to think Iryna's notion had merit. "I was very close to writing a document to Victor asking him to release us," Ruslana says, "but first I went to see him and explain the situation. I told him our thoughts. I wasn't worried he would scream at me, but what he said was totally unexpected. He said, 'Ruslana, I respect what you think you should do, but if you ever want to come back to my team you will be welcome.' Now I was crying, and I said no, I don't want to write any documents. I want to sail with Victor. I expected something harsh from him. I was not ready for what he said.

"I was worried about betraying Victor when Iryna suggested leaving him as coach. Then when he was so understanding, so different from what I expected – I will remember that for the rest of my life." Ruslana took on the experienced Olena Pakholchik as crew after Larisa retired. The two worked very well together, and started winning.

An excellent Ukrainian men's 470 team was developing at the same time. Evgeniy Braslavets and Igor Matviyenko came out of Dnepropetrovsk, Victor's home city. In fact, Evgeniy echoes Victor's story of representatives coming to the school and offering the kids participation in the activity of their choice. Evgeniy, who is now a professional sailor racing Dragons for United Arab Emirates – he won both the World and European Championships in 2015 – recalls that a coach came into his class and asked who wanted to go sailing. "I had no idea what this means, sailing," Evgeniy says. "I thought maybe we will build small sailing ships. I said okay, sure, I will go with friends. Then I realize we will not build, we will sail."

Evgeniy started sailing Optis in 1980, and showed natural ability. Before he was done with the class, he was two-time Russian national champion. A coach from the National Team selected him, and he jumped directly into the 470.

"At the time," Evgeniy says, "Victor was one of the best 470 coaches in USSR. He was like a super star for me. There was a regatta in Sochi, a training base at the time. I went to him, introduced myself, and said I wanted to train in his group. He said okay. He did not help us immediately. There were five or six teams in his group and you had to fight all the time for his attention. If you were doing better than others, you had a chance. It was like a family of small wolves. He was like a father. We were diamonds in the rough. Victor was the master who could find these diamonds and polish them."

By 1991 when the USSR dissolved, Evgeniy and Igor, and Ruslana and Olena, had become Victor's primary teams. "He was always tough," Evgeniy says. "He was on top of the mountain urging us, forcing us to come closer, climb higher. You had to want to be there. It was the big dream. It was also hard work: put your boat on top of the van, jump in, drive, train, go running, rest, same the next day, then a regatta, then on to the next event. Once we raced in Germany. Friends asked what I had seen. I told them the highway, the yacht club, some apartment, and the sea. But most important, after dinner we would sit and talk with Victor for hours. And he would say now it is time for tea, or maybe he had found a good bottle of wine, and it wasn't really allowed, but we would have a bit of wine and some cheese, small things like a father would do. He wasn't a teacher like at school. He was more like a friend."

The New World

Ruslana's gold medal at the European Championships in 1993 was remarkable considering the equipment she was using. Her old boat was from Switzerland, sails were hand-me-downs from JJ Isler, the centerboard and mast had been collected from France. But she was that good. Support from the Ukrainian hierarchy was sorely lacking. "We thought after her win at the Euros we would have more support," Victor says. "There was a little bit more, but not enough." So when he was contacted by Jim Young, head coach of the Swiss Olympic Sailing Team, Victor was ready to listen.

Young hails from Oshkosh, Wisconsin, now lives in Colorado. He was on the US sailing team in the 70s (Tornado). He's won more than 20 national and North American championships in a variety of classes. In the 1980s he coached the US Tornado Olympic team, and in 1990 began coaching in Switzerland. When Anna Maria Gregorini took over as Chairman of Swiss Olympic Sailing, she made Young head coach.

"I wanted authority to hire my assistants," Young says. "Anna Maria agreed. My specialties were the Tornado catamaran and the Finn, but I had never connected with the personalities of the sailors in the 470. Those guys are different. They tend to be young, immature. That's why older 470 sailors do well. Paul Foerster won his Olympic gold medal when he was 42. So I was looking for a 470 coach. Most coaches put buoys in the water and run lots of short races. I don't do that. I prefer full motion drills without stopping, forcing sailors to react and get their heads out of the boats. In the run-up to Barcelona I had seen one coach doing similar training. I didn't have a name, but found out it was Victor Kovalenko. I ran into him in early 1993, introduced myself, said I needed a coach, and asked if he were interested. He was shocked and amazed, asked why me? I told him I'd seen him work on the water. He asked if I needed his CV. I said no, I've seen your work. He said he'd think about it, came back and said yes a day or two later."

It had to have helped that Jim Young spoke Russian, because at the time, Victor's English was in a formative stage. Talk about a fortunate coincidence. Jim was in college during the Vietnam years and had joined Reserve Officer's Training Corps (ROTC) to avoid the draft. That enabled him to extend his schooling. One of his majors was anthropology. For his linguistics requirement, he wanted a non-Western language, and chose Russian. He became fluent at one point.

"I told Victor to get to Switzerland any way he could," Young says. "He arrived a few days later. I educated him about the Swiss, how there is a huge amount of social pressure in the culture not to stand out, an attitude that has to be changed with athletes, and about the ins and outs of Swiss banking. He was astounded when I paid for dinner with a piece of plastic."

Anna Maria Gregorini's first impression of Victor was positive and lasting. "He was humble, very engaged in his work," she says. "I was immediately convinced he was good." She was so taken with him that on one of his first trips to Switzerland, Gregorini put him and Tatiana up at her mother's house, which turned out to be a novel experience for the mother and Tatiana. Across the impenetrable language barrier, the two women came together in the kitchen, preparing borsch, along with traditional Swiss food. "They had a great time," Victor recalls. "It's amazing how people can get along without language. They opened their hearts and communicated. They have all remained friends ever since.

"Jim Young was great," Victor says. "He's intelligent, and has helped a lot of people in sailing. He was a mentor for a long time. He helped me explore this new world in many areas, in coaching, taught me Compuserve on the computer (!), and other technologies. I got my own credit card. We had competitions on the lakes, and with some salary from the Swiss I bought a very old Volvo 240, a miracle, very good for transporting a 470 on the roof—a little better than the Panda. The Swiss were very organized, everything was structured. I brought the Ukrainian team in as a sparring partner and it all worked well. The Ukrainians had more talent and experience, but it was beneficial for both teams."

It was common for countries, especially European countries within driving distance of one another, to use international sparring partners. No country has enough depth in any class of boat to provide the level of competition needed for teams to attain Olympic quality. "The biggest competitor you have to beat to get to the Olympic Games is your own country," Jim Young says. "As US coach for the 1984 Olympics, I had my

Tornado sailors, Randy Smyth and Jay Glaser, working with a training partner from the Netherlands. Randy and Jay took silver. I knew if I hired Victor as a coach he would bring in his Ukrainian sailors to train with us, and that would be very beneficial. As it happened, Evgeniy Braslavets and Igor Matviyenko ended up traveling with Victor and Chris Rast through much of the next four years."

Chris Rast, who has dual citizenship – he is American on his mother's side – was Switzerland's best 470 sailor at the time. Young says Rast's American influence made him less prone to the normal Swiss inhibitions to stand out. But he was still waffling about an Olympic campaign. "One the things that makes Victor great is he has the necessary soft skills to figure out the right approach to various athletes," Chris Rast says. "Through talking with them he figures out what makes them tick, and how to tickle the maximum out of their potential. He came out of coaching women, and coaching women is more difficult than coaching men. A lot more soft skills are involved. I know. I've done it. It's a psychological game. With men it's way easier. Men are more focused.

"Victor understood I was wavering. I remember one talk we had in 1994. I was trying to figure out what to do in sailing. He said it's like jumping off the high board. You are not going to jump a little bit. You can't turn around and grab the edge. You jump, and you are going."

Rast jumped. He and his crew, Jean-Pierre Ziegert, were not an ideal combination. But in a small country like Switzerland, the choices are limited. Rast, as Young recalls, was aggressive and willing to push himself harder. The problem was that Rast and Ziegert argued constantly. "JP had sailed around the world on *Merit* in the 1989-90 Whitbread Race," Victor says. "He was a difficult character." The combination of Young and Kovalenko didn't exactly calm those waters. "Victor and I often communicated in a mixture of English, Russian, and Spanish," Young says, laughing at the memory. "It drove the Swiss sailors nuts. Most Swiss are multilingual, but because they are Swiss they can only speak one language at a time. Victor and I were talking in this polyglottal mess of words to make sure we understood each other. It angered the sailors, especially Rast and Ziegert. Ziegert yelled at us a couple times : `You Can't Do That !' That was Victor's initiation to the Swiss."

In 1995, Victor got his second close look at Australia. After the 470 World Championships that year, Australian teams had the option to bring out training partners for the summer. The men selected the Greek team (they had won the worlds), while the women chose the Ukrainians. Victor also brought Chris Rast and JP Ziegert along.

To qualify for the Olympics, a Swiss team had to place in the top ten in the world championship of its event. "We started working with Chris and JP in 1993," Victor says. "It was a tough job. There were only three years to the Games, and they needed a lot of experience. The 470 is a complicated boat." The team progressed, and on their last chance to qualify in a regatta at Porto Alegre, Brazil, they finished 8th. Morgan Reeser — who had won a silver medal (470) at the 1992 Olympic Games — says that Rast qualifying for the Olympics by finishing 8th in Brazil was Victor Kovalenko's greatest achievement. "Chris has become a great talent," Reeser says, "but in 1995 he was not. He'd never been in the top 25. The odds were really against it, but there he was."

Thanks to his freelancing, Victor attended the 1996 470 World Championships in Brazil with the Swiss team because Ukraine had no money to send the team. He had met with his Ukrainian directors in 1995, told them about the great potential of his team, how Ruslana and Olena had been on the podium in all their regattas for two years. Impressed, they asked him what he needed for success. He told them money for sails, and help sending a container to Brazil. "They said `oh yes, we are behind you a hundred percent,'" Victor recalls. "`We will organize a container. You will be at the Worlds.' But nothing happened."

Ruslana and Olena had won silver at the Worlds in 1995, and still Victor had had to beg the authorities for boats, sails, lodging, and food to support his team. Victor went to Pride, a paint company in Ukraine, and pled his case. "This was not their job," Victor says, "it was the job of the sport system in the country, but Pride bought us a VW van, a boat for Evgeniy and Igor, sails, trapeze harnesses, dry suits, and we were a Pride team. We had good results. If not for their support, no Olympic Games for us."

The Swiss ended up sending five classes to the Olympic Games in Atlanta in 1996, but they sent no coaches other than Jim Young and two "officials" for moral support (Gregorini had left her position at the Swiss Olympic Committee by then). "The press focuses on the medals at the Olympics," Jim Young says, "but the real target for most athletes is to be in the top eight `certificate positions.' Chris had a shot at a certificate position, and for the Swiss to say no to Victor made him angry. He'd worked long and hard with Chris. It wasn't easy. The door was still open for him to go with the Ukrainian team, so he did."

Victor's Ukrainian sailors had been racing hard and doing well. Evgeniy and Igor had been climbing up the men's 470 fleet in regatta after regatta. Their 4th in the 1995 World Championships in Canada was a sign they might peak at the right time. And Ruslana and Olena were on a tear. Leading up to the Atlanta Games they had won the European Championships in 1993, 1995, and 1996 (they would go on to win the Euros in 1997, 1998, and 1999), and they had placed second at the World Championships in 1995 (they would also win the Worlds in 1997, 1998, and 1999).

Rast and Ziegert finished back in the fleet at Atlanta in 1996. The Ukrainian 470 sailors won two medals. Ruslana and Olena won bronze. Evgeniy and Igor brought home gold, but not without being convinced to use a new mainsail. "Ruslana had a new model mainsail," Victor says. "She won the 1996 Euros with it, and she was fast. Evgeniy wanted to try this new main even though he also had good speed. He was not as fast as Ruslana, but to change mains just before the Games is a big risk. We decided it was worth the risk, but to make it happen we needed a special approach. I asked the head coach to play a game. He told Evgeniy he did not have permission to change sails, told him he was comfortable with his sail, successful with it, and it was a huge risk to change sails 2 days before the regatta. He said the sail had to be totally familiar to him, his use of it automatic. The plan was to force Evgeniy to convince the head coach that the sail would be better for him because if you just gave him the sail, said `use this, it is better,' and then if he had a couple bad days, he would blame it on the new sail. The sail could create lack of confidence, a disruption of the flow, breed harm. But if he very much wants to use it…

"So we gave it to him to test. He said probably he would use it in the regatta. Probably was not good enough. The head coach said no. I said to Evgeniy you must talk to the head coach, prepare your arguments, convince him you want to use it. He told the coach he was confident the new main would be better. Confident is much better than probably. The head coach then said okay, but this is your responsibility. He was happy to have the sail. After two days of the regatta he was in first position."

Victor had also done a little work behind the scenes for Evgeniy. First he had argued against going to Atlanta for the opening ceremonies of the '96 Games, saying the drive from Savannah (the sailing venue) to Atlanta and the need to stay overnight would destroy the team's focus on performance.

He won that one. Then he suggested Evgeniy as team flag bearer for the Savannah ceremony. The team boss preferred the Soling crew, a powerful fellow who could carry the flag in one hand, impressing the world with his strength. Victor argued it was more important to benefit the team than impress the world. When the boss wouldn't listen, Victor called the chief of the Ukrainian Olympic mission in Atlanta and explained the situation. Persuaded, the chief called the boss. "He was angry," Victor says. "He told me I achieved again what I wanted. Evgeniy was very proud, and won a gold medal. Afterwards I thanked the boss for supporting me to make him happy as well. We are one team."

Politics

The even bigger news was that competing in the Olympics for the first time as an independent nation, Ukrainian athletes won a total of 23 medals in all sports, surpassing the overall performance of countries like Canada, Hungary, Spain, Great Britain, Brazil, and Japan. Ukraine was an amazing 9th in the medal count. The country was ecstatic, as expressed by the thousands who showed up at the railroad station in Kiev to welcome the athletes home. A full-on state event had been organized, with many dignitaries, including President Leonid Kuchma, standing proudly on a podium with the athletes, their ranks of medals glittering in the sunshine. A bevy of young women were presenting flowers on cue. A band played rousing, patriotic tunes. The ceremonies were precisely planned according to who would speak when, and for how long, and the nature of the subject matter. Finally, as protocol dictated, President Kuchma delivered his remarks. As he concluded, he asked if anyone else would like to say something. With the exception of one man on the podium, everyone was silent, understanding the President's query was politic, good-naturedly insincere. In the silence, and to the disbelief of the athletes and dignitaries, Victor Kovalenko was heard to say yes, thank you, he would like to say a few words.

"I walked to the podium, stood next to the President," Victor says, "and I said this was a special moment for all of us, but our mission is not complete. I said to the athletes, when you go home, don't put your medals in the bank or in the safe. Bring your medals to the people, show them to the workers and students and farmers to make them happy and proud of what we have done. You can tell them that half a year ago we were standing at the same bus stop together, or in the same queue to buy milk. We are not people from the moon, we are part of our country, Ukrainian characters made from the same tough material as you."

Victor says he spoke from the heart. "I cannot change my fundamental self," he says. "I had to speak. It was the biggest achievement in Ukrainian sport, it put us on the map." And in fact his teams did take their medals to the people. "It was fantastic for us," he says, "to talk with people, look into their eyes, see how they touched the medals, people who had no hot water in their houses, not enough food, to touch the Olympic gold medal and say it was a miracle." But his superiors saw it as a political ploy, an opportunity to impress the President and land a top job in the sports system – perhaps one of their jobs! Already gearing up for the 2000 Games in Sydney, Victor had met with the director of the Sunflower Oil Company and had been given a van that could carry two boats, one inside and one on top. And the politicians had pledged their support, but Victor knew better. "I was suspect after the speech," he says. "They thought I was trying to get their jobs. I was dangerous."

An indication Victor was right was the message delivered to him in the form of the award he was given for his coaching efforts. While his athletes were each given the Order of the Cross (for bravery), and all other sport managers, directors received medals for their work, Victor was issued a paper certificate reserved for middle level bureaucrats. In a culture where medals count heavily, the insult was unmistakable, and extremely upsetting to Victor.

Initially, in the aftermath of the Ukrainian sailors' success in Atlanta, there were indications that better support would be forthcoming from the country. But the feeling was short-lived. Soon, despite what his teams had accomplished, Victor found himself banging his head against all-too-familiar bureaucratic walls. "That," Victor says, "helped me decide to accept the Australian invitation."

CHAPTER 8

Holistic

It was John Harrison who asked Victor Kovalenko if he would like to become the 470 coach for Australia to prepare the team for the 2000 Games in Sydney. He was Australian Team Leader at the time. That conversation took place in August, 1996, in Savannah, Georgia, right after the last race of the Olympic Games. They met in the athletes' lounge. After Victor quickly said yes, thank you, Harrison asked him when he might be ready to start work. "I told him ten days," Victor says. "I just had to fly home, kiss my wife, and pack my bag. I said if we are to do well in Sydney we must start tomorrow."

Australian interest in Victor had started as early as 1987, at Kiel Week. Among the women 470 sailors preparing their first Olympic campaigns that season was Jenny Lidgett (now Danks), from Australia. Larisa Moskalenko's bronze medal at Kiel helped spotlight the Ukrainian team, and Danks had made an effort to seek out Victor. It was a brief meeting. "We were very aware of the Soviets," Danks says, "because they were so separate from the rest of the teams. They were a little like the East Germans because they were never allowed to talk with us. It was feared they would learn too much about the West."

Two years later at Japan's Shishido Cup, when all the teams stayed in the same big hotel, Danks got to know Victor. "He was the first holistic coach I had come across, or that sailing had ever come across," Danks says. "Victor realized there was so much more to being an Olympic gold medalist or world champion than just being a good sailor. You had to be physically fit, nutritionally fit, and mentally extremely fit. Being a good sailor was a given. He had a motto : enjoy the life. At end of day he would say go do things for your own personal development. Sit under a tree, look up at the clouds, be calm and happy.

"Later on, at a regatta at Medemblik, Holland, I got bad case of food poisoning. I was vomiting out of control. I would have been inclined to stay in bed, miss the race. But Victor came and got me, took me to a bar on the main street at 9 o'clock in the morning and had me drink a whole glass of whiskey. He believed whiskey would kill the bug that had given me food poisoning. I had never drunk whiskey in my life, but there I was sitting in this bar in Holland in the morning with everyone pulling sails up across the street and he's making me drink. Sure enough, it settled my stomach, relaxed me. I went out and raced. My Australian coaches never would have done that.

Danks' strong feelings about Victor's value as a coach were confirmed during the summer of 1995, when he and his Ukrainian team had been brought to Australia as sparring partners. That's when relationships were forged that would eventually lead to Victor making a commitment to coach Down Under.

Victor might have been ready to move to Sydney in ten days, but it took the Australians a year to put the deal together. They had to find the money, organize a permanent working visa, complete other mounds of paperwork, and come up with a comfortable way to integrate Victor into the coaching staff. Their national coach at the time, Buster Hooper, was not fired. "He was supportive," Victor says. "He said 'invite this guy and he will do a good job.' He was thinking of Australia, not himself." Jenny Danks agrees. "Buster was a great coach. He didn't take umbrage. He felt he had done all he could. He was fantastic for us. We adored him. But having exposure to Victor was different. I think maybe Buster realized Victor was in a different league. He learned a lot from him."

As a member of the board of Yachting Australia at the time, it was Danks who had been pushing for them to go after Victor. She had gotten some private coaching from him prior to the '96 Games. She had missed bronze by one point that year, and had seen the efficacy of Victor's approach. "In early '96," Danks says, "Victor brought the Ukrainian team to train with us in Melbourne along with a couple of Swiss guys he was working with. He said with fitness, all you need to do is your chin-ups, sit-ups, and triceps dips. He said you don't need a gym, just a playground. So we'd find a playground and do chin-ups on the monkey bars. He had me competing with a Ukrainian girl and I swear I've never been so determined to beat anyone. I can remember it was blowing clappers, 30 knots plus. Sailing had been canceled, but no rest for the wicked.

"He taught us self-discipline. After each race we had to write a report, and after each regatta, a regatta report. That was new to the Australian way of thinking."

Victor has always required written reports from his sailors. He says it helps the sailors more than him. "I can't change them by telling them something they did wrong," he says. "It has to be their experience. So when they write about a race you can see their abilities to analyze their decisions, their thinking, and criticize their mistakes. This helps prevent making the mistake again because they wrote it down. They'll remember it forever. Athletes are their own best critics. I had them also do camp reports, what they learned, the positives and the negatives, what could be done better. Sometimes I asked them to analyze my activities. Not all of them," he says with a smile.

With Victor, when his sailors were on the water – whether training or racing – they were always in race mode. "You would have discipline,"

Danks says, "you wouldn't waste a moment. In Kiel, the race course was an hour and a half away. At the end of racing, blowing 20, you'd think my team mate Addy Bucek could sit in the trapeze and relax, cleat the main, but Victor made us sail home as if we were racing. He was a meter behind us in the coach boat the whole way. We were spent, having raced all day, but for Victor that was an opportunity to sail home practicing our body kinetics to keep the boat flat and fast the whole way. That kind of self-discipline was new to the Australian way of training, or doing anything."

Danks also learned about Victor's personal discipline, and his loyalty. When he was in Australia in 1995 getting paid to help the Australian team, the sailors felt he was giving all he had in the way of both coaching and friendship. But when they turned up at an international event, it was a different story. "I bumped into him at the Olympic Village in Savannah prior to the 1996 Games," Danks says. "I went bouncing up to him as my normal self and this brick wall went up between us. I thought, who is this ? What have I done ? I'd spent all this time with him and considered him a close friend, and now this wall. But Victor was there for Ukraine and not giving anything to me, no confidence, no friendship, nothing. It was a real shock.

"The board poo-pooed me," Danks says. "I felt like a token female. But after the '96 Games were over they went after him."

While he was waiting for the Australians to complete their preparations, Victor had kept busy working with Ruslana and Olena, and Evgeniy and Igor. The men suffered a bit of a slump after their gold medal performance in Atlanta. They would eventually rally, winning bronze at the 2000 Games in Sydney, and winning both the European and World Championships in 2001. But in 1997, Ruslana proved her Olympic medal was no fluke. She was dominant, winning her 4th of five European 470 Championships, her first of three World Championships, and singled out for sailing's ultimate accolade: ISAF World Female Sailor of the Year. Such an honor reflects handsomely on a coach. And of course Victor's son Vladimir had won the junior 470 national championships the previous year. Victor would be leaving Ukraine on a roll.

Sydney

On October 14, 1997, a year and a month after he agreed to take the Australian job, Victor moved to Sydney. After evaluating the enormous task ahead of him, he had arrived alone. Moving to Australia was a dream come true for Victor. With support flagging in Ukraine, the timing was perfect. He had to make this amazing opportunity work, and in only three years. He knew it was a long shot. He knew there were many endless days ahead, with very little time for family or anything else other than sailing. After a long discussion, he and Tatiana decided she and Vladimir would wait until after the Sydney Olympic Games were finished before they moved to Sydney. Thanks to Victor's accomplishments in the Ukrainian sports world, they were living well in a spacious, three-bedroom apartment, and owned a small summer cottage on the Dneper River. Tatiana could keep teaching, and the delay was okay with Vladimir, who at age 16 had a full, teenage life and was not looking forward to being uprooted. Unspoken was the possibility it could all go bad and Victor would be the one moving after three years – back to Ukraine. Tatiana could visit Victor on holidays, and he would be able to visit when the team was traveling in Europe.

When he arrived in Sydney, Victor was picked up at the airport by one of the coaches, taken directly to the waterfront where the Australian 470 sailors were practicing, and put in the boat with the team's head coach, Ian Brown. Belinda Stowell, a round-the-world sailor from Zimbabwe who was new to both Australia, as a citizen, and to dinghy sailing, remembers that day.

"He'd flown in from Ukraine with his gold aviator sunglasses," says Stowell, who today is the head coach of Western Australia's sailing program. "I looked over during the session and Victor had fallen asleep, with his mouth open, catching flies. We were that exciting for him. The guy was really impressed with us. Of course he was fully jet lagged. We went in, and I'll never forget that first meeting with him. His English was very broken, but he already had that power when he talked. Everyone was drawn in, listening carefully. He told us we had to be like frogs. That was his first analogy for us. He said we mustn't sit on a rock and deliberate, we had to jump in the water and be committed. Later on he named my boat *Frog*, and gave me a little frog pin."

The next day, Victor met his boss, Tracy Johnstone, who had taken over as High Performance Manager of Yachting Australia just a few months before. Tracy was a big boat sailor who had earned her stripes by surviving several years working as personal assistant to Syd Fischer, arguably Australian yachting's saltiest and most celebrated (and accomplished) senior curmudgeon-yachtsman. Tracy hadn't been enthused when she'd heard Australia was getting a coach from Ukraine. She favored nurturing national coaching talent. But the results for Australia in the 1996 Olympic Games (one silver, one bronze) had not lived up to expectations. Personnel changes that followed had included the hiring of Phil Jones and Johnstone. "Phil had good insight," Tracy says. "He realized we were limited in finding Australians with enough expertise to drive a hard program.

"I was uncomfortable meeting Victor. I'm always cautious with a new person : who is this bloke ? He turned out to be everything I thought he would be : well-presented, ironed shirt, neat pants. Conservative, was my first impression. He was intense, reserved, not at all into self-promotion. His English wasn't so good, but he always got his message across. He pressed me for details. There was no social chit chat. He wanted to get working. That impressed me because I'm a worker. I felt he was here to get a job done."

It was Phil Jones who had officially confirmed Victor's hiring. In 2015 Jones was the interim CEO of Athletics Australia, the country's governing body of sports. A fit man, he gets around Sydney on a bicycle. In 1997, Jones had been CEO of the Australian Yachting Federation. He had to leave town for three weeks just as Victor arrived, and invited him to stay at his apartment until an accommodation could be arranged. "When we returned," Jones says, "Victor advised us to be careful with the kitchen knives. He'd spent his evenings sharpening them. My wife cut the end of her finger off with one. He said in Ukraine they always had sharp knives."

Tracy Johnstone arranged a room for Victor at the HMAS Penguin Australian Royal Navy Base on Hunter's Bay, just north of Sydney Harbor. Part of the base was unoccupied, and it provided a perfect headquarters for the sailing team. "The accommodation wasn't much," Johnstone says, "but the man is frugal. He could live off the smell of an oily rag. He was willing to live in a minimalist environment to establish a relationship with the sailors and the program. He understood he needed to be cautious, so it worked well. But here was this Ukrainian guy sleeping in the middle of our Navy base with full security all around and badges required, eating in the mess hall with Navy personnel. No way that could happen now. He integrated, that's his nature. He's an intuitive character. He saw where he was and did what was needed to survive. You had to trust the man. He read people and situations really well."

Vladimir Kovalenko says that's always been his father's strength. "He can quickly find the key to any person," Vladimir says. "He can start a conversation with anyone. He can subtly convince people to go to the subject they know. That's what Father does."

Jenny Danks says she's never met anyone who makes friends faster. "He can be standing in an airport line," Danks says, "and see some guy wearing a North Sails hat, and he's got a new friend."

Victor had been hired by the Australian Yachting Federation for $28,000 a year, a pittance in 1997, but an improvement on what he was making in Ukraine. The 1997 sailing budget for all classes was $500,000 USD, also a pittance (in 2014, the budget was $8 million). Victor says he wore a necktie to AYF meetings, carried a dictionary, and understood about 20% of what they were talking about. "I knew sailing words," he says, "tack, jibe, in, out, but the bureaucratic words I couldn't understand. Even now, in Australia with my better English, when I listen to politicians I only understand 60%. But with politicians 60% is all you need. The rest is BS."

His first accommodation at the Navy base was a small, windowless room with a mattress on the floor. He stood the mattress up every day and used the room as his office. Two weeks later, he was moved to the senior sailor's mess hall up the hill. His room had a great view of the harbor, and the base had an excellent gym, and tennis courts. For the first year there, he was not charged for the room. The last two years he had to pay $40 USD a week, with three meals a day included.

"I loved the base," Victor says. "At night they served wine with dinner. It's where they trained Navy Seals." While he was there, a group of

US Special Forces arrived. They stayed next to his room, put sleeping bags on the floor. "It was interesting to talk with them. I watched them practice. They were into team building, talking about the importance of trust while operating in extreme conditions. They know better than anyone what it's like to make decisions under pressure of time and in tough situations, with bullets flying. That's very valuable stuff.

"I don't talk to my sailors about pressure," Victor says. "I work in advance for them to be aware of the pressure, work at showing them how to control themselves and understand they are under pressure. Because the pressure is always there. In each race, each regatta, they will encounter a different psychological state – different motivation, attitude, expectations, preparation, and different results. The guy leading has five bullets in six races. What is his state of mind when he wakes up in the morning and comes to the club ? What is the attitude of the person with bad results, or the person who has five seconds. They all have different attitudes and approaches.

"Take three sailors after three races. One has 1-1-20; another has 20-1-1; the third has 10-6-6. What is common among them ? They all have 22 points ! The difference is the attitude they carry into the next race. The guy with 1-1-20 is upset. The guy with 20-1-1 is wow, fantastic ! The guy with 10-6-6 says okay, I am progressing."

Them and Us

It was obvious from the start that the two worlds of Ukraine and Australia were going to need some time to resolve their considerable differences and find common ground. The differences had to do with the controls and restrictions under which Soviet citizens had, until very recent years, grown up and learned to function, and the wide-open, friendly skies, surf's-up nature of Australians. Victor Kovalenko couldn't have found a culture that was more contrary to the Soviet way. Even among first world democracies, Australia has a reputation for being at the far end of relaxed.

It began the first day of training. To set the tone, Victor told his new sailors one of his favorite analogies. It's about tanks. He told them that Ukrainian tanks are better than American tanks because when Americans build a tank they take their best soldier and build an environment around him that has everything he needs. He has all the information at his fingertips, he is comfortable, and the machine is easy to operate. Then they cover the tank with armor and put a gun on the top. When the Ukrainians build a tank they get the biggest gun they can find and build a tank under it. Then they open the hatch and shove a soldier in the hole and force him to adapt to the environment. It might not be comfortable for the operator, but the Ukrainian tank is the better tank. Victor went on to explain the moral of the story: an Olympic campaign has nothing to do with making it easy for yourself because you cannot build a campaign around your lifestyle and what you want to do. The right way is to force yourself to fit the mold if you want to be the best.

That little speech was followed by Victor's approach to fitness. Fitness is embraced by the Australian life style. One doesn't surf or play rugby or even cricket, ride bicycles or ski, without being fit. But Victor's training methods included some routines that were quite different. While the chin-ups and running were old school, the hanging chair was another matter. The idea was to sit in a plastic classroom chair suspended from the ceiling by four lines — one to each corner of the seat — and using only your body (no legs) try to get it swinging. The lines were crossed to make moving the chair more difficult. That was followed by sitting on a bench with 20 cans of soda and placing them upright on the floor one at a time, then placing them back on the bench one at a time, on the clock of course. The idea was to improve balance and coordination. The sailor/athlete is different than all other athletes in that his playing field never stops moving. All his moves, like in the hanging chair, are executed on a randomly-unstable platform. Compared to a 470 dinghy in a strong wind, speeding along on a confused seaway, that chair will seem easy.

"Some found Victor's program too tough, and bailed," Phil Jones says.

The common ground was the quest for Olympic medals. With Victor, winning an Olympic Gold medal is unsurpassed as an accomplishment. "It is the top of the mountain," Victor says, "the highest recognition in life. It is not only extremely hard work, but you have to change yourself and expand the limits in your sport to win. It is higher than the Nobel Prize, different. Nobel winners have no idea they are being considered, because the Nobel Prize is a judgment by others about someone's work. In sport, people have to perform – compete and prove they are the best under incredible individual pressure." But even among a self-selected group of sailors who were committed to winning medals, Victor's approach was a hard sell. He still puzzles over Australians' desires to have things in life other than Olympic gold medals.

"Victor started talking about medals right away," Belinda Stowell says. "There was lots of eye rolling, because there were no real contenders other than Jenny and Addy and me in our ragtag group. They all thought he was nuts to talk about medals. But I never thought he was nuts. That's why I was there, to win a medal. But I had no clue how a 470 should be sailed. I looked at the top crews sailing perfectly, the boat upright, the timing perfect, and remember thinking if I want to win a medal I have to be at that level. I had watched Ruslana and Olena sailing, and a year or two later Victor arrived and is asking me why I wasn't more like Olena. I advised him I was going to try my damndest to be that good, but I was never going to be her."

Stowell and her skipper, Jenny Armstrong, had met on *Elle Racing*, an all-women round the world race boat out of New Zealand prepping for the 1997-98 Whitbread race. When their syndicate ran out of money, they decided to dispense with all the crew between the cockpit (Jenny) and the bow (Belinda) and start sailing dinghies together. Neither woman was a stranger to dinghies. Armstrong had done a near-miss Olympic campaign in Europe dinghies in 1992, finishing 4th in Barcelona. Stowell had won some silver in the 420 class. They had a go in a 470 to see if they liked it. "We laughed our heads off sailing around Sydney Harbor capsizing," Belinda says. "But I declared to myself in 1995 that I wanted to win gold in Sydney.

"I remember in 2000 Victor and I were sitting on a rock on Lake Garda. Jenny Armstrong and I had just won the European Championships. Victor was being so honest, telling me that when he first arrived and saw us we were so bad he was hoping we'd quit so he could go back to Ukraine and work with his gold medalists. I laughed. He said he gave us minimal exercises we had to do four hours a day for six weeks. But we wouldn't go away. He told me after four weeks he was thinking maybe there is something interesting about us.

"Then he had us doing windward-leeward courses with so many tacks and jibes, 2-3 hours at a time, over and over, and rotations around a mark, ten each way. It wasn't boring, not if you couldn't do them. And he played tennis with us, got us inventing many different games with balls thrown at walls to improve our reactions. We had a work ethic. We were prepared to trust him. We always had trust from the moment he walked in. We stood the test of his system. He always said thank you for trusting him."

It helped that Belinda was a committed athlete who was not overcome by Victor's physical program. If anything, he had to keep her from overdoing it. She loved the land boat, spent hours perfecting her movement through the boat on tacks and jibes. And the fact she had grown up in a 3rd world country (Zimbabwe), where even necessities are not always available, helped her understand Victor's background, and connect with him. For her, the psychology was the tough part: Victor's conviction that changing a big section of her personality was an essential element of an athlete's Olympic package.

"It's about how you react to situations, and behave," Belinda says. "He needed the right window of opportunity so I could see the need for that change. He has the ability to understand the athlete completely. He says he's three steps ahead of everyone and that's probably the case. You have to stand up to him at times. He kept suggesting I sail with someone else, and I refused. I think he appreciated that. He's a tough task master. He burns a few people along the way who don't have the character to handle ultimate pressure. He drives at a high level. Everyone wants to be there, but there's only going to be one boat that ends up at the Games. He'll test you in all sorts of ways. The winning spirit in the boat will win the test. He'll pat you on the back and look after you when you're down, but he's very hard on the way up."

Victor had been hired to coach both men and women, as he had been doing since 1993 in Ukraine. He finally put a stop to it in 2008, when he focused exclusively on the men's teams. Looking back, he wondered how he had coached both for so long, paying full attention to two teams often on two different courses that were so diverse in personality and needs, and also regarding how they might be doing. Maybe the men would win and the women would finish 15th in one race. He had to share the men's enthusiasm and keep them focused, then change channels to help the women who always wanted to know how the other boat had done (or vice versa). "I would have to tell them," Victor says, "and now they were even more upset."

In 1997 he inherited three men's teams: Tom King and Mark Turnbull; Nathan Wilmot and Daniel Smith; and Lee Knapton and Malcolm Page (Knapton would leave and Cameron Hooper would become Page's skipper). King and Turnbull were the de facto first team, King (with crew Owen McMahon) having competed in the '96 Games in Savannah (they finished 23rd). Mark Turnbull, with a few national championships of his own, teamed up with King after that.

"I might have been brash," Turnbull says, "but I thought we were good. Physically I saw no reason we couldn't win gold. Those with experience knew it took more than that. We had never been exposed to the discipline of the Eastern Bloc mentality. It comes from a hard background. The way to escape the rigors of normal life in those countries is to go into sport. The main thing Victor brought was discipline. His way or the highway. Many teams dropped out because he runs such a tight ship. It's frustrating. You have to live and breathe with him. At the time you might not agree, but a week or four years later you understand.

"He had a bunch of strange land activities," Turnbull says. "There was the suspended chair you were supposed to get swinging, a tough chore because of the way he tied it, and spinning your head in a circle 50 times in one direction, then 50 times in the other direction, the idea being to overcome motion sickness. I don't think it worked. And he had this watching eye. We were always under observation. We learned to deal with it, live with it."

"He was famous for his walks. He'd come up to you in the boat park, put his arm around your shoulders, and say `you will walk with me.' It might last half an hour, an intense session because you've done something wrong, or maybe he wants you to do something different. Everyone had these walks. Even my girlfriend, Jo. People not used to him can be frightened by him. He can be intimidating. He came up to Jo and said `you will walk with me.' Tom King shook his head, said that could be the last you'll ever see of her. They came back. She looked shell shocked. Not for any particular reason. Just because Victor was being Victor. For those of us spending a lot of time exposed to his passionate, persuasive approach to the sport, it was normal. We were used to it. But Jo was unprepared for one of Victor's `you will walk with me' conversations. He had to set parameters for those who could influence the team. He needed control over that. And there was nowhere to hide."

Tom King got off to a shaky start with Victor because of his determination to finish his engineering degree at university. He'd deferred his studies three years to sail in the '96 Games, and felt if he didn't finish in 1997 it might never happen. King told Victor he'd rejoin the team full time after his final exams at the end of 1998. That did not go over well with Victor, who by his standards was already getting started a year late to prepare for the Games in 2000. But King was undeterred. He got his degree and returned to training as planned. "It took a full six months before we established ourselves in Victor's mind as worthy of his full commitment," King says. "We had to prove we were worth it. Thankfully one of the other teams created uncertainty about their commitment, and we seemed a more reliable partner going forward."

While it wouldn't have changed his mind, King would later understand Victor's insistence on a four-year program. "Victor held the somewhat unusual view that the primary determining factor of boat speed was how the sailors were trimming and using body weight to force the boat to go fast," King says. "He wanted us to be constantly seeking to accelerate the boat by maximizing how and when we applied body weight to the boat and against the sails over every wave and in anticipation of every gust of wind. Tuning – mast rake, step position, rig tension, sails, trim – impacts speed, but in Victor's philosophy the biggest factor was how we worked the boat. First he had to impart that philosophy to us, and second he spent hundreds of hours following us around forcing us to work on those techniques until we appreciated what they were doing, and until they became second nature to us."

Victor also reversed the roles of skipper and crew. In a two-man dinghy, traditionally the skipper was responsible for boat speed, trim, and tuning, and the crew, who has better vision of the course from the wire, was responsible for collecting information and making strategic decisions. Victor thought the crew, heavier, and with more leverage from the trapeze, would have a bigger impact on making the boat go fast. That left the skipper to make strategic decisions. The advantage to that is the skipper has the helm in his hands, and can react instantly to something.

"We spent many hundreds of hours refining the skills of using wind and waves," King says, "keeping the boat flat, capturing all the power possible out of the wind. Victor's sailors not only learned to go fast, but to sail fast in crucial situations where fractions of speed really matter, like coming off the starting line with someone on your lee bow and being able to sail accurately and fast in order to hang there – things other people couldn't do."

Mark Turnbull recalls how he and Tom King worked harder and harder to impress Victor because of the lack of feedback they were getting, and how that served to toughen them in a useful, but slightly bothersome way. "When there's so little feedback," Turnbull says, "you try harder. There's a lot of maturity involved with everyone who does an Olympic campaign. You are in tight confines with a single goal. Every decision for four years is based on the question of will this help me attain my goal of an Olympic medal? It doesn't make you the nicest person. You have to be very selfish. I had to learn that. Tom had it. He can be aloof, but focused. I had to quickly get that focus. And with Victor, you are doing it for higher powers, for honor and glory and country, not personal gain. Not for money, and not because you love it. You started because you love it, and you're good at it, but you end up trying to fit into that Ukrainian tank every day – if you are comfortable on the boat you are probably doing it wrong. It's supposed to be hard. To be fast you are contorting your body into positions that aren't any fun. It's a war. The toughness has to be there. You get insular and close with those you trust."

Victor hadn't been on the job very long when he raised a few more eyebrows by bringing in his old Ukrainian team as a sparring partner for the Australians. It had to be difficult for the Ukrainians, losing the coach that had produced their first two medals ever, in Savannah. Ruslana was openly crestfallen, losing not only a coach she trusted and relied on, but a man she considered family. Evgeniy Braslavets was more stoic. "It was not a big shock when he left for Australia," Evgeniy says. "That's life. We make a good result in Savannah, but Ukraine doesn't understand how it worked. So if he has a good opportunity, why not? We were upset a little bit, but that's life. We could not say no, Victor, you must not go. He always searched for possibilities, so why not? It would be different after he was gone. He protected us from the outside world in Savannah, from that pressure. It was harder on us without him."

But training is training, and taking advantage of Australia's summer instead of being locked in Ukraine's bitter winter was a huge benefit for the Ukrainian team. And as sparring partner, the team would be privy to Victor's guidance, a situation Tracy Johnstone puzzled over. "Our initial reaction was that we were getting used," Tracy says. "We thought he was double-dipping, giving away technical advice to two opposing teams. It wasn't quite Hoyle. There were all these questions going around. I struggled to explain it, said it would be okay while I questioned it myself. But at the end of the day Victor was ethical, professional. He delivered great value to our sailors. Looking at the bigger picture, it was good strategy, the right thing to do."

"I said this will make our whole group faster," Victor says, "and if our group is fastest in the world then one of them will be fastest at the Games. Ukraine was not happy I was coaching Australia. The Australian Federation was not happy I was working with Ukraine. But it was a great opportunity. Both teams trusted me. In reality, I manage relationships. We moved toward the Games as one team."

A Third Team

Then a Mexican team arrived in Sydney. It had started with an email from a man named Manuel Villarreal Medrano, asking if Victor would coach his son, Manuel, who was on the Mexican sailing team. Victor dismissed the email. Then he got a letter from Villarreal who said he was coming to Sydney and wished to meet. Victor thought it would be easiest to have a meeting and tell him politely but firmly, no. He admits to a touch of profiling. "I was expecting a big guy with a mustache and a large hat who would come and push me around," he says with a laugh. Instead Villarreal turned out to be an elegant, educated man who had just sold a business that produced disposable diapers, detergent, and candy. He had also created the Mexican chapter of the 470 class, contacting the class headquarters and paying the dues. He got Victor's name from 470 paperwork that noted he was in charge of training. Villarreal outlined the situation, said the sailors loved what they did, and wanted to make sailing more visible in their country. He had decided to take a business sabbatical, and going for the Olympics in Sydney was his choice of projects to occupy his time.

"I had a feeling he was a good man for us," Victor says. "My mind said no, it would be too much, too big a group, the Mexican team was too young, it meant more work, more problems. But my intuition said this man with his passion and big heart would help us a lot." Victor also liked the son, Manuel, and his crew. Both sailors were helpful and positive.

From a practical standpoint, the Mexican team would fill a void in Victor's program. In training, the Ukranians were hammering the Australians every day. That put the Australian teams in a constant position of attacking. They needed to also know how to defend. The Mexican team would provide that element, while having the opportunity to develop and learn at the same time. It turned out that Victor had briefly encountered Manuel, the son, at a regatta, and had noted that while he was small in stature he had a strong will. But Victor made him and his crew earn their place in the process.

"Once we had moved to Sydney," Villarreal says, "Victor said over coffee to tell my son he could watch training from 500 meters, that he should not come any closer or try to talk with Victor. He wanted to watch him sailing in Sydney's rough waters. A few weeks later, over another coffee, he said Manuel could come in closer and listen to what Victor was telling his sailors, but that he mustn't interrupt. So little by little he was let in, and became a training partner of the Australian team. Victor was very careful."

Manuel Villarreal Medrano is a wealthy man, which could also be a help, but Victor puts Villarreal's commitment to helping the overall effort far ahead of any monetary contributions. When Victor was given a large motorboat by AYF, and an oversized trailer that constantly blew bearings as he was driving around Europe, Villarreal flew in to help solve the problem. When Victor had two hernia repair surgeries in 1999, Villarreal jumped in the motor boat to handle the lifting of marks and anchors. And he proved to be a good messenger. "As a coach, I try to be invisible, not dominate, and sometimes it would not be effective for me to send messages to the sailors," Victor says. "So I would ask friends or maybe officials to tell something to Jenny and Belinda, or Tom and Mark. Villarreal understood how to put things, and he was in the motor boat with me and understood what I saw."

Back home in Mexico, Villarreal had run a company with 1400 employees. As a leader he had stressed the concept of total quality, one who was concerned with his workers' "minds, spirits, and emotions," as he expresses it. "The idea of delivering messages made me interested in Victor," Villarreal says. He knew Victor was Ukrainian, so he was also guilty of a bit of profiling. "I thought his Russian background would make him militaristic, strict," Villarreal says, "and I found the opposite. He was very close to what it had taken me many years to learn: how to treat people so they liked the job. I asked him how he did it. He said you have to live it. When I first went on the boat to help him I did things very fast. He said to slow down, because my body language will transmit how I was feeling – that whatever my attitude was would be communicated to the sailors.

"He said be careful how you move, what you say. If someone made a mistake and we were far away, Victor would be very mad, cursing, saying he was going to kill that guy. By the time we approached the boat he was smiling, cordial, very helpful, asking what did they see, what did they learn. That surprised me. Before we took to the water he would always ask the sailors what they wanted to do that day, what they thought the weakest points were, what aspect they should be training on. After sailing he would ask what they learned that session, what they learned from others. He never said 'what mistakes.' He let them tell what they did wrong and they would learn from that.

"If someone was complaining about the boats or the crew, he would exchange them. My son once said a certain boat was much better. So Victor said okay, tomorrow you will sail that boat." He did, and found no noticeable improvement.

Travels with Victor

In most Olympic classes, there are five or six important regattas every year that a contending team must attend. The European and World Championships top the list, and they are never in the same place consecutively. Half a dozen World Cup regattas (so designated by World Sailing), in addition to test events at the Olympic venue (Rio de Janeiro in 2015-16), can count heavily in world rankings, and for qualifying when an Olympic year is imminent. Travel has always been a part of competitive sailing. The time sailors and coaches with world class ambitions must spend away from home is daunting. In his career, Victor has spent an average of six months a year on the road. Moving to Australia made it all that more difficult for him. Wherever one flies from Australia seems to take around 20 hours, whether it's the European continent, or North or South America. Once on the ground, with a boat under tow, it's business as usual.

Belinda says the team always picked her to travel with Victor because no one else had the patience to deal with Victor's uneasy relationship with the road. After the repeated breakdowns caused by failed bearings on the overloaded trailer, Victor's confidence with any trailer was blown. As a result, he would stop every hour or so to let the bearings cool off, often pouring water on them. "It took us 17 hours once to make a 10-hour trip," Belinda says. "I definitely took one for the team."

It's also a coach's duty to care for the health and welfare of his team, and Victor has always been very active on that front. His own physical state seems to be impeccable at age 65, and is tended with care. Every day begins with a half hour of exercises strenuous enough to break a sweat, followed by a modest breakfast of freshly extracted fruit juices (including a bit of ginger root), perhaps a boiled egg and an assortment of cheeses on fresh bread with a bit of Manuka honey, and green tea. And always there is the little dish containing a Brazil nut, a walnut, and a macadamia nut, Victor's secret formula for staying fit and healthy. He'll often ask while chewing up the nuts with a friend, "Can't you feel the goodness going into your body?" To those who register distaste for any of the nuts, Victor says, "Then you can take medicine instead." When we have had dinner together, at Victor's suggestion we most often order one appetizer and one entrée to share as a way to combat overly large restaurant portions.

Victor believes exercise works a lot better than medicine. "The best medicine is blood," he says. "Blood brings oxygen to muscles and damaged tissues. If people have a knee problem, they run to the doctor. He gives them medicine, or a special bandage, or surgery, or antibiotics – a huge mistake. The best treatment for a knee problem is more exercise to strengthen the knee, exercise that brings blood to the damaged area. Biking is the best. And blood is good for the brain, for cleaning the mind, burning out stressful hormones. If you are tired or angry, do a bit of exercise to get the blood going. Walking, running, or biking early in the morning is when you absorb the freshness of the universe. After 8am, it's too late."

His way of dealing with illnesses on the road is even more aggressive. For Jenny Danks, the prescription was drinking whiskey at 9am to combat food poisoning. Belinda Stowell tells a similar story of being treated with a triple shot of whiskey for stomach cramps with less rewarding results. "I was drunk in the debrief that day," she says, "but still had the stomach cramps." Another time Tom King had a chest cold. Victor said he must rub Tom's chest with vodka. Then Tom set fire to the vodka, and Victor was rubbing Tom's chest with a prickly woolen jumper. "Jenny and I were rolling on the floor laughing," Stowell says. "Another time he prescribed hot milk with a tablespoon of butter and 5 drops of iodine for some ailment I had. I was in a hotel in Palma drinking this disgusting concoction. But I trusted him, figured I may as well drink it down the hatch. It didn't help at all. Tell him you've got a cold and see what he comes up with. Let me know if he suggests gargling with your own urine because that's been suggested. At the time, Jenny asked if you did that hot or cold. It made iodine with milk sound good."

Peter Conde, a former world class Laser sailor from Brisbane (Conde placed second in the Laser Worlds in 1979) who now races Etchells competitively, is High Performance Director of Yachting Australia in 2017. He's Victor's boss. Conde says he once met Victor at a café for breakfast. His voice sounded nasal that day. Alarmed, Victor asked Peter Conde if he had a head cold, and moved his chair back. "He told me if I ate some garlic, we could talk," Conde says. "Otherwise he was gone. I went to a nearby fruit stand and got some garlic. Eating a clove of raw garlic for breakfast was his condition for sitting at the same table with me."

Phil Jones has to chuckle when Victor's health philosophy is mentioned. "I've seen him order a warm Coke with ginger chopped in it," Jones says. Victor also had a plan for helping Jones' son strengthen his immune system that involved immersing his feet in cold water. "It must be a gradual process," Victor says. "Once a day for 5 seconds at first, then ten, twenty, then twice a day, then you graduate to ice water for longer periods. I have seen this work very well on several people."

"Victor sometimes has ideas that don't work," Peter Conde says, "but that's just part and parcel of the genius that is Victor. And there is genius involved. He doesn't know everything about everything, but it doesn't stop him from having a go. He'll abandon ideas then forget they were his, move on to new things."

Contenders

The picture for success with the Australian women's 470 team went from bleak to cautiously optimistic in Victor's mind in 1998, when Jenny and Belinda finished 7th at Kiel Week. A top-ten finish at Kiel is an accomplishment, and after only one year of training it was not only unexpected, it was remarkable. In between Kiel and the World Championships in Spain that year, Stowell developed shoulder problems. A doctor suggested surgery, but that would have meant the end of the team. Instead, Stowell was seen banging her shoulder against the mast a couple times a race to snap it back in place after it had dislocated.

In Spain, there was more good news as both the men and the women finished 8th in the World Championships, the year's most important event. It was a dog fight within the ranks as Tom and Mark dueled successfully with Nathan and Dan, and Jenny and Belinda fought off Jenny and Addy. Both struggles were a portent of things to come. But the good results did wonders for both teams.

"I was finally beginning to be able to deal with my emotions at the level of a world-class athlete," Belinda says. "I was always hard on myself. I lacked confidence, always feeling I had to do more, that I couldn't win because I hadn't done enough. Victor could plant seeds of belief early, seeds that led to changes in your behavior. It's part of his drip-feed system. He said he'd waited 14 months to have a conversation with me on a particular topic. He'd make you believe you were a world champion before you were. The power of that was amazing. It cleverly changed your behavior.

"Victor changed my life, changed how I see things and how I operate. He gave me confidence I never had in my own athletic ability."

Tom King might say the same thing. Victor generally puts his sailors in one of two categories, "foam," or "iceberg." By foam, he means a chunk of Styrofoam floating on the water that is instantly affected by the slightest breeze or ripples. "Foam" indicates an excess of natural talent in a sailor you can easily see. The iceberg describes a less visible but often deeper talent. "Foam is all about the water," Victor says. "When the wind is blowing the foam flies across the water with the wind. When the wind blows, the iceberg stands like a fortress, he is not blown by the wind. He stays strong against wind and storm. That is real talent." Victor saw Tom King as an iceberg. Tracy Johnstone agreed. "I used to write in my diary whenever I was able to coax a smile out of Tom," she says.

King had finished his engineering degree at the top of his class. He says he has always had an intellectual approach to sailing, a desire to understand why it works, understand what makes a boat go fast, understand the logic behind racing strategies and weather analysis. "That's different from having the wonderful feel for boats or wind that, for instance, Nathan Wilmot has," King says. "Nathan was a totally gifted young sailor, very different, and also a difficult human being. He had an extraordinary talent for making a boat go fast. I had a strong base for being a good sailor, and it got me a long way in the sport. But the biggest challenge for me was to let go of trying to be so logical at everything and trust my instincts. Because it is all so complex out there that your instinctive decision-making is more accurate and quicker… if you are good at it."

Getting good at it takes both belief, and practice. The more you trust your instincts, the more you can rely on them. It takes time, and experience to fuel the instincts, and Victor was the keeper of the clock, an often frustrating situation for the sailors. "I like to know the big picture," King says. "But Victor doesn't open up about what he is trying to do. Twelve months before the Sydney Games we finished 5th in a big regatta. That was an okay result, but we weren't fast. Other boats had an edge. We needed help to go faster, and he said don't worry, by

the time the Games come you will be fast. That wasn't the answer we
wanted. We wanted to go faster that afternoon ! He wouldn't help us,
said we must trust him, by the Olympics we would be fast enough, and
that was true. A lot of effort went into it, lots of time was required on
the water. But at the time he was dealing with the psychology of racing
at a high level without a speed advantage.

"He was able to take me from analyzing everything to trusting
my instincts," King says. "But I couldn't do that until I had a base
of knowledge and training and confidence in my own understanding
of things. He said don't over think it. If your instincts are there, do it.
When we did that, we raced extremely well. Mark said when we were
in that zone he didn't dare speak for fear of disrupting it."

"That zone" where it is all working, where perfection itself is
threatened, is where every athlete – every artist – strives to be, dreams
of being. That zone is an altered state that remains elusive to most,
and is an occasional moment of mystical joy for the best. The great
ones live there much of the time.

CHAPTER 9

Selection

Because Jenny Danks and Addy Bucek had come so close to a medal in 1996, and because Jenny had worked hard to secure Victor as Australia's 470 coach, Jenny and Addy had decided to go for it again in 2000. Given the unknown quantity of Jenny Armstrong and Belinda Stowell, Victor had urged Jenny and Addy to mount a campaign for Sydney. Danks had had a baby in 1997. As soon as she was recovered, she and Addy took to the water. But Jenny and Belinda proved to be a handful. When it was all over, the two teams ended up in a dead heat for being selected. Jenny and Addy lost in a countback, in which each team's scores for the qualifying regattas are listed best to worst, and at the point where there is a difference the tie is broken in favor of the boat with the best score. A countback is a tough way to lose any regatta, brutal when Olympic selection is in the balance. It's even worse when the Games in question will be held on your home waters. Danks was advised she could challenge the decision and have a reasonable chance of winning if she raised the issue of Armstrong's (New Zealand) and Stowell's (Zimbabwe) origins. Instead, Danks congratulated Jenny and Belinda, said they deserved to go to the Games and wished them well. "Victor," Danks says today, "came into my life one Olympics too late."

It wasn't quite as simple for the men. Tom King and Mark Turnbull had started the 1999 season with an 8th at the World Championships in Melbourne, making them the top Australian boat. Their rivals – the foam to Tom's iceberg – Nathan Wilmot and his crew Dan Smith, had finished 23rd. But King says his decision to take time out to finish his degree was still behind the fact that Victor wasn't giving them his full attention until they finished in the top ten in the World Cup regatta at Hyères, France, in 1999, about a year before the Games. Until then, Tom and Mark had registered a less than stellar series of finishes on their European Tour.

"Before Hyères," King says, "we had a week off in Austria. We did some hard thinking, laid out a plan. We'd been looking at the American Paul Foerster and decided we had to be at a professional level a step above what he was doing. After that, our preparation was better, we were on the water early, and we focused on the details."

Then after one regatta Wilmot and Smith behaved badly. A car was damaged. Alcohol was involved. "At that point," King says, "I think Victor realized we were his best chance to go all the way."

Selection for 2000, which was ultimately subjective, was based on the results of three regattas: Kiel, 1999, and two regattas on Sydney Harbor. A panel was established by the Olympic Committee to select the team, but it would rely heavily on the scores, and what Yachting Australia recommended. The coach's opinion along with mitigating circumstances (perhaps a regatta had been sailed in extreme conditions) would also be taken into consideration.

King/Turnbull were way ahead on points. They had finished 4th at Kiel, while Wilmot/Smith had sailed a bad regatta. Wilmot/Smith did better in the smaller, Sydney regattas, but there was no way for them to make up the points. King/ Turnbull were selected. Wilmot/Smith immediately challenged the decision, citing their better performance on Sydney water where the Games would be held (they beat King/Turnbull by one point), but mainly citing an assertion by Victor that they were the best team. It was Daniel Smith's stepfather, Ross Fenton, who initiated the challenge. The sailors went along with it.

The rules of the game included a legal process for challenging selection. However spurious the basis for challenge might appear, the process had to be served with hearings, depositions, sports attorneys and a barrister. King says it cost them around $10,000 and took six weeks. Having finally been selected after long years of preparation, having gone through anxious months of trying to get back into their coach's good graces, and having been uncertain of the outcome until the final regattas, the modest celebration of their success (the relief) turned out to be premature. Legal process can develop a life of its own, with the issue at stake often being lost in the progression of argument. Thoughts of training and continuing to prepare for the most important regatta of their lives had to be set aside while the challenge was addressed. "The grounds for appeal were so absurd," King says, "but we had to be concerned about the outcome, had to give it our best shot. It was very upsetting at the time."

It was impossible for the aura of the Wilmot family's sailing history not to impact the proceedings, at least in the media. Nathan's father had competed in the 1984 Olympics. An uncle had competed in the 1988 Games. Another uncle, Hugh Trehane, had been the tactician aboard Australia's winning America's Cup challenger (Australia II) in 1983. There was a certain preconception in Sydney that there was a certain logic to Nathan following in the family's illustrious wake.

The outcome of the hearing rested heavily on Victor's testimony. "Nathan's father, Jimmy, who is still a brilliant sailor, asked me to be a witness for them," Victor says. "I was supposed to be the expert." He was also the coach of both teams, and as such, he had to be feeling the squeeze. But as usual, Victor let the facts speak for themselves.

"They asked me what I thought of Nathan as a sailor," Victor says. "I said he is very good, he was winner of this and this and this. Next question: have you told Nathan and his family that he is a great sailor and he will have a chance to be a medalist at the 2000 worlds? I said yes. That means Nathan is good, you have confirmed he is a fantastic sailor. I said yes, I said this, but he is Brilliant Sailor Number Two. Brilliant Sailor Number One is Tom King, confirmed by his results. There was a battle between the two of them, and Tom won."

Case dismissed.

"I made peace with Nathan eight years later," King says. "He is a talented yachtsman, and was an immature prat as a human. At the Olympic level, personality traits get exposed. It's Victor's job to mature you into an athlete with the strength of character to make an Olympic champion. Nathan didn't have that at the time. Victor supported us. I might not have had Nathan's talent, but I had maturity and experience."

Later, Victor would expound upon his testimony. "Tom won the World Championship once, in 2000, and a gold medal the same year. Nathan would go on to win the Worlds three times [he was second twice and third once], he won the European's twice, and an Olympic gold medal in 2008, in addition to many other regattas. But in 2000, Nathan was number two."

During the challenge, Victor's approach to keeping King and Turnbull focused was to increase the intensity of training. "Pushing athletes is my job," Victor says. "If I don't push them enough I betray them. If I push them too much, they betray me." After the challenge was dismissed, Victor saw marked improvement in the way his number one team was sailing. In the final training races they sailed inside the harbor with the Olympic decor on the sails along with their names. The passengers on every ferry that passed them crowded the rail yelling AUSSI AUSSI AUSSI – OI OI OI ! ! The whole city was cranked for the Olympics, and especially the sailing because it was Australia. The pressure was palpable.

As the Olympic Games approached, Victor became concerned about King's obsession with the accumulation of spare parts against breakage. He sensed a bit too much anxiety coming from his thoughtful engineer/skipper. So when all was ready, and Tom and Mark had moved into their Olympic accommodation, Victor showed up one evening with a bottle of wine. He thought it was important to draw the line between preparation, and competition. "I said `Tom, let's celebrate the finish of your preparation.' And Tom said `no no, I am an athlete.' I said `Tom, don't worry, you are ready, you will perform great, I am confident.' The idea wasn't to drink the whole bottle, just a bit of wine. Tom was under pressure. If I had said don't drink, it would have put more pressure on him. You are ready, that was the message." Victor also brought King a book that evening, a book that is a favorite of his friend John Bertrand, the winning America's Cup skipper in 1983. It's called *Jonathan Livingston Seagull*, about the renegade bird who lived not to eat, like his brethren, but to explore the limits of flight.

2000

The last dinner before the Games was held at Manuel Villarreal's lovely rented home on Pott's Point on Sydney Harbor, with a great view of the Harbor Bridge. The house was lavishly decorated for the occasion. The food was delicious, the music stirring, and there was a memorable display of fireworks. "The atmosphere was incredible in Manuel's house," Victor says, "a mood created that bridged into the behavior of the athletes. In sport we are always looking for these bridges to build confidence and a winning spirit."

At the dinner, Manuel told the two leading Australian teams if they won medals he would buy them tickets to Mexico. If the medals were bronze, they would fly economy class. If silver, business class. If gold, first class. A year or so later, on the occasion of his son's marriage, the tickets would arrive as promised, and hotel accommodations in addition. "It was an incredible wedding," Victor says. "The reception for 500 people was in an old monastery lit by a thousand candles. There were so many flowers, music, costumes and masks. In the ladies room they had slippers so the women could rest from their heels. Manuel's attention to details like that was the catalyst of our success in Sydney."

Sydney was as successful as it gets. Victor says the training partners he put together in the lead-up to Sydney were the best group ever assembled. The collection of medals that would eventually be amassed by the Ukrainian and Australian boats was impressive. Competing daily against the Ukrainians, who were arguably the best in the world at the time, lifted the Australians to world class quality. And while they would finish back in the fleet (23rd), the Mexican team registered two single digit finishes in Sydney.

King/Turnbull fought off their exemplar from the USA, Foerster/Merrick, to win the gold medal. On the women's course, Armstrong/Stowell hung tough to beat the USA team of Isler/Glaser, who took silver, and Taran/Paholchek (UKR) who won bronze.

It was a blow for the Ukrainians, who had to have been favored going in. Three days before the Games Victor's multi-national group was still training together. At the Games, the Ukrainians ran into the same stone wall Jenny Danks had encountered in 1996: Victor was suddenly and exclusively Australia's coach. This time there were a few cracks in the wall. The issue of nationality, and the longevity of intimate relationships with Ruslana and Evgeniy, could not be dispatched in a day, even by someone with Victor's professional aplomb. "At the Games," Victor recalls, "I said to the Ukraine team, `sorry guys, I have to be with the Australians.' But I told them if they need help, let me know.

"Ruslana was a little bit fragile because she was nervous about Jenny and Belinda. Jealous. Half way through the Olympic regatta she was leading. If she'd kept her confidence she would have won the Games easily. She was number one. But she started playing politics. She'd come to the boat park to talk with me, speaking in Russian, making the conversation appear even more personal and confidential. We did not talk about sailing. We talked about life, anything, it didn't matter because she was trying to show Jenny and Belinda she could talk to me and make them think I was guiding her, telling her secrets, trying to shake their confidence and trust in me. It was a game. But the game was against Ruslana. Jenny and Belinda didn't care because they were playing their own game. They were tough. She destroyed her own confidence by playing this game."

Victor says Ruslana departed from the model that had served her well, a model based on the confidence that no matter where she is in a regatta, she can still win. "Many times she followed this model and after some bad races, came back to win," Victor says. "She would say I am not leading, I am in 4th position, but I am okay, I can always win. She would not even come to the board to check the results."

Victor did help Ruslana at the Games. She came to him before the last race, went to his hotel, said she had to talk. "I said to her `Ruslana, I am Australia's coach, this is my team.' She said `no, you are my coach as well, I am your athlete.' I said okay. We talked. That day she had gotten a 1st and a 15th in two races. She was upset. I told her imagine for a second you got a 15th and a 1st. You would have the same number of points, but you would be on fire because you won the last race. Only your imagination makes the difference. She hugged me."

Before the last race, he suggested to her (and also to Jenny and Manuel) that going left after the start toward Bradley's Head, a well-known landmark in Sydney Harbor, would protect her from the current and also allow her to pick up a favorable shift. "After the start, Ruslana said to Olena they would tack to the right," Victor says. "Unbelievable! Olena wouldn't let her, saying no, coach said to go left. They argued. Olena won. They went left, finished second and got the bronze medal. Jenny and Belinda won the race, and got the gold."

The Ukrainian men, Braslavets/Matviyenko, got off to a fast start and were second after two races. "There is a big difference between coaching the men and the women," Victor says. "Ruslana trusted me a lot. Evgeniy trusted me too, but he always had doubts, he had his own agenda." Three disqualifications put the Ukrainian men out of contention. Even so, they rallied to finish 6th overall.

Having helped produce the only two sailing gold medals won at Sydney, Victor's stock could not have been higher. The celebrations in Sydney were over the top. "We went wild on the VIP boat when they won," Tracy Johnstone says. "The Minister of Sport rang Phil Jones and myself just after the win to congratulate us on the work we had done. At the awards ceremony the team was ecstatic, but there was also a feeling of completion, and relief. Victor's appointment as head coach was inevitable."

The celebrations in Ukraine were mixed. Ukrainian officialdom was reeling a little after the coach they had casually let go had just produced two gold medals for a rival country. In the Kovalenko household in Dnepropetrosvk, while their patriarch's incredible success was being celebrated, thoughts about the enormity of the upcoming move to a strange, unknown land was a cloud lurking on the horizon.

CHAPTER 10

Anniversary in Dnepropetrovsk

During the year leading up to the Olympic Games in Sydney, Victor Kovalenko had spent a total of 14 days with his family in Dnepropetrovsk. Three of those days were in high celebration of his and Tatiana's birthdays, and their 20th wedding anniversary. The first week of August, 2000, had been perfect timing for Victor to fly to Ukraine after his team wrapped up a European training trip with the French National Championships. It had been an exciting trip full of promise for the team; a series of regattas highlighted by the testing of a new generation of Ziegelmayer 470s that Victor had a hand in conceiving.

He had called his friend Sebastian Ziegelmayer, who was building a very competitive line of 420 and 470 dinghies (and Optimists) at the time, at his company in Hamburg, Germany, and told him he had ideas for how to improve the boats. Victor had asked Ziegelmayer to fly to Australia. Ziegelmayer wasn't very enthusiastic about making the trip until Victor told him that if he didn't like his ideas, he would pay for Ziegelmayer's ticket. The details are still secret, but the basic concept involved lengthening the boats by 1.7 cm (within maximum dimensions under the rules). Victor also had ideas for making the hulls stiffer or more flexible in certain areas. "You could tell the boat was a little hard going upwind in the waves," Victor says, "and downwind as well, a little bit stiff. I thought we needed to make the skin and structure a little softer, more flexible, like a dolphin. If you race a dolphin against a torpedo, the dolphin will win."

Ziegelmayer flew to Australia, listened to Victor, and ended up paying for his own ticket. The new boats that resulted had been tested for the first time in Europe, 2000, and the sailors had been pleased with their performance. With the team shaping up well for the Sydney Games, the three-day celebration in Dnepropetrovsk was well-timed.

"It was a great party," Victor says. "We chartered a big ship for my birthday. Two Ukrainian ministers were there, and the Deputy Chairman of National Security, all good friends. They were regretting I was in Australia, but they were happy for me. Tom King and Mark Trumbull had won the Worlds, then the Holland regatta and Kiel Week, and had been second in Hyères. Jenny Armstrong and Belinda Stowell had been first in Hyères, had won the Europeans, and had placed second in the Worlds. Our Australian team was ranked #1 in the world!"

They danced and toasted Tatiana's 40th birthday, Victor's 50th birthday, and their wedding anniversary with more than 100 friends from all over the Soviet Union as they cruised the Dneper River. The party started at 10 in the morning, and finally concluded at 3am. The next day Victor returned to Sydney for a final round of training before the Olympic Games, then just six weeks away.

Reunion in Sydney

Tatiana had visited Victor several times when he was living alone in Sydney. In 1998 she had stayed for a month, turning heads when she would walk across the Navy base from Victor's accommodation in the mess hall on the hill in her bikini, on the way to a swim in the harbor. "It is a nice country," Tatiana says. "I liked it as a tourist. But I couldn't imagine living here. The culture and the people are different. They smile all the time. In Ukraine, if you smile people ask you what happened, because life is hard."

Her imagination was tested in the Fall of 2000, when she and her son Vladimir arrived to take up residence. It was a severe test for both of them. "It was a hard immigration for a person my age," Tatiana says. "I had no friends, no language, no job. It's very hard for me to stay at home. Some women enjoy it. Not me. I was all the time working in Ukraine, studying and working. And Victor was working, away much of the time. I started to cry every morning every day for six months because I wanted to go back to Ukraine. I had everything there, a good apartment, a nice job teaching elementary school, and all my friends and family. In Australia when he was away, I was alone. I never unpacked my clothes. After two years, I said maybe I will put my clothes in a wardrobe."

Victor said he never knew how distressed Tatiana was. "She was very strong, never showed me she was unhappy. She told me years later she was crying. I asked her why she did not tell me. She said it would have been a bad distraction for me."

After four months, Vladimir — now 20 years old — returned to Ukraine, leaving Tatiana even more isolated. Like his mother, Vladimir was lonely. He was also distraught, confused by his new surroundings. He knew no one. He had flushed under patronizing, uniformed smiles when he had mistakenly gone to the police station for a driver's license. He had a steady girlfriend in Ukraine, and his quality of life there was excellent. There was the large, three bedroom apartment, a car, and the house on the Dneper river.

"One day Vladimir came to us," Victor says, "and said he had decided to go back home. He said he would continue his law studies and get a job as a security guard. I said okay, I will buy you a ticket, but it is a one-way ticket. If you decide to come back, you must pay your own way. I told him no problem, you can go, but my wallet will stay in Australia."

Vladimir's plan of having the big apartment in Dnepropetrovsk all to himself and his girlfriend was dashed when Tatiana's sister refused to give him the key. Instead she said he could stay with her family. He agreed because it was his only option. "He couldn't find a job," Victor says, "and his studies were not easy. The relationship with his girlfriend went bad. I think she was pushing him to come back so they could live in the big apartment with financial support from Australia, have a good life." Victor smiles. "But we said no. After six months he contacted Tatiana, said he'd made a mistake and wanted to come back."

Vladimir's English was quite good. In Ukraine, Tatiana had provided a private tutor for him. But it was not at the sophisticated level the study of law would require in Australia. He went to work. His first job was in the coffee shop of a bookstore in a building owned by Bell Properties, arranged by Victor through a sailor he had befriended named Chris Meahan. Meahan was on the board of Bell Properties, and had helped Victor and Tatiana purchase a good apartment. Victor had built what he calls his "dream house" in Sydney, but it was very far from the water. He was trying to upgrade, and had found an ad for an attractive place with a stunning harbor view that was going to be auctioned.

Victor and Tatiana knew they could not afford the apartment under auction, but had decided to have a look anyway. Later on, Victor called Chris Meahan hoping he could help find them an apartment. Victor showed him the ad. Meahan laughed, said the place was being handled by Bell Properties. Meahan introduced Victor to the mortgage system, organized all the paperwork, took the apartment off auction with a phone call, and marked it "sold." By comparison, finding a job for Vladimir in the coffee shop was easy for Chris Meahan.

Since then, Vladimir has gravitated toward his consuming interest: cars. When not racing boats in Ukraine, he was racing go carts, and doing well. As his father says, "He's a great driver and he loves cars, knows all cars, is mad about cars. He is meticulous with cars, is always upgrading his cars. He had a job selling Jeeps, then lost it through office politics. He was sitting home, depressed, helping me a little but thinking about cars. I said you need a job, it doesn't matter what job, but you mustn't sit home and get depressed. So he went to work at a car wash. For three days he did wheels. He was upgraded. Two weeks later he was shift manager. In less than a year he was manager of the car wash. He has a good work ethic, he's organized, a good leader."

Today Vladimir is Operational Manager of Australian National Car Parks, a large organization that manages car parks for businesses all over Sydney with the latest in robotic technology. The job has a certain tense, high security feel to it that Vladimir savors. It has to do with a number of people who are intent on hacking the systems and parking for free. When challenged, these people can get nasty. Vladimir has an increased watchfulness about him when he strides through one of his garages. The lens of a tiny, protective CCTV camera can be seen on his jacket.

Desperate to find a positive direction, Vladimir's mother enrolled in a beautician's course. "If I don't study something," Tatiana says today, "my English will not improve. I studied two and a half years to be a beautician. I never worked at the job, but I had to do assignments and pass exams, and my English improved as a result. I had to study to improve myself, and beauty is not bad for women. If you study all the time you will never grow old."

What finally gave Tatiana the break she needed was when she was asked to work for Yachting Australia. She still struggled with the language, and said they had to teach her everything, but YA Performance Director Peter Conde says she was determined to learn to do the job perfectly. At

YA, Tatiana is an administrative assistant, collating results for all national and world regattas, and working in support of program managers.

Everywhere, Nowhere

After his big success in Sydney, 2000, Victor Kovalenko's contract was extended through another Olympic cycle by the Australian Sailing Federation (now Australian Sailing). They also offered him the job of head coach of the Olympic sailing team. "First I thought this is probably not a good idea," Victor says. "It's like if you appoint a good surgeon as director of the clinic, you will lose a good doctor, and not get a good director of the clinic."

Victor's instincts, as usual, were right. But he took the job assuming that, as in Ukraine, the head coach had the biggest power. He didn't know that in the Australian system, the high performance manager was boss of the team. For an entire year, he didn't realize the high performance manager was above him in the organization. "I was dedicated to my job, thinking, analyzing, making reports, reading athletes' reports, trying to do everything I could to be first to step into the future," Victor says. "When I came from the airport, I didn't drive home until after I had been to the office to talk with administrators. I did this for four years. It was draining. But after one year I discovered I had to report to the high performance manager, Susan Thompson. She said I am not working under you, you are working under me. And I said wow ! My enthusiasm went down a little. But we got along. I wanted to help the team, not fight. And she was a good operator, a good sailor."

Today, only the budget for swimming – for many years Australia's marquee sport – exceeds sailing's $8 million budget. But in 2000, the $500,000 didn't begin to cover what was needed. Athletes had to buy boats, sails and gear, and cover their travel expenses. There was an inadequate medal incentive scheme. In addition, there was political infighting about where sailing should be positioned within the hierarchy of the national sports organizations.

"No one really represented us," Victor says. "As head coach I spent far too much time and energy in too many directions trying to make the system work. That time and energy came out of the team. And the Federation did not help us financially to get equipment needed to compete. It was a chain reaction, especially in the Olympic year 2004. There was not only a financial effect on the team, but a psychological effect. Everyone was expecting new boats and equipment. We were world champions in the Tornado and the 470. Armstrong and Stowell were Olympic gold medalists. The Laser was good, our board sailors were good. We had a strong team. We expected very good results. In Athens we were close, but no medals. It was a big letdown. As head coach I was not working in the right directions. I was spread between management and head coaching and 470 coaching and it was a huge big mistake. It had a big impact on me personally and on the whole team."

Tom King had retired after winning gold in Sydney. Victor tried to persuade him to continue training for Athens, but King had always planned to stop Olympic sailing after Sydney. He'd borrowed money to get to the Games, and with no monetary rewards forthcoming for winning a gold medal, he needed an income. Nathan Wilmot's partner, Dan Smith, had gone into coaching. Victor put Malcolm Page in the boat with Wilmot. Page had exhibited talent as a young sailor, winning the Manley Junior nationals — a nine foot dinghy with jib and spinnaker — when he was 13 years old. When Victor arrived in Sydney in 1997, Page was sailing in a 470 with a skipper named Lee Knapton.

"Victor was very hard, initially," Page says, "very black and white, the Eastern European mentality. He was elusive, secretive. Sometimes we'd feel he wasn't on our side. But I was young, naïve about the Olympic situation. Over time I learned, and he learned a lot about us, about how Australians think. Since then he's gone more Australian, and we've also understood what it takes. What we needed was his thoroughness and 'no excuses' attitude."

The new team clicked. After Sydney, Wilmot/Page had steadily progressed up the world championship ladder, winning bronze in 2001, silver in 2003, and gold in 2004 on the way to being selected for Athens (they would win the Worlds again in 2005). Page was Chief Marketing Officer for World Sailing in Southampton, England, until he was drafted as Chief of the US Sailing team in late 2016. He is Australia's most decorated sailor, winning two Olympic gold medals, and nine World Championship medals (six gold, two silver, one bronze). But in 2004, he and Wilmot would strike out in Athens.

"You've heard the rap about how the Olympics is just another regatta," Page says. "That's what they drum into you anyway. Well, it isn't just another regatta. There's more pressure, more expectation, and you say it won't affect you but it will. You get the uniform, everyone has one, all these funny colors and flags, you're living and eating in a village with the other competitors…it's different."

Page says he should have insisted they do penalty turns on Day One of every Olympics he has been to. "We didn't do one in Athens, and we got disqualified. It was such a dubious infringement that if it had happened in the World Championship there would have been no protest. There's a certain tolerance in the fleet for near misses. But in the Olympic Games if someone says protest, even when there is not an incident, they will conjure something up to try to kill you because it is the Olympic Games: win at all costs."

On Day One, Race 1 at Athens, Wilmot/Page had a close crossing on port tack with a starboard tack (right of way) boat. There was no contact, and infringement was debatable. But if a degree of doubt can be raised, the starboard tack boat will always prevail in a jury room. "I said to Nathan three times we should do turns because we can't win a protest on port." Page says. "And he said no, we are not doing turns. Ashore, he said what will we do? I said withdraw. I normally did the protests, and I wasn't doing that one. It was a message to him as well. He said okay, and we withdrew from the race."

Page says, in hindsight, that Wilmot took too much risk after that to get back in the game. Wilmot agrees. "Athens was just one of those weeks," Wilmot says. "I sailed stupid." Victor says if Wilmot had sailed more conservatively perhaps gold would have been beyond reach, but bronze or even silver could have been his. "Nathan goes by the seat of the pants," Page says. "All guts. He's a brilliant talent. He just gets in the boat and goes. I didn't know how to handle what happened to Nathan and me on day one in Athens. I did the best I could with what I knew at the time."

Victor was having trouble getting through to Wilmot as well. He frequently stresses the critical importance of timing of the messages he sends to his sailors, how he sometimes must wait many months for just the right opportunity. "But in the motor boat between races," he says, "you must send a message right then because it will be important for the next race. In general there is more trust from the women. Like the men, they want to know why, the big picture, the reasoning, the benefits, but they are accepting. Sometimes men don't accept what you say. They follow their own agenda. They might say okay, but they don't do it, or they do it half way. You say to yourself, I can wait. Then they come back and say they have no speed or can't point, and you say let's do this. They do it, and everything works. With Nathan you sometimes had to wait a long time.

"He had a strong character. It was not easy to deal with him. He was very selective about messages, selecting the ones that were comfortable for him. I had to be very patient, accurate with timing, wait for a good mood when he would accept a message that was productive for him… maybe it would not be so comfortable, but one that would make a big difference in his life perception and his performance. But if he said yes, he meant it 100%. Many others said yes, and did not mean it."

The women, Armstrong/Stowell, fared no better. Observers say theirs was not a happy boat, and Belinda Stowell agrees, stressing the difficulty of trying to repeat a gold medal performance with the same partner; figuring out what elements of their sailing style to keep, and how to raise the bar on others. "It's incredibly hard," Stowell says, "because you change, you both have different things going on in life, you're on different pathways. The decisions we made outside sailing put pressure on how we operated. And Jenny had been involved in an Olympic campaign for 16 years. She was hankering to be a mom. I had decided to go into coaching."

There was more. Stowell had partnered with Australian Laser sailor Michael Blackburn, who had won a bronze medal in Sydney behind gold medalist Ben Ainslie (GBR), and silver medalist Robert Scheidt (BRA). Meanwhile, Armstrong had married Blackburn's Laser coach, Eric Stibbe. The ebb and flow of what turned out to be an uncomfortable coach-sailor relationship between their two partners couldn't help alter the relationship of the women on the #1 boat.

The fact that Victor was spread too thin at Athens had an unfortunate effect on the proceedings. His English comprehension wasn't up to speeding through the reams of administrative papers he was receiving. He was bogged down with demands from the other Australian coaches and teams, and was required to handle delicate political situations that arose. "Instead of being able to work with us 24/7," Stowell says, "and focus his mind on making the 470 go fast, which is one of his great strengths, he was distracted. He was pulled in many directions. In his own words, he said he was `everywhere and nowhere.'"

The team had lost the high-spirited cohesiveness it had displayed at the Sydney Games. In Sydney, the men's and women's teams worked together, helped one another, and pulled for each other to win. That was not the case in Athens.

As far as training with the women, which both King/Turnbull and Wilmot/Smith had done prior to the Sydney Games, Wilmot/Page were unreliable enough that Armstrong/Stowell hired Mat Belcher and Nick Behrens to train with them. "Nathan is one of the most talented sailors I've ever sailed with," says Stowell, who sailed a couple regattas with him in the course of their training [Page sailed with Armstrong at the same time]. "I really like him and get on well with him. He has a great sense of humor. We had laughs, played bat and ball and ran together. But he was a young lout, opinionated, and you knew right away if he didn't like you. He wore his heart on his sleeve. If he decided he wanted to be bad, he could make the whole team negative. Jenny stayed in the same house with him once and said he was great fun to be with at home, but the moment he got in the car he turned into a monster. He'd carry the black cloud over the whole team." But the talent Wilmot brought to the race course seemed to be worth whatever it cost.

"It was because of pressure," Victor says. "Nathan would get emotional and flail away. But he is very special, and he needs a special approach. I was trying to support him and explain him, be positive. Top caliber people are very fragile. You do not want to harm them because their ego and ambitions are also tools for winning."

The final blow to the Australian 470 team in Athens was a case of flu that broke out the day before the Games. The team had a policy: when someone became sick, he or she was to be immediately isolated. Instead, team members had hidden the illness until it became obvious. "In Sydney," Victor says, "the spirit was good. In Athens, it came apart. The relationship between the two boats was not good. I was busy as head coach, as leader of the whole group, and I did not pick up the small details of what was happening with the team. I could not pick these things up in time, or monitor what was going on — keep up with the delicacy of the relationships. In general, the relationships within the team were not there. The personalities did not match. I was trying to be a shock absorber between them, but it was not good."

At the Athens Olympic Games, Wilmot/Page, who were ranked #1 in the world, finished 12th. Armstrong/Stowell finished 14th.

CHAPTER 11

Gold Medal Plan

Tatiana says when her husband returned from Athens, he looked like he had aged 15 years. At the airport in Sydney, Victor had encountered John Coates, Australia's Chef de Mission for the Games in Athens. Coates had been President of the Australian Olympic Committee since 1990. He dismissed Victor's apology for sailing's lackluster performance, and told him he had his support. Later, Australian Yachting Federation president Andrew Plympton told Victor he still had the Federation's trust.

Phil Jones, who was then CEO of the Yachting Australia – the man who had hired Kovalenko in 1997 – said Victor asked him if he should resign. "I said I would accept his resignation only if I were really stupid," Jones says today. "But for him to come away from Athens with no medals was complete and utter failure for Victor. He took a while to get over it."

The confidence expressed in Victor was reassuring, even gratifying, but he knew that to turn the program around, many things had to change. "After the failure in Athens," Victor says, "money was critical, how to obtain more money. But most importantly, we did not have the support of the Australian sailing community. They were too easily satisfied. They took it all for granted. They said we are winning, no problem. They were too relaxed. They said we have world champions in many classes, why worry? The reality was we had no new sails, boats, masts, not enough final preparation, and all our support staff was volunteers." The volunteers even included Andrew Lechte, from North Sails Japan, who Victor considers a key to the team's medal performance in Sydney. "Andrew worked for nothing," Victor says. "He stayed in my room in Athens, sleeping on the couch. He was one week with us. He worked every day on the sails. I bought his meals."

"From time to time in high performance sport we get it wrong," Phil Jones says. "In the lead-up to the 2004 Games the system was not functioning properly. There was too much politics. There were distractions with other issues, not the focus on the performance outcome there should have been. And there was a bit of overconfidence going into Athens. We had to rebuild the program."

Victor had immediately begun work on the third major document of his career, a detailed report to the Australian Yachting Federation about why sailors had come up empty in Athens. After the Olympics, Victor had taken his team to the big Sail Brisbane regatta a few hundred miles north of Sydney. It turned out to be a fortuitous trip. In Brisbane he met a local sailor named Peter Conde. For many years Conde had frequented Etchells' podiums. John Bertrand, the Finn sailor (Bronze medal, 1976 Olympics) and America's Cup skipper who would finally wrest the oldest Trophy in sports from the New York Yacht Club's clutches in 1983 after 132 years of consecutive victories, had asked Conde to trim the mainsail on *Australia II*, the 12 Meter that would win the Cup. Much to Bertrand's disappointment, Conde had elected to follow the corporate business career he had mapped out for himself rather than sail on *Australia II*. He worked for the prestigious Boston Consulting Group, specializing in corporate strategy, business or product line strategies, and organizational issues for large banks of consumer goods. Conde eventually set up his own consulting group.

In Brisbane, Victor was drawn to Conde, whom he had met in passing on his first trip to Australia in 1991. Victor had been intrigued by Conde's organizational background and sense of business strategy, intriguing philosophies that were complimented by Conde's prowess as a sailor.

"I spent many years witnessing Victor's tremendous achievements as a coach and in 2009 was lucky enough to experience this first hand when Victor coached the Etchells team of John Bertrand, of which I was a crew. Victor's experience, skill and enthusiasm for the sport are what makes him such a great coach. For me though, the keys to Victor's success are his human qualities. Victor has the ability to connect with people no matter what their background. It's this ability to connect that produces such amazing results."

Sir Ben Ainslie

14 | Victor on 470 Trapeze
15 | First time in Australia
16 | Gulf War alert in Israel

17 | Touring Europe
18 | Celebration in Dnepropetrovsk, UKR

19 | Gold and bronze in Atlanta, 1996
20 | World champions

21 | 470 road sign in Ukraine

23 | Olympic Waters Qingdao (Wilmot Page)

24 | Gold for King/Trumbull
25 | Gold for Armstrong/Stowell

26 | Celebrating in China, 2008

27 | Flipping in Weymouth
28 | Celebrating gold

29 | Australian Olympic Sailing Team London 2012
30 | Leading the fleet

31 | Belcher / Ryan – Last race, last reaching leg
32 | Silver in Rio 2016

33 | A good day in Rio

14 | Victor on 470 Trapeze – With Valentin Arefij at the helm (1983).

15 | First time in Australia – Victor's first trip to Australia was to coach his Ukrainian team in Brisbane, in 1991.

16 | Gulf War alert in Israel – Victor (center, wearing mask) with his Soviet Sailing Team and friends during an alert in Israel when the Gulf War was ongoing (December, 1991).

17 | Touring Europe – In 1991, Victor and his 470 women's team of Larisa Moskalenko (right) and Olena Pakholchik (left) put 25,000 miles on this overloaded Fiat Panda, driving to regattas all over Europe.

18 | Celebration in Dnepropetrovsk, UKR – Victor and his 470 men's gold medalists Evgeniy Braslavets (right) and Igor Matviyenko (left) are celebrated at the rail station in Dnepropetrovsk after the 1996 Olympics.

19 | Gold and bronze in Atlanta, 1996 – Ukrainian teams winning Gold (m) and bronze (w) medals. From left to right: Olena Pakholchik, Evgeniy Braslavets, Victor Kovalenko, Ruslana Taran, Igor Matviyenko.

20 | World champions – Coach Kovalenko with his three-time women's 470 World Champions: Ruslana Taran (right) and Olena Pakholchik (1997).

21 | 470 road sign in Ukraine – The Ukrainian sign reads, "World Champions from Dnepropetrovsk" (1996).

22 | Sydney Olympics 2000 – After the final race at the Sydney Games, 470 gold medal winners Tom King and Mark Trumbull (AUS) exchange congratulations with USA's 470 team of Paul Foerster and Robert Merrick, who won silver.

23 | Olympic Waters Qingdao (Wilmot/Page) – Nathan Wilmot and Malcolm Page training on weed infested waters in Qingdao, 2007. This photograph shot by Victor was published in 22 countries.

24 | Gold for King/Trumbull – Australian men's gold medalists at the Sydney Olympic Games, Tom King and Mark Trumbull, lead the fleet on a downwind leg.

25 | Gold for Armstrong/Stowell – Australian 470 sailors Jenny Armstrong and Belinda Stowell on the way to a gold medal at the 2000 Sydney Games.

26 | Celebrating in China, 2008 – Australian teammates hoist Victor in triumph after Nathan Wilmot and Malcom Page won gold in Qingdao.

27 | Flipping in Weymouth – Mathew Belcher smiles happily as Malcolm Page backflips off their 470 after winning a gold medal at the 2012 Olympics in London.

28 | Celebrating gold – Victor, Mathew Belcher (left) and Malcolm Page celebrate gold in London after four long years of hard work.

29 | Australian Olympic Sailing Team London 2012 – Achieving 3 Gold and 1 Silver medal.

30 | Leading the fleet – Belcher/Ryan leading the fleet at the Weymouth Portland World Cup 2015.

31 | Belcher/Ryan – Last race, last reaching leg – going for the Silver medal in RIO 2016 - Umpires in the background.

32 | Silver in Rio 2016 – Mathew Belcher (left) and Will Ryan celebrate their silver medal result of a contentious Olympic Games in Rio.

33 | A good day in Rio – Mathew Belcher and Will Ryan training in the Rio Olympics, 2016, with Christ the Redeemer atop Corcovado visible in the background.

An official meeting to analyze the Athens situation and open discussion about how to rebuild the program had been set for Melbourne. Outstanding sailors like Bertrand and Simon McKeon (skipper of *Yellow Pages*, the triscaph proa that held the sail-powered speed record from 1993 to 2004), had been invited to attend.

"The theme of the meeting was how to take the sailing program forward to its highest level," says John Bertrand, who in 2015 was President and Chairman of the Board of Swimming Australia. "It was a discussion that reminded me of the philosophy behind our *Australia II* America's Cup win when we decided we were in the business of figuring out what the game would look like in 20 years' time, and apply that thinking to the now—unleash the thought process, take the blinkers off, and try to project forward to a level people have not achieved before. The winged keel development that propelled our America's Cup win came about as a result of that kind of thinking."

At the meeting, Victor gave his report on the system failures in Athens, not sparing what he considered his own inadequacies. "Mainly he was keen to get people's thoughts from around the table," Bertrand says. Bertrand first met Victor at the Sydney Olympics in 2000, when Bertrand was working as a mentor for several sports, sailing among them. "Victor is the most natural sports psychologist I've ever come across," Bertrand says. "He has an amazing feel for people, and for competition at the highest level. He is a true student of life. And he is so tuned in to the concept of performance. In Sydney we'll walk along the waterfront and stop to look at the butterflies and birds to see how they fly. He marvels at what can be done with wind swirling around a foil we call a sail, or with a hull going through the water, and with humans operating all those controls. That's Victor's world, to always push further, higher, faster."

No concrete plan came out of the Melbourne meeting. But a clear set of philosophical guidelines for how to best move ahead was established. There was also unanimous agreement on Andrew Plympton's suggestion that Peter Conde would be the person who could hammer the concepts into a working plan. "Getting Conde on board was a stroke of genius," Bertrand says. "He was the right man at the right time."

"At the meeting," Conde says, "it was decided I would use my consulting skills to develop a plan for the high performance sector of Yachting Australia. I come from a professional services background. Various problems I had tackled were not unlike this situation. These are bright people, experts, coaches and sailors who need to be treated properly. Our approach was to establish a culture, build on it, and reinforce it; establish a set of values we worked towards. It involved personal responsibility up and down the line for the plan's execution. We created a lean operation, with everyone working hard for a cause.

"I worked closely with Victor to get that going. It was called The Gold Medal Plan, a bit of a grandiose title given there were no medals in Athens. There were a lot of influences on the plan we developed, but Victor was a key. My role was to pick his brain and assemble his insights into a workable system. To begin with, the role he was asked to play in 2004 was unfair. There was no performance director on hand. He had to manage the program and coach at the same time. That was mission impossible.

"Victor's not the easiest guy to work with, but we have a trusting relationship. It works. Give him a problem that needs solving and you know he's working on it 24/7. His insights and expertise were critical for what I did."

Peter Conde says there was some anxiety about sailing's national funding being cut after Athens. But he, Phil Jones, and Andrew Plympton went to the Australian Sports Commission (ASC) with the Gold Medal Plan. The ASC provides financial support to nearly one hundred national sporting organizations to deliver both participation and high performance results. ASC is accountable to the Minister of Sport, and Parliament. "They liked the plan, and increased our funding by 22%," Conde says. Next, Conde and company initiated the Patrons Program, run by a volunteer citizens group that has raised as much as a million dollars in an Olympic year. In short order, the financial package was looking much stronger.

Talent and Troubles

On the water, Victor had put together a new women's team he thought had great potential. He first became aware of Elise Rechichi as a sailor when she was 13, racing Optis. She had finished in the top three (and first girl) at the Australian Opti Nationals in 1996, when she was just 11. A diminutive youth from Fremantle, Western Australia, Rechichi's initial interest was gymnastics. But as she told the *The West Australian* newspaper in 2015, "My parents took me out of that and I had all this extra energy so they sent me to the furthest place they could find for me to burn it off, and that was the middle of the Swan River." In a sailboat, she might have added, at age seven, and that marked the beginning of a stellar career. That she had extra energy is an understatement. While she was polishing her racing skills on the water, she learned to fly. She also played the saxophone.

Rechichi's partner in the 470 was Tessa Parkinson, another Fremantle native who had also started sailing at age 7. Taller, heavier, and another committed athlete, Parkinson was the perfect match for Rechichi. As a team they were progressing well until the Fall of 2005, when Rechichi slipped on the wet ramp while launching their boat for training in Qingdao, China, site of the 2008 Olympics. She wasn't injured, but in the splash she ingested a small bit of water from the extremely polluted harbor. Before long she became ill with what was described as "gastric trauma." It brought her life to a standstill. She was sleeping 18 hours a day. When she was awake, she was often passing out from low blood pressure, hallucinating, and suffering dehydration. She was in constant pain, unable to walk up a flight of stairs.

By March, 2006, Rechichi's doctors had come up with a medication that began to alleviate her symptoms. A few months later, she began sailing a half hour at a time. The team director sent her an invitation to training camp. She declined. "She said she was still seriously ill," Victor says, "unable to be a normal person, that she was still sleeping most of the time and could not stop. It was dangerous. I called her. I said I know you are ill, in trouble, but you should come to camp, be in a different environment with the team, see your friends, the coaches, and be a part of us. I told her never mind fitness tests, she could progress at her own speed. She said alright, and she came. Slowly she got motivated and began to heal."

And heal she did. In 2007, at Thessaloniki, Greece, Rechichi/Parkinson took the bronze medal at the European Championships.

At that same regatta, Wilmot/Page suffered a disaster. They had gotten a slow start at the Europeans. Usually, for them, that meant a bad outcome. Breaking this pattern, they had settled down and worked their way back into the regatta. Entering the medal race, the final race that's half as long as the rest of the races and counts double, Wilmot/Page were fifth overall, meaning they had a shot at winning the regatta by doing well in the medal race. From the start through 90% of the medal race they were in front by a wide margin. The result, as Malcolm Page says, was in the bag. Then the wind went bananas, going through a massive gyration the likes of which Victor says he has not seen before or since. First the wind died completely. After a disorienting series of light puffs from several different directions, it filled 180 degrees from where it had been blowing. The boats in the back of the fleet finished at the top. Wilmot/Page, who were just 150 yards from the finish line before the unlikely shift, came in 8th, and did not make the podium. "We got screwed," Page says. "It was heartbreaking."

"It was an enormous test from heaven, from the universe," Victor says. "A big punch for Nathan and Malcolm. I was shocked. You could not believe it, a complete turnaround, a billion to one. In my notebook I wrote, 'Mega Bad Luck.'"

After that race, Victor found Wilmot in the sailors' lounge with his Shit Index threshold at the red line, moaning about his bad luck to whomever would listen. His beer consumption was fueling the fires of frustration. "I went to him," Victor says, "I said listen, nothing happens in this life without reason. It's either a serious test, a warning, or a penalty. You know this. If it's a penalty, it means you did something wrong to the universe, you created karma. If it's a test, you must pass it. You must be strong. Instead of staying here and complaining and drinking more beer, go home, focus on the next event. Don't worry about this. If you complain about the universe and drink more and show weakness and struggling, you have not passed the test. Nathan said okay, went to his hotel, had some rest, listened to music."

The men's difficulties had begun long before the 2007 European Championships in Thessaloniki. Six weeks after the disappointment in Athens, Wilmot and Page had put their heads together with Victor at his apartment and decided what they had to do to make the podium in Qingdao, 2008. After going over the more predictable items (improved boat speed in lighter conditions), Victor steered the discussion to one of his favorite subjects: the nature of those who have won gold medals, and the necessity of bringing about changes in one's self in order to achieve that goal. "All of us change ourselves all the time," Victor says. "If we set serious goals. For athletes in pursuit of gold medals, it is tough because as their vision of the world changes, they have to be disciplined. They could have a much easier life, but their chosen life is tough and demanding. They have to keep their bodies and their minds in good shape. They have to follow certain routines. Because their ultimate goal is to bring something new to the world, that's what they are doing. Not only for people to say 'Wow!' but to change their self-perception. Maybe you can get silver or bronze by chance, with some luck, but Olympic gold, oh no, this is a reward from the universe for all your work, all those years, your dedication, for who you are. There is something unique about gold medalists, both for their abilities, and with their personalities. If a person is arrogant or rude to his competitors, then he is not deserving from the universe. The competitors will know. Ask them who the champion will be and unless they say 'me,' they will pick out a certain special person, and usually they will be right."

The person Victor fixed on that evening with Wilmot and Page was the Athens 470 gold medalist from the USA, Paul Foerster, who had finished 2nd behind Tom King at the Sydney Games. Foerster was as well-known for his quiet determination and strength of character as for his talent on the race course. In the preparation for Athens, he had told his sailing partner Kevin Burnham that his wife's pregnancy was the priority. If she happened to deliver during the US trials, as supposed, he would be with her, not in the boat with Kevin. Burnham could only shrug and agree to Foerster's conditions. They were practicing in Houston, Texas. For the last three weeks of the pregnancy, every day after racing Foerster would drive to the airport and fly to Dallas to be with his wife. He would fly back in the morning, and hop in the fully-rigged boat. As luck would have it, the baby was born three days early. Foerster/Burnham went on to win the trials.

That evening at his apartment with Wilmot and Page, Victor asked Wilmot if he thought Foerster was deserving of his gold medal. Wilmot said yes, by all means, and was enthusiastic about what an admirable figure Foerster had become in sailing.

For a while, it seemed as if Victor's message to Nathan Wilmot about how champions comport themselves had been delivered. Wilmot/Page won the 470 World Championships in 2005, and took silver in 2006. But leading up to the annual World Cup regatta in Miami in January, 2007, the situation in the boat had become uneasy. In Miami, it came apart. Victor says Wilmot was "wild," not on the boat, but ashore, staying out late, losing his professional edge, losing his focus on what mattered.

"We were tolerant, trying to understand Nathan," Victor says, "but if the support is too tolerant, people will lose touch with reality, try to dominate in the boat, lose discipline and self-control. It's a progression. You cannot stop it sometimes. I was trying to talk with him in Miami. I was trying to explain the pressure of leadership and the trials. But sometimes you cannot see the trigger. He was aggravated by all of it, not able to stop being rude to Malcolm."

Malcolm Page says after Miami he confronted Nathan, his friend and fellow sailing pal from childhood. "It was business," Page says. "We had agreed that night at Victor's that we were going to work on three things. Two were about how to be a better sailing team. One was about Nathan personally. I said we weren't doing it. I didn't care about going to another Games and stuffing up. I said I know it's going to hurt us short term, but we'll get over it. We've been mates forever. But we can't keep going like we are."

Victor agreed. In his mind, Nathan had crossed the line. He approached High Performance Director Michael Jones and suggested Mat Belcher's crew, Nick Behrens, be replaced with Malcolm Page. Victor was certain it would be a gold medal paring. Jones was supportive.

Belcher/Behrens had been sailing well. Since he had received his national team scholarship in 2001, at the age of 18, Belcher had been plunged head first into the Olympic life, Victor-style. For almost a year, he had lived with his coach, traveling, sailing, and talking. "Victor helped me a lot," Belcher says. "I remember wanting to watch TV, and he wouldn't let me. He would turn on a sailing video, or give me a sailing book. It was quite a culture shock for me. Intense. I didn't know him. He was a lot harder back then, more difficult to understand. But it was important to acquire that discipline from someone who believed in you, who kept encouraging you. I was at a tough age, going through a transition period when you are not sure what you want to do. Party, I guess. Be with girls.

"But Victor knows his athletes well. He knew how to speak to me, support me, push me. And he knew when to back off. The time we spent together balanced me as a person. I ended up spending more time with Victor than my friends. But I got on well with him. He was a huge influence, a big factor in guiding me to discovering who I am and helping me establish my principles. You're a kid and you have these Olympic and world champions traveling with you, Tom King and Jenny Lidgett, who were big influences on me as well. It was a cool time, traveling the world with the Olympic dream fresh and exciting."

Belcher had first sailed with his brother, Daniel, as crew. By 2004, the Belcher brothers had risen to the number two team behind Wilmot/Page. For his second Olympic campaign (2008), Belcher sailed with Nick Behrens as crew. Behrens is a Tasmanian who had skippered the #3 Australian 470 in 2003. By 2007, Belcher/Behrens were very close to beating Wilmot/Page. A few weeks before Miami, the team found out that because of a shipping delay, Belcher's boat was not going to make it in time for the regatta. They were talking about chartering, but Victor suggested Mathew fly his boat from Australia for the regatta. It was an outrageous suggestion. They could have bought a new boat for what the shipping would cost. But Victor persisted. *All of the money*, one mustn't forget, is part of Victor's three-part requirement for *sailing for glory*. "I told him it was better to spend the money to have his own boat and get valuable points at this world cup regatta," Victor says. "He was in good shape, sailing well. He said `okay, I trust you,' flew the boat in and finished 2nd. Nathan finished 7th. After this regatta, Belcher/Behrens were ranked #1 in the world, and had a psychological advantage over Wilmot/Page."

But the plan to replace Nick Behrens with Malcolm Page was foiled – by Mat Belcher. Knowing Belcher as well as he did, Victor might have known that would happen, having had a strong influence on the principles Belcher developed along the way, but he was blinded by the light: so convinced the Belcher/Page pairing would result in a gold medal that he had supported the plan.

"Victor had always wanted me to sail with Malcolm," Belcher says. "He knew our sailing styles and personalities would fit. Nathan and Malcolm weren't getting on, and there were ten years difference between Nick and me. It was all open, Malcolm had said yes, but I had made a commitment to my sailing partner. I just couldn't bring myself to say no to Nick and swap. That was it, pretty much. If I'd said yes it would have guaranteed Olympic selection for me.

"I know Victor wanted me to have the courage to say yes," Belcher says. "I think he felt I let him down by not agreeing to take Malcolm. Maybe it

THE MEDAL MAKER — A BIOGRAPHY OF VICTOR KOVALENKO

was that Eastern Bloc mentality that says you are there as an individual, and whoever your partner is doesn't matter. It's harsh, really harsh. My relationship with Nick, my commitment to him, didn't matter."

Peter Conde knew Mat Belcher from Brisbane, where they both lived. They are both members of the Royal Queensland Yacht Club. "Mat and Nick were using me as a sounding board during this time," Conde says. "What stood out was Mat's absolute integrity. The deal was, here's a gold medal, but to have it you have to dump the guy you've been working with. It's incredible that Mat was able to look at all that and say he wasn't going to do it."

"That's Mathew," Victor says today. "It is his nature to be loyal, honest. He is a tough guy. If he is racing and he touches the mark there is no question he will do turns. I'll say to him `no one saw this, I did not see it,' and he'll say, `I saw it.' That's why people trust him. He is honest. He would never lie in the protest room. Sailors and judges respect him."

Today Victor looks back at that situation in 2007 and says it was a huge test for all four sailors and for himself, a test of all their relationships. "And it was a big message for Nathan," Victor says. "He went through some big changes. He wrote a letter to Malcolm and me, promised he would make some corrections, continue to sail with Malcolm, keep going, and win the Games. We said okay, we have no choice. We started to work again as a team. It was a really tough time."

Nathan Wilmot has a different perspective on the situation that is somewhat confounding. We spoke at the Middle Harbor Yacht Club in Sydney in February, 2015, where he was doing some coaching. "I never thought me and Mal weren't going to the 2008 Games together," Wilmot said. "We'd had a bad season, ups and downs, then I got sick. We took a bit of a break. We were still seeing each other, figuring out what we had to do to win gold. We were good mates. I don't know if Victor was doing anything, or if there were talks between him and Mat and Mal. It was a non-event, really."

Belcher/Behrens had continued to train hard. In particular, they had worked on a suggestion of Victor's and developed their own technique for sailing fast. The details are still under wraps, but the technique had to do with the dynamics of sailing the boat (a refinement of pumping) in connection with a specific sail configuration. The development presented a difficult decision for Victor. "I had a big temptation — it was very difficult working with Nathan — a big temptation to keep this new technique secret," Victor says. "If I had kept it secret from Nathan, that would have given Mathew an opportunity to win the trials. But the way I coach, and with my life ethics, I could not do this. Both sailors trusted me, considered me their coach. I could not betray my sailors by keeping the new technique a secret. And Mathew never said `this is my secret, keep it from Nathan.'"

Chances are, honor and ethics play a bigger role in sailing than in other sports. In refereed sports where officials (and video replay) have the final say, a player would never disagree with a call in his favor even if he knew in his heart it was incorrect. It's just not done. But in sailing, many are the stories of skippers doing turns or dropping out of races after committing a foul that no one else — not even the skipper's crew! — has seen. There are sailors who cheat, or at least stretch the rules, no question. But for the most part, honor on the water is upheld by most of those who race sail boats. The late Danish sailor, Paul Elvstrom, said that winning is empty if you have not maintained the respect of your competitors. Victor often insists that racing sailboats is a gentleman's sport. On any team he coaches, he makes sure of it.

Wind against tide

The year 2007 would be difficult for both teams. Mathew Belcher was in a relationship with Frederike Ziegelmayer, daughter of the 470 builder in Germany. That was initially complicated by Victor's lack of enthusiasm for the pairing. "He was never keen for me to date Rike," Belcher says. "It was unknown to him that one athlete/sailor would date another. He never understood that situation." Frederike wanted to sail for Australia, but she could not untangle the intricate bureaucratic road blocks and ended up sailing for Germany. In Victor's eyes, that created a potential international leak of performance secrets that was unsettling. And as Belcher got older, he was dealing with some career anxiety. "I had spent a lot of time, worked hard, and had done well," he says. "But in the meantime my brother had finished law and business degrees at Columbia University in New York. I'd spent eight years of my life sailing and was still working on a bachelor's degree. I thought Jesus, I'm not making much of my life…is this what I really want to be doing?"

In addition, Belcher suddenly found himself ignored on the water. "After I said I wouldn't trade crews I realized Victor had to spend his time with Nathan and Malcolm to prepare them for China," Belcher says. "All his focus and attention was to get that team back on track. We got no support at all. It's the most difficult year I've ever experienced. Not to blame Victor. I'm sure it was difficult for him to manage. And that's how the system is." But by the end of 2007, Mat Belcher had hit the wall. He decided he needed a break, and stopped sailing for 18 months.

The breakup of the Wilmot/Page team lasted six weeks. When they resumed racing, the results were not encouraging. At regattas in Palma and Kiel they suffered from both break downs and bad luck. The way Mother Nature had pulled the rug out from under them at Thessaloniki, blind-siding them 150 yards from the finish line and erasing a sure victory, had to have made them consider the possibility they were being penalized for upsetting the universe. But Malcolm Page says after the intense wave of disbelief and disappointment had subsided, the overall effect of Thessaloniki was positive.

"Thessaloniki galvanized us," Page says. "If it had happened a month or two earlier, or even at a different time in that regatta, it might have had a different effect. Maybe the tension had to be built to a certain level to make it work for us. One of the things that came out of the meeting we had with Victor after Athens was that we had no measuring system. We couldn't separate fact from emotion. People say sailing is complex, but when you break it down into little parts, it's amazing how you can pull out exactly what you need. What was our wind strategy, what about the current? Did we not execute the game plan because of a bad start, or because we didn't have confidence in our plan? Or was our plan wrong? When you break it down you can pinpoint where your mistake was. Then you look at several regattas and begin to spot trends.

"Here's what you have to remember: you haven't lost your skills! People forget that. Emotions start to run away with you. But hold on. We've been number one, we can do it again. Maybe that's what we did remember after Thessaloniki. If not for that weird wind anomaly we would have won the medal race by a mile. And the regatta. What happened was beyond our control. Victor had preached that when we were just starting out. Having control is what you want, but when you can't be in control, have the wisdom to accept it. And half way through the Europeans at Thessaloniki, Nathan had told Victor he was confident with our speed in lighter wind. That was another key thing that happened, a breakthrough with our speed in light air, one of the things we had agreed to work on.

That made us know we had our shit together.

"When you are weak, and you get hit with something like that last race in Thessaloniki, you crumble. But when you are strong, it can refocus you. We rolled into the 2007 World Championship in Cascais, Portugal, and won it in strong winds, our specialty. Then we won the test event in Qingdao in drifting conditions. We felt like a complete team again. The Euros in Thessaloniki turned out to be the first indicator that we were ready."

Victor recalls the four-day drive from Greece to Cascais for the Worlds in 2007 with Nathan and Tessa Parkinson. They put a mattress in the back so one person could sleep while the passenger talked to the driver to keep him awake. Driving was a two-hour shift. Most nights they drove, but one night they stopped at a hotel, had a good meal, a swim in the pool, and a restful sleep. "It was a fantastic trip," Victor says. "We talked about sailing, life, everything. After 4 days we said oh, we have arrived.... There was not enough time to talk, we could have used one more day on the road."

As defending world champions, Wilmot/Page dominated Sail Melbourne in 2008. But at the World Championships (also in Melbourne), they had a relapse. After a 4th and a 6th, they sailed too riskily and finished off the podium. Hoping for a more positive prelude to the Olympics, Victor took the team to the 470 European Championships in Garda, where more drama ensued.

"Wilmot/Page were 46th after the first day," Victor says. "We had big conversations. I told Nathan he could see this as a big test for him. Then they qualified as one of 35 boats for the finals. They just made it. They sailed well and made it into the medal race of ten boats. And they won the regatta. It was the biggest comeback for Nathan in his life. It changed him, gave him new confidence, new ability to deal with himself."

Qingdao

Conditions for the 2008 Games in Qingdao were light and variable with lots of current, providing seductive opportunities for teams to take risks. Elise Rechichi and Tessa Parkinson had finished 3rd in both the European and World Championships that year. Half way through the Olympics, they were leading, bringing Victor to full attention.

"Coaching Elise was a big trick," he says. Victor says it's more difficult to work with sailors after they have won gold medals. He calls gold medal winners "tigers," saying those next to them must be ready to be scratched. But he says Rechichi was a tiger before the Games. "I always called her Tiger," he says. "Before the Games I bought her a little figure of a tiger.

"She always needed a challenge, but it was difficult to find challenges for her. She was always trying to prove she was right. That was her biggest drive, proving to the world, and to me, that she was capable of doing the job. Before the Games she said to me many times, 'you don't believe we can get a medal.' I told her no, I trusted her abilities. But I had to be very careful with her because if she knew in advance I thought she would be the gold medalist she would put enormous pressure on herself, lose her aggressive, competitive edge. She would become more vulnerable. In the Games I focused on one race at a time. Then at some point she realized she was leading. That was the moment when pressure came. She became very nervous and very fragile. If I had allowed this moment to come earlier it would not have been good. I always said 'no no no you are good,' and she was saying 'no no no you don't trust,' and I said 'of course you will do it.' But I made it so she had to convince me. It was a very difficult game with her. She is so talented, so bright."

Victor won that game, and Rechichi/Parkinson won a gold medal.

Wilmot/Page sailed smart, and on the conservative side. Going into the medal race, they had not won a single race, but their consistency had paid off. Their lead was such that it was mathematically impossible for them to lose the gold medal, even if they finished last in the medal race. "We had watched what Foerster and Burnham had done in Athens," Nathan Wilmot says. "They had been consistent. That's what we worked on. You can't have a 3rd followed by a 20th. If you have two 6ths instead you will win gold. In China we knew if we had single digits all week we would go into the medal race with a chance to win it all. And we did it. We never had a bad race."

They had sailed so well they didn't need to sail the medal race. When Victor began talking about tuning and strategy the next day, they were distracted. "They had been celebrating a little the night before," Victor says. "Their attitude was, `we are champs, we don't care !' I said yes, you had a great regatta, but you have not won any races because you were very disciplined all week. This is your chance to win an Olympic race. Sail with complete freedom now, take as much risk as you want, just enjoy it, go out and win this race !"

With Victor, Wilmot/Page re-tuned the boat, discussed conditions, current, and strategy. They had a good start on starboard, and graciously dipped two boats on port because the two were still in the hunt for medals. They were in the best possible situation, sailing such an important race with absolutely nothing at stake. Instead of a nail biter, the medal race was pure fun for them. The pressure was off, decisions came easy. They led the fleet out to the sea breeze on the right, were first at the top mark, and won the race. "It was an amazing race," Victor says. "It confirmed they were the best in the world. They were so happy."

"We had our arguments," Wilmot says of Victor, "but I have a lot of respect for him. He has made 470 sailing one of Australia's most successful sports. There were hard times, but you have to take your hat off to him. It was interesting working under him. I learned a lot. You can't argue the results. But for me, winning a gold medal was more relief than anything else."

CHAPTER 12

Unfinished

On an Olympic sailing race course, there are dozens of small motor boats zooming around on official business. There are mark boats, the coach boats of thirty or so different teams, and a variety of media boats. In Qingdao, China, during the 2008 Olympics, anyone familiar with the Australian team situation would have quickly raised his binoculars for a closer look at the driver of a film crew boat on the 470 course to make sure what they thought they had seen. Sure enough, it was Mathew Belcher.

During his absence from the Australian team, Mathew Belcher had been finishing his degree work at university, taking exams, and racing a Moth. He'd done well at both his studies and his sailing, finishing 3rd in the Moth World Championships — a notable achievement in that hot international foiling class — and winning the Moth National Championship. "I hadn't spoken to Victor very much, or the team," Mathew says. "But I was into hydro-foiling, and loving sailing again." Belcher got a call from Michael Jones, High Performance Director of the Australian Olympic Sailing Team at the time, asking if he'd like to come to the Games, drive a media boat.

Belcher said yes. "It was good money," he says, "and great fun filming Nathan and Malcolm on the course every day. Before the Games neither Rike nor I were comfortable with the idea of going back into sailing. But I had come so close. It was something unfinished in my life. On the last day of the Games, after they had won, I told Mal I wanted to come back, asked him if he would come back with me. I think it was understood that after the Games Nathan was going to stop. But no one had said anything. The next morning I met Mal at Starbucks. He said to give him a couple months."

Malcolm Page had a talk with Victor. "I told him he had a chance to be Olympic champion for a second time." Victor says. "There is only one other sailor in 470 history who has two gold medals. I said to Malcolm, 'trust me, let the three of us dedicate four years of our lives to prove to ourselves and to the world we can do it.' We would do this 2012 campaign with only one goal in mind: to be Olympic champion. Not silver, not bronze; not to try to win, but to win."

Victor's focus on the project he was proposing would be even more intense than his customary 110% effort. For the first time since 1993, he would not be coaching both the men's and women's 470 teams. Victor likes to say the Olympics should be a holiday for the coach, that the coach has done what he can and now it is up to the athletes to perform. But it happened that both teams racing in Qingdao needed his full support and attention. Trying to monitor both race courses took super human effort. Victor had made it work in Sydney, and again in Qingdao, but somewhere along the line, one team was going to get short-changed. It was inevitable. Victor knew the effort had spread him dangerously thin. As head coach, giving up the women's team was something he could do while still keeping an eye on the process. And he relished using the extra time that would afford him with the men's team. In all his years of coaching, it's safe to say Victor had never had such high expectations for a team as he had for Belcher and Page.

"Mathew is judicious, balanced, very good at making decisions under pressure," Victor says. "He has proved this many times. He is incredible. He could be Prime Minister of Australia, anything he wants. Because when all else is in place, making decisions under pressure is the most important thing a sailor does. Or a prime minister for that matter – anyone in a position of responsibility.

"Mathew was a huge factor in Nathan Wilmot's gold medal, a big contributor. If Nathan had not had Mathew as a sparring partner, Olympic gold would not have been his. Nathan was emotional and erratic. I could more easily find the key to him and use emotional treatments. Mathew is more logical. If he has something in his mind, it is more difficult to change."

Victor can also be effusive about Page, who had compiled a 3-2-2-1-1-1 record in six, 470 world championships – and a 1st at the Europeans – all with Wilmot, in addition to their Olympic gold medal. "Malcolm's contribution to our success in the 470 group was enormous," Victor says. "His strength of character is number one, and he never gives up, never ever. He is the best fighter in the history of our group, the leader of our group for many years in many areas. He is a very special guy."

Domination

Together, Belcher and Page became a team that came very close to the ideal Victor imagines. "If you motivate a team properly," Victor says, "open the sailors' hearts, give them a dream, this dream becomes their goal. They just need a catalyst. The minds and hearts of athletes are not bottles we have to fill. It is an elemental process. We only need to start a fire, make a spark, and poof! All great athletes – Beckham, Ronaldo, Messi – have coaches who tell them to jump, run, shoot, but all are different, and all are difficult. The coach has to be their assistant and advisor. But they must say `you are my coach, you have to tell me what to do' before the coach can say 'okay, I will tell you.' The coach is the fire starter, and once you start the process you cannot stop it because now they have a new vision of life, gaining confidence, taking on more and more challenging roles. When they stop playing a sport they continue to want more challenging things in their lives."

A few weeks after Qingdao, Page went to Gold Coast, Australia, Mathew Belcher's home waters. It only took a few days of sailing a 470 together for the two of them to be convinced. They did a relaxed program in 2009, just getting warmed up. They were 5th in the Worlds that year, an indicator they needed to train harder, do more events. Mathew says his parents were cautious after what he had been through. "From their perspective, they had one kid who had finished his MBA and who had a top level job at McKinsey, a business consultant firm in New York City, and the other kid was still screwing around with boats," Mathew says. "There was no money in it. My parents were funding a lot of it. I was lucky to get $20,000 a year from the Federation, and that barely covered plane flights."

Mat and Mal enjoyed one another's company in the boat. Victor had been right about them being good partners. Although after he later found himself in the same position, Mat understood how hard the pressure of trying to repeat a gold medal was on Page. It's not easy to dedicate four years of one's life to obtain what is already on the shelf. Perhaps galvanized by Mat's return to an Olympic campaign, his (now) wife Friederike followed suit in 2010, and rejoined the German team. "I remember the day I told Victor about Rike," Belcher says. "I told him over the phone. Later, Mal told me he'd spoken to Victor, and Victor had told him, 'we've just lost our gold medal.' He was worried I'd spend more time on Rike's campaign than ours."

Belcher says the World Championships in 2010 happened to be the first event after Friederike became active with the German team. "I knew it was the most important event I would ever do," Belcher says. "I knew if I didn't win that regatta it would cause a lot of problems. If I didn't win, Rike would be the reason. But we won it, and then it was okay." Belcher/Page won it going away, by 21 points over the second boat (France), with five firsts and two seconds out of 11 races. They won the Worlds again in 2011, with six firsts; and again in 2012 with five firsts. Victor's word for what was transpiring with this team: domination. It's one of his favorite words. In Victor's mind, the ideal team is so prepared, has been so dominant in regattas leading up to the Olympics, that from the outset the rest of the competitors are resigned to fighting for the silver medal.

That was the situation approaching the London Olympic Games in 2012. Beginning with the 2011 World Cup regatta in Holland, Belcher/ Page would begin a remarkable, unbroken streak of podium finishes in major regattas that would be carried on by Belcher/Ryan after Page retired (It would finally be broken at the regatta in Weymouth, 2016 – more on that later). Belcher recorded an even more amazing streak: he won the first 18 of those regattas.

A coach is the ultimate spectator of an athletes' performance. No one understands the perfection the competitors are striving for better than the coach, the expert who constantly urges them in that direction. And no one in the house or on the race course has a better seat. Every so often, the great athletes come tantalizingly close to touching their impossible goal. When they do, the coach is momentarily transported, and never forgets. "I have seen it with Ben Ainslie, watched his reading of the waves, boat, and conditions. He was so fast the fleet looked ten years behind him. I watched Tom Slingsby in the medal race of the Laser World Championships in Perth, 2011. His style was incredible. The next year he was Olympic champion. And in our last training day before the Olympics in London I was watching Mathew and Malcolm sailing upwind in 15 knots into a narrow wave angle and it was incredible. They were using four different styles at the same time. It was all about body kinetics. And I said this is the best sailing style I have seen in my life."

But no one was mentioning domination after the first day of the 2012 London Olympics (sailed in Weymouth). With a third and a ninth in the first two races, Mathew Belcher found himself in a most unfamiliar position on the scoreboard. He could sense the fleet ready to seize every opportunity to keep him from advancing. "We'd been on such a run we hadn't had many of those bad moments," Belcher recalls. "At the World Championships that year we'd won six races in a row. Half way through the event we'd won the regatta. This was kind of a first for us. I saw Victor at the end of day one and told him we've never been in this position before. I didn't know how to handle it."

Malcolm Page is ten years older than Mathew Belcher, and with a gold medal to his credit, Page was providing a lot of experience and guidance for his skipper. But Belcher admits he was slightly stunned by his first Olympic race. "I had won three Worlds," Belcher says. "I didn't realize this would be different. I recall coming off the start thinking `I'm in the Games, don't fuck this up.' It almost paralyzes you, the pressure. My body felt rigid, it was hard to focus. I thought I might drop something, like the tiller extension, or the mainsheet. It was a really interesting moment. I was in a race, subconsciously making decisions because boats were coming from all directions. But I felt like I wasn't really there. My mind was wandering. It was a good couple of minutes before I began to free up."

They rounded the top mark, and hit it — also a first. They did penalty turns (720), dropping to 6th place as a result. But they came back to finish third, not bad with a penalty. "Victor was very supportive," Mathew says. "He could sense it had been a tough moment for me, and he knows Day One in any big regatta is critical."

Belcher says he had a good start in Race 2, and accelerated well off the line. They thought their number was called for being over early, premature start (OCS—on course side). They quickly went back and restarted, and were now dead last in the fleet.

"The wind was strong," Belcher recalls, "and we were confident that in those conditions we are good fighters, we never give up. We got back to fifth. To this day, that was the best strong wind race I've ever sailed. We passed 23 boats. It was amazing. We got around the last weather mark and were setting the spinnaker. I was excited. Both of us were feeling it, and were a little distracted. The set took longer than it should have. The dynamic wasn't quite right. The spinnaker filled, and until the last second neither of us saw the Italian boat coming in from leeward. We were clearly going to hit them at speed.

"We blew the spinnaker halyard and basically did a 180-degree turn in 25 knots of wind with the spinnaker flailing. We completely rounded up. Malcolm was able to get on the wire, and we were sailing upwind. We infringed upon the other boat, but we didn't hit them or capsize or rip our spinnaker. I'm confident in saying that not another team in the world would have been technically able to do what we did without capsizing the boat.

"We had to do a 720 (two turns). We lost four boats and finished ninth. It took an hour to sail back in after the race and it was pretty quiet in the boat. We'd been in some difficult situations, but I knew exactly what Malcolm was thinking: this is either gonna go downhill quickly, or we're gonna be alright. He didn't say anything, really. Ashore, Victor took me aside. We talked for some time. I don't remember what he said, but I knew it was going to be alright. I know Malcolm didn't have the same feeling."

To add salt to the wound of a bad day, it turned out that Belcher/Page were not OCS. "They *thought* they were OCS," Victor says four years later with a rueful chuckle.

The start of a dinghy race with 28 of the best crews in the world jockeying for position is a Zen exercise that takes confusion to a new level. Boats are inches apart, with teams roll tacking and jibing and running the gamut of extraordinary boat handling skills, while desperately avoiding costly fouls. Meanwhile the countdown clock is resonating in teams' brains as they struggle to achieve the position they want on the starting line while trying to time their acceleration to perfection. As Victor is fond of saying, "A second late is no good. A second early and you're dead." In the confusion of Race Two, Belcher/Page had thought they were dead and went back to restart. The logic is that it's better to restart and hope to pass a few boats than be disqualified and receive points equal to the number of boats in the race. One of the worst moments in racing sailboats is turning around to restart after being called OCS, while the fleet rockets off in the opposite direction. At that moment, one really does feel dead.

"Most teams who get an OCS shrug and say okay, is not our race," Victor says. "But Mathew and Malcolm said 'no no no, we will fight.' They passed all those boats, they were 5th at the top mark, then they set the spinnaker and met the Italians. Yes. They did a 720. To have so many problems and finish in the top ten is amazing! They are great sailors, strong characters. I didn't need to give them sympathy. Before London I had been working with Mathew for 12 years. How many times did we have difficult situations? We know those moments. We also know this, that you can't lose a regatta in one day. You can't lose your character or your skills in one day. A lot of people shook their heads, thought Mathew and Malcolm were finished. No, they were not finished.

"After racing I was reminding Mathew about these things, and about how we always fight to the end, never give up. In my notebook, the biggest section is psychology. We have very advanced psychological principles that cover many different situations."

Belcher says he had the best night's sleep of his life. "Even though the British team had registered a 1-2 that first day," Belcher says, "Victor made me really calm. That talk with him after the first day was a defining moment. He made me feel like everything was fine. Without him I don't know how we would have finished. But we won five of the remaining eight races, finished with under 20 points, the lowest score we'd ever done. We used the 9th as our throw out, and spent the next four days catching the British, slowly. We'd win, they'd be 2nd or 3rd. We finished 4 points clear."

After that frightful beginning, the gold medal in London turned out to be one of those 18 straight regattas won by Belcher. Domination.

The problem is that to dominate, coach and team must pull out all the stops, reveal secrets; show their hands. "By dominating," Victor says, "Mathew and Malcolm — now Mathew and Will Ryan, his partner since London — show new standards of sailing to other people. Four-time gold medalist Ben Ainslie, after winning the Olympics in 2000, was sailing only two regattas a year because he was so much in front. Mathew sails all regattas, and improves himself and Will, and improves the fleet as well. It's like when Bob Oatley [founder of Australia's famed Rosemount Vineyards] became the predominant wine maker in the world. It was said that Chardonnay would never be the same after a certain vintage he released. Mathew is doing the same thing with sailing."

When asked about the pressure of keeping a long winning streak going, Victor shakes his head. There is a long pause as he struggles with how to express his thoughts. Then he talks about how the number one USA 470 team (Stuart Macnay/David Hughes) won back to back regattas during the 2015 season. In the next regatta, they finished tenth, because even after winning just two regattas the pressure was disabling. Suddenly they needed to change channels, become comfortable as winners, be confident they could continue to sail according to their game plan and not let a raft of new expectations influence their decision making. How to keep the pressure created by the media, their teammates, friends, parents, and their own psyches from having an effect on their performance (and their lives) is a confounding dilemma. It takes incredible strength of character from the sailors, constant and incisive guidance from the coach, probably a good sense of humor on all sides, a bit of time, and some luck.

Even after having accomplished it, the very idea of winning 18 straight world-class regattas boggles the minds of Victor, Mathew, Malcolm, and Will. Victor shrugs when talking about it. "Some of the wins were well-deserved because we sailed well," Victor says. "The overall strategy was good, the sails were right, the starts and tactics were good, the sailing technique top class. But we are not that brilliant all the time. Some we won because of good luck. This is not track and field," Victor says, "this is sailing. A boat can come out of nowhere and hit you, bam, and you are finished. In many situations we ask God not for good luck, but to protect us from bad luck."

In today's world of high-end sailboat racing, the top third of any fleet is so advanced, so keenly aware of technology and sailing styles, that even the slightest increase in speed from any team is painstakingly analyzed. Not so long ago, sailors like Valentin Mankin and Paul Elvström pioneered fitness and extreme practice schedules as key elements of winning. Now everyone is fit, and well-practiced. Then the teams with the best sails had the advantage. Mast development took over, and those with the best masts – mast/sail combinations – prevailed. Now all the top teams are quite equal, clustered on the learning curve which has become very steep, working desperately to find some small thing that has been overlooked.

Victor compares it to detectives revisiting the crime scene for the nth time, trying to find the hidden clue that will break the case.

To review, the 470 is only a 16 foot boat with a mast and three sails (including the spinnaker), a rudder and centerboard, two shrouds stretched over spreaders and a forestay, and a tangle of control lines. Everything must measure in to one-design parameters. Even so, when every millimeter counts, the combinations of trim are in the thousands. Add the constantly changing, subtle dynamic positioning of two human bodies reacting to the instabilities of the two mediums (wind and fluid) in which this sport is practiced, and the possibilities become infinite.

After winning his gold medal in the Sydney Olympics, Tom King made the startling statement that he saw more room for improvement in his sailing than at any point prior to that. "The more time we spent training with Mat and Mal," King said, "the more opportunities we saw to be better at what we were doing. That was exciting. That's why we spent so much time with them, because it's not a static process of maintaining a level. It's finding ways to be better and extending your advantage. Making improvements is limitless in every aspect of this sport, in tactical and strategic frameworks; in fitness; in techniques to make the boat faster on every angle of sail; in equipment and the refining of masts, hulls, foils.... Incremental gains in all those things add up to a lot. Most of it is in technique by virtue of making the boat go faster by what you're doing as you're sailing it.

"The differences you can achieve in a 470 are staggering," King says. "Different teams have different styles. We were very good at making the boat go low and fast upwind. Other teams have a tendency to pinch and sail slow and high upwind. You can set up the boat to make it work with your strengths, to give your team a full range of options. As a heavy team able to sail fast, we had to use longer spreaders to make the mast stiffer sideways to give us a high groove sailing upwind when we wanted it. And we used a mainsail that was slightly fuller, slightly rounder toward the leech.

"In the same way that the mast bends and the sails flex from pressure on the rig, giving you responsiveness to changes in wind and waves, the centerboard flexes as well. In the three Olympic Games of 1992, 1996, and 2000, the men's 470 gold medal was won with as many different centerboards – maximum, medium, and minimum thickness – because each of those teams had different styles. The thickness of the centerboard and the amount it flexes changes the boat's response to gusts, acceleration, and the way the boat points upwind. Using different centerboards is like using different mainsails.

"It's great when you get all the pieces together that work for you. You go out there knowing that in any given condition you are going to be somewhere near the pace. That's where the advantage of Victor's sailors really originates. He's forced a bunch of athletes to go through a process of learning how to sail the boat fast constantly. When that becomes second nature because you've done enough of it, you are in a hugely advantaged position because you are quicker most of the time."

That doesn't mean that a new concept of sailing the boat, once spotted, can be immediately employed or even properly diagnosed by another team. It often takes considerable probing to understand the innovation, and plenty of practice to make it work. "Mat has some good downwind techniques that are completely different," Victor said in mid-2014. "He does a lot of pumping to stay on waves. His competitors see something is different, but what exactly it is they don't know. Centerboard position makes a difference. There are many details. You need the whole package to make it work, and the technique varies with the wind and the waves."

That was 2014. The techniques teams are using today have evolved even further, and continue to do so every week, every day of practice. With thousands of top sailors, coaches, boat builders, sail makers, and technological experts of all nationalities working day and night to stretch performance envelopes, and new, space age materials constantly appearing on the scene, techniques for making boats go faster come and go at a frantic pace. Initially, all this development is done in secret. When it involves gear or equipment, as it did when Victor contributed suggestions to Sebastian Ziegelmayer for improving the 470 hull, it's impossible to keep those innovations off the open market for very long. Business is business. "When we discover something," Victor says, "we make agreements with those who supply us with masts, sails, hulls. We ask them to give us an advantage, keep the technology exclusive for us for one or two years before they make it generally available." But the dynamics of actually sailing the boat are secrets perhaps Victor, even more than other coaches, is determined to keep locked away for as long as possible. Where Victor grew up, keeping secrets often meant survival. In Olympic sailing, secrets often mean success.

That's why when Nathan Wilmot went off to coach in Great Britain after winning his gold medal in Qingdao, Victor was most unhappy. Nick Rogers, who had won silver medals for the UK in the 470 at Athens and Qingdao, had asked Wilmot to be his coach for the London Games. "I know my going to the UK really upset Victor," Wilmot says. "But there was nothing we were doing here that was that different. There were a couple of Victor's `things,' and I couldn't share everything. I had to respect him in that way." Rogers fathered a child during the campaign and lost some focus on sailing. Wilmot then worked with the women's team (Mills/Clark), coaching them to a silver medal in London.

CHAPTER 13

Big Boats

In just a few years, Victor Kovalenko had made quite a splash in Australia's athletic world. In 2008, following his team's double gold medals in the Beijing Olympics, he was named Australia's coach of the year. In 2012, he was awarded the Medal of the Order of Australia (OAM), given as recognition of achievement and service to outstanding Australians from all walks of life (Australian citizenship had been bestowed upon Victor in 2003). In a country where sailing matters, his Olympic accomplishments drew not only praise, but fostered associations with business leaders eager to expose their management teams to Victor's contagious, winning ways.

Audi was one such company. A speech Victor gave to 45 of their directors and managers was typical. He spoke to them about how to compete, and how to be unpredictable. "I told them," Victor says, "that like our sailors, they are one team, the best in the world. Audi was our sponsor beginning in 2005. I told them we carry their logo on our sails and chests, from boatyards to restaurants, that we are ladies and gentlemen who promote their product, that we are both winners, the best sailors, the best cars as we fight BMW. During my talks, I often pause four seconds. If there is dead silence, that is good."

Victor also attracted a variety of grand prix big boat skippers who were bent on winning. Among them was the late Bob Oatley, the wine king in a wine-rich country, one of Australia's 50 wealthiest men and most notable sailors. His boats were a succession of yachts called *Wild Oats*. Oatley was eight-time line honors winner of the challenging Rolex Sydney to Hobart Yacht Race, and *Wild Oats XI* set an elapsed time record for the raced in 2012. Oatley owned the Hamilton Island resort on the Great Barrier Reef, and a villa on a cliff in Sardinia. Neither Oatley or Kovalenko could remember exactly where or when they met, but it was mutual respect at first handshake. Their backgrounds are similar. Oatley's success was also self-made. And he started sailing by rigging a hunk of fabric on a canoe so he wouldn't have to paddle, a story reminiscent of Victor's childhood experience with his father's skiff boat on the Dneper River.

In the 1940s, Oatley was selling trade goods in Papua, New Guinea. He saw an opportunity to specialize in coffee, and made it work, which more or less summarized Oatley's hands-on method of operation. After planting Shiraz grapes in 1969, he had seen the wine trend shift to Chardonnay. Quickly, he had grafted Chardonnay stock on the existing plants, and went on to create an award-winning series of vintages. When he realized his harvester's construction made it impossible to access critical moving parts, he cut a hole in the structure. At first outraged, the French manufacturer subsequently incorporated the new port into its design. Bob Oatley was known as a hard-working innovator. In Victor, he saw a kindred spirit. The fact Oatley always refused to work on Wednesdays so he could race on Sydney Harbor was surely a contributing factor to the friendship that developed between the two men.

Oatley turned 87 in 2015. Deteriorating health had slowed him considerably. He was no longer sailing on *Wild Oats*, but he still showed up at his elegant company headquarters on Pacific Highway, St. Leonards, NSW, five days a week. Enormous black and white photographs of various *Wild Oats* and his other boats taken at dramatic sailing moments, decorate the walls. He sat quietly during much of a chat I had with him and his son, Sandy, in the Australian summer of 2015, but he missed little. "Victor and I, we have a lot in common," he said at one point, his eyes steady on mine. "He's determined. He works hard. Hard!" The eye contact sustained. It was steely, underlining Oatley's strong, personal value of the ethic.

He and Sandy talked about Victor, laughing as they recalled an after-sail celebration on one of their powerboats with him and Tatiana and Vladimir, when Victor stuck glow sticks in his socks and was dancing on the afterdeck. "He sailed on *Wild Oats* for the delivery back from Hobart one year," Robert Oatley said. "A few days after they got back he gave me a written analysis of the crew. That's how he spent his time at sea." Bob Oatley passed away in January, 2016.

Martin Hill encountered Victor at Sydney's Middle Harbor Yacht Club, where the national 470 team was training. That was in 2000, when Hill was competing in the Sydney 38 class. A lot of excellent sailors have come out of Middle Harbor, and Hill had several of them on his crew including Malcolm Page, Laser silver medalist Michael Blackburn, and Nathan Outteridge, who would go on to win five 49er world championships, a gold medal (49er) in London, and a Moth Worlds. Page was the connection to Victor, who Hill engaged on a part time basis as the team's coach.

A trim, youthful looking man in his 50s, Hill is a former Commodore of Middle Harbor. At this writing he is president of the International Farr 40 Class. As founding director of HillPDA, he is an esteemed property consultant in Sydney. He developed Estate Master Property Software, widely used globally to assess the risks of property development. An organized man with confidence in data and procedure, Hill was intrigued by what he had heard about Victor's approach. Hill became a patron of the Australian sailing team in 2005, and for the next two years he adopted Victor's Olympic-style training program aboard his Sydney 38.

"He took us on with passion," Hill says. "He didn't like the spinnaker pole being on deck. One of the first days he sailed on board he suggested we lash it to the boom, Etchells'-style. That didn't go down very well with the crew: 'Who is this guy?' He had different ideas, a dynamic approach he brought from smaller boats. He takes you aside and gives you the basic elements of sailing: preparation, speed, and eventually psychology. As for speed, he got us to move weight first, then adjust the sails, and last of all, move the rudder because the rudder is a brake. He had us turning marks over and over. Downwind on short courses he had us jibe once, then twice, then three times before we doused spinnaker and tacked around the mark. He increased the level of difficulty until we broke. The better you do, the more the level rises.

"From his coach boat he took hundreds of photographs of everything, sail trim, crew positions. He's a superb photographer. He was fascinated by the way the bow was piercing the water."

Hill and his crew won the Sydney 38 National Championships in 2006.

On Hill's Farr 40 it was more of the same. "We wondered where are the notes, the coaching notes like the computer programs the other Farr 40s had," Hill says. "With Victor that information is happening, but you are the person doing it. He gives you a series of questions, and you have to provide answers. You learn it yourself. He leads you down the path, but you do the exercises and figure out the process. It's a different style. Not like when Tom Slingsby [Laser world champion, ISAF Rolex World Sailor of the Year (2010) and Laser Olympic gold medalist (London 2012)] told John Bertrand he was steering too much through tacks. It was never like that with Victor. He did give me a lot of attention about the journey I am on, and about the importance of communication on a forty-footer, with so many people in different roles.

"Victor's way is more like growing you as a person," Hill says. "Anyone at any level of success has to admire him. He provides you with a set of tools to help you adapt to whatever you need. It's easy when it goes your way. He helps you be ready to deal with a situation when it goes bad. I actually enjoyed the training more than the racing. During training we tried things, made improvements. In racing we simply did what we had been trained to do."

Many successful people who sail big boats acknowledge they apply their business philosophy to sailing. Martin Hill is the reverse. "The analogy of communication on board the boat makes you think," he says. "These are vital communication skills I have taken to my business. And Victor has shown us that predictability isn't set in stone. You have to beware of pre-learned stuff, like weather forecasts. Because pre-learned stuff can block identifying change and the creative opportunity it presents."

Marcus Blackmore met Victor sailing. "I asked him to get involved in my Farr 40," Blackmore says. "He said he hadn't been on big boats very much. I said it's a one-design, same as a 470 only bigger." Blackmore is CEO of Blackmores, the largest nutraceutical empire in the Southern Hemisphere. He's a large, robust man with a stable of boats that includes a TP52, and a new Southern Wind 82 for superyacht regattas. Marcus' father Maurice, a pioneer of naturopathy in Australia, started Blackmores in the 1930s. Marcus took the reins in 1975, at age 28. Specializing in supplements and vitamins, and with a strong presence in China and nine Asian countries, Blackmores grosses $3.5 billion a year.

The first year Marcus Blackmore raced in the big Hamilton Island Regatta, he had Victor coaching his team. "He got on the boat," Blackmore says, "and told the crew, `okay, there'll be no alcohol for the week.' Hamilton is great racing, but it's also a party. I took Victor aside and said I thought that was a bit rough. The next day he tells the crew, `okay, the second drink is one too many.' The guys stuck to it. They had respect for Victor. And we won the regatta.

"I also race a Dragon," Blackmore says. "I got Victor out to coach us for a day. He gave the three of us a little lecture beforehand, and in the space of three hours I learned more about sailing a Dragon than I had in the rest of my life. He sets up things for you to do, and you keep repeating them. We all walked away with a great deal of confidence about how to sail the boat.

"I've never run into a more positive individual," Blackmore says. "He came by one day. It was pissing rain. Miserable. He said no no, it's a good day. I asked him how so ? He said, `It could be your last.'"

CHAPTER 14

One more

It wasn't long after Mathew Belcher and Malcolm Page had won their gold medal in London that Belcher decided to try winning another one. His decision had a lot to do with the bond he had formed with Victor Kovalenko. "He has such an influence on me, and understands what drives me," Belcher says of his coach. "And I have to do what motivates me and what I believe in. I had so much to learn. The list was huge, and the details were interesting to me. It had taken so long to get to where I was…we were defining new areas of 470 sailing…and no men's team had ever been so dominate. I wasn't sure I could leave that."

Listening to Belcher talk about having so much to learn echoes Tom King saying he never saw so much opportunity for improvement as after he had won his gold medal. It's that kind of focus, that sustained quest for perfection that is unique to Olympic athletes and those who coach them. When it comes to evaluating ultimate accomplishment, Victor has said he puts Olympic gold medals ahead of Nobel prizes. He is accomplished at infecting athletes with his passion for gold medals. When he recognizes a sailor with great potential, who is also committed to sacrificing heavily to realize that potential, his campaign is very seductive.

"Coming into London," Belcher says, "we were still trying to get to the stage of performing consistently at the top. That last year was about building confidence, developing rhythm as a team, working on communication styles, just getting used to winning comfortably. And we were close to the cusp of new ideas, working on different dynamics, understanding how to sail the boat faster. With Malcolm leaving, Will Ryan was ready. As a new team, Will and I reached where we were in

London very soon after the Games. And we had almost four years left to work."

Will Ryan met Victor in 2008 at Middle Harbor Yacht Club on Sydney Harbor. Ryan was working on Martin Hill's Farr 40 when Victor came aboard as coach. Victor says he took one look at Ryan and saw the ideal 470 crew. The calm, friendly, intelligent nature of the young man was equally impressive. Victor quickly enrolled Ryan in an Olympic training group that met at Middle Harbor at 6:30 am, a schedule that allowed participants to get to their real jobs on time. Ryan had sailed for fun in 470s a few times, but he had purchased a 49er. He soon learned that because of his size and weight he had a more competitive advantage in a 470.

"Victor was impressive," Ryan says. "I remember him jumping into a 470 on land and showing us how to handle the spinnaker pole and sort out other movements. It had been a while since he raced competitively, but he was both fluid and fast, and could repeat moves over and over. He was very nimble, and always fit."

Ryan says he spent the first four years on the team figuring out how the 470 program worked. In 2009 it was suggested he and his skipper, Tom Brewer, sail in the 470 nationals in Port Lincoln, a 1500 mile drive west from Sydney. Victor arranged for Will to drive his car so they could have a good, long talk. "There were lots of questions from Victor," Ryan recalls. "He asked me what my favorite car was. I chose something conservative, practical for a sailor. He shifted my thinking to something more fun. Victor delivers messages that way, slowly, so a long car trip is an ideal situation for him."

Ryan remembers seeing lots of sharks during that regatta, providing excellent incentive not to capsize. He also remembers the brief moment his boat momentarily got in front of Belcher/Page during one race. "To beat them," he says, "I realized it took a lot more than being able to pick the right wind shifts. You had to be a lot fitter than I was, and I thought I was fit already. Over the next few years I realized you had to be somewhat selfish in order to pursue your dream. You had to be professional in all aspects relating to the campaign, relying on the people around you, and remembering the sacrifices you'd made to get to where you were. You had to be doing the best thing for you and that dream."

Victor preaches it, and all the teams that have helped produce the Australian 470 dynasty are quick to praise the progression of dedicated sailors who have helped create such an impressive string of satisfying results. Each successive Olympic qualifier has learned from the team ahead of them, and then, working with Victor's constant creative input, advanced the game on its own. Shortly after the Port Lincoln Nationals, Will Ryan teamed up with skipper Sam Kivell. Mathew Belcher and Malcolm Page say that Kivell/Ryan's effort as their training partner was a significant factor in them winning the gold medal. It was that close participation in the training for London 2012 that enabled Will Ryan to make such a smooth transition into the boat with Mat Belcher.

"Will was patient and passionate," Victor says, "waiting for his opportunities, working very hard. I caution him about working too hard. After sailing all day he goes to the gym, or for a swim, or a long bike ride. He's very good on the bike, rides miles and miles. Will is amazing, a great sailor."

Mat Belcher says that by the end of 2013 he and Will had learned all the skills Malcolm and he had going into London. "As we get ready to sail in Rio in 2016," Belcher says, "Will and I have more experience than Malcolm and I had because we've had more time together. What we learned from London we were able to put into practice quickly. Our preparation for Rio has been more detailed, more refined than our preparation going into London. We're focusing on much smaller details of our campaign."

Going into London in 2012, Belcher/Page had good boat speed and they were winning races. But Belcher feels there was no consistency about it. "Sometimes you don't need consistency," he says. "You just keep making good decisions at the right time. But we've broken into a new area. You have to understand yourself, the type of decisions you are making, and what kind of sailor you are, and merge all that with your partner. You have to use each others' strengths and find each others' weaknesses so you can build a strong partnership, and that takes time. Once you get there, you can't guarantee your performance, but you can avoid a lot of the mistakes you would normally make.

"But the fleet…as Will and I have transitioned into a different style of sailing, so has the fleet. We've brought the fleet with us."

Showing their hand

Mathew Belcher was selected as the 2013 ISAF Rolex World Sailor of the Year, the highest accolade there is for a competitive sailor. It was a great moment for Belcher, and also for his coach. Belcher was the third sailor coached by Victor to win the award. The first two were the Ukrainian 470 team of Ruslana Taran and Olena Pakholchik in 1997. Because Belcher established his record with two different crews, he alone received the award.

Looking back, Victor wonders if what they did was such a good idea. "Before the London Games," Victor says, "Mathew and Malcolm had won eight straight regattas. Then we won the Games. Then Mathew and

Will won every regatta in 2013. If we had not sailed that year at all we would be in a much stronger position to win in Rio. But we began sailing right after the Games because we had to bring Will on track and start winning. At some point we should have said that's enough winning, we're okay, we have the speed. But we thought Mathew had a good chance to win sailor of the year.

"If we had not sailed so much, the top teams – USA, Croatia, France, Great Britain – would be swapping victories and everything would be fantastic, everyone would be having an interesting life in the class. But because we were dominating, they all realized another level exists, and we are not there! They said we have to work two times harder to get to that level. They started to follow Mathew and Will every second with cameras, even during races. Maybe their own boat was in 15th, but they were filming Mathew and Will because they need to know why they are in front."

At times it got testy on the water. Victor says some coaches, like his long-time friend Dave Ullman, who coaches the USA women's 470 team, are always gentlemen. Other coaches shrugged and closed in on Mathew and Will in their motorboats during races, saying it was their duty to find out what the Aussies had going. Once during a test regatta in Rio in 2014, Morgan Reeser, then a USA coach, was pushing the limits. "What he was doing wasn't cool," Belcher says. "He was on the race course, influencing boats on the course, coming in close. We'd been putting pressure on Victor to get the guy away from us. Victor was as upset as we were. He sent the guy a message. He hit him with his motorboat, unintentionally of course. There was no damage. They were both rubber boats. There was no escalation. Reeser realized we were upset and stopped it."

Victor says he doesn't recall the incident. He does recall that the aggressive American coach made Belcher angry. He laughs. "They finished with five bullets and won the regatta." But early in 2014 he was seriously questioning the value of domination: did it function to show other teams they had no chance, or did it simply encourage them to work harder? Should we try to win everything again," Victor mused, "or be more quiet and win the Olympic Games?" Other factors took that decision out of his hands.

Distraction

On May 4, 2014, Mathew Belcher was named skipper of Team Australia, the America's Cup Challenger of Record. Team Australia's principal backer was winemaker Bob Oatley. As a friend and shipmate of Oatley, Victor was involved in the decision to select Belcher. Victor was thought to be line for the team's coach. At that point he was an advisor. "We did this," Victor says. "We put Mathew as skipper. It was a big step for him. And then we discovered the America's Cup is not what we thought it was."

Victor had asked friends and associates who were America's Cup insiders for advice about signing on as coach. They cautioned him, said what he was doing with his Olympic team was much more exciting and interesting than what he would be doing with the America's Cup. "There would have been much more money, one more zero," Victor says. "They said it was my choice: more money, or more interesting work.

"We were expecting the America's Cup to be a higher level of the sport, higher than Olympic sailing, fantastic, amazing. But we found their level was two steps below Olympic sailing. Olympic sailors make a difference in the America's Cup, and Team Australia had none. Who won the last America's Cup? Ben Ainslie and Tom Slingsby. John Kostecki was not doing well.

Even Tom Slingsby wasn't effective with him. But when Ainslie came on board the atmosphere changed. You could hear it in the communication: Tom to Ben to Tom to Ben. Spithill's job was speed, driving fast. Eventually, that afterguard won the day.

"Sailors from Team Australia were getting up at 5:30, going to the gym, sailing five hours…we were shocked by their approach. It was absolutely unprofessional, a model of a 1980s campaign. We expected new technologies, unique equipment, but there was nothing. Each America's Cup needs a completely different approach, and this syndicate was two steps behind. One crew on board was a family friend who thought he knew everything about sailing. *Ho boy!* They all thought they were great, but it was not true. I would rank some of them at level four out of ten. Some I would rank six, some eight — no, seven-and-a-half. And who is this Mathew Belcher? They thought of him as a kid from the 470 class who couldn't be trusted. Mathew has a black belt in sailing. He is an Olympic champion, six-time world champion, a world sailor of the year. When he took his break from the team he jumped into a Moth and won the Nationals in that very competitive class. He got third in the Moth worlds! He is not just a talented man, he has a system behind him that makes him unbeatable."

A system. Victor's three-part tenet about racing for glory (that "capricious lady") consists of all your time, all your money, and *the best possible support system*. Mathew Belcher is the latest "caretaker" (Victor's word) of the dynamic system Victor started in Ukraine with Larisa Moskalenko, Iryna Chunykhovska, and Olena Pakholchik. It gained momentum with Ruslana Taran and continued with Evgeniy Braslavets and Igor Matyivenko. The system moved to Australia in 1997, survived severe culture shock, and flourished with Jenny Danks and Addy Bucek, Jenny Armstrong and Belinda

Stowell, Tom King and Mark Turnbull, Elise Rechichi and Tessa Parkinson, Nathan Wilmot and Malcolm Page, Sam Kivell and Will Ryan, and a dozen or more others who were tireless and challenging sparring partners for all those medal winners who learned from those before them, then passed the baton of knowledge and experience to the next team that ran with it, continuing to grow, develop, and explore new ideas and techniques. Victor has always been the master of the system, reliable, understanding and inducing change in his athletes, leading by example. Much of the time he meets his own, self-imposed challenge: the need to not only see the future, but be the first to get there.

"Mathew was in the bubble of the system," Victor says, "and he absorbed it like a fetus absorbs everything from its mother. All the sailors before him and those who sailed as his training partners, his coach, his wife, his friends and family—all this was the system around him. He absorbed philosophies, spirit, experience, and knowledge to create his own internal system."

But it was the America's Cup. Being named skipper of a boat competing for the oldest active trophy in sports is a very big deal for any sailor, even Mathew Belcher, whose coolness under fire rivals that of an astronaut. Even he couldn't help but be a little bit impressed by his selection, and being Mathew, he took it seriously and went to work. This created still another problem for Victor, because here was a change perpetrated upon his athlete – a distraction of significant magnitude that Victor had had a hand in creating – that had to be added to Mathew's coaching profile (Will Ryan's as well, because Will was a shoe-in to be selected for the America's Cup team as well).

Change is one of Victor's mantras. Change, both internal (how the athlete with Olympic dreams must change him- or herself to realize that dream);

and external, (the surprises life holds in store). The internal changes are more manageable because they involve well-considered resolutions, and the acquisition of behavior patterns (habits). The individual is in charge of internal changes. Self-discipline is the prime facilitator. Having helped direct the course of internal changes, the coach observes closely, and lends a hand by delivering the right messages along the way at the right time.

External changes arrive helter-skelter, and require prudent and often instant reactions that (one hopes) have been fine-tuned by the internal changes. External changes include the thousand situations encountered on and off the water during a regatta; illness; death of a friend; falling in love; winning and losing; having a child; or being named skipper of an America's Cup boat.

"To move Team Australia to the next level was going to take a lot of time and energy," Victor says. "Mathew was not only going to the boat and sailing, he was talking on the phone for hours before his own 470 regattas. Before each race he was on the phone talking with Iain Murray (CEO, Team Australia), talking, talking, solving problems. That's why we lost the Palma regatta (March 2014) – we were third – and why we lost Miami."

Team Australia was short-lived, as it happened. On July 18, 2014, four and a half months after they had become the challenger of record, Team Australia pulled out of the competition. "The challenge was initiated," Bob Oatley told the *Sydney Morning Herald*, "with a view to negotiating a format for the 35th America's Cup that was affordable, that put the emphasis back on sailing skills. Ultimately our estimate of the costs of competing were well beyond our initial expectation." The cost of a series of international regattas, the elimination of San Francisco as host city, with the contemplation of Bermuda as host, were high on the list of Team

Australia's reasons for withdrawing. Oatley's brief foray into the Cup had reportedly cost him a cool ten million.

Mat Belcher registered disappointment. Looking back at the situation a year later, he said it had been a crazy time. "I don't know how we got through it. I was studying a bit, working on a masters degree, the America's Cup campaign was starting up, and there was the ongoing Olympic campaign on top of that. It was Mission Impossible, yeah, but what an opportunity to do everything you love doing, to try and balance all that. There were times I was really pushing things to the limit. I couldn't even show up for prize-giving at World Cup regattas because I had to be on a plane to Australia for America's Cup stuff the next day. But the Cup didn't go through, and I'm still married, which is good.

"Agreeing to do the Cup was a hard decision we made as a group — family, friends, and Victor," Belcher says. "I've been in sailing 16 years, and you're not sure such an opportunity will come back again. But we were fortunate with it not going ahead. It didn't seriously effect our Olympic campaign. It would have been heartbreaking to lose both."

Victor says if the Cup campaign had kept going, his team's chances of winning a medal in Rio would have been reduced to 5%. "The Cup is over," Victor said in March, 2015, "but Mathew is still affected by it. The level of fatigue he got from it — the psychic drainage — remains. The trace effects are very strong."

CHAPTER 15

Manly

It was February, 2015, mid-summer in Australia. Walking, I entered the crowd collected on a corner of one of Manly's main drags near the ferry to Sydney just as the light changed against pedestrians. A woman in a late model BMW accelerated so hard she squealed her tires. At the same time she blasted her horn at a straggler who hadn't quite made it to the curb. "Foreigner," someone in the crowd muttered. "Must be," said another, and we all had a friendly chuckle.

Manly, near where Victor and Tatiana live, is a lively beach suburb a 30-minute ferry ride across the harbor from Sydney. Manly is a low, island-like promontory connected to the mainland by a wide causeway where the town of 50,000 begins. On the southwest side is Manly's harbor, part of greater Sydney Harbor. A 15-minute walk takes you to the northeast side, and the busy beach where the Tasman Sea breaks. Magic names, parts of the Southern Pacific Ocean.

In Manly, one quickly gets used to people walking on the street dressed only in a bathing suit carrying a surfboard, or maybe boarding a bus with surfboard in hand. There is an open, attractive park bordering the harbor shaded by big old trees, and a variety of interesting restaurants and shops off a wide promenade that runs the length of the town.

It was19 months before the Olympic Games in Rio. Victor was at home for a few days before the start of another training camp for his team. "Home," for the past 14 years, is a bright apartment on the second floor of a small, modern building with a spectacular view of the Sydney Heads that mark the entrance to the harbor. It's an immaculate place with hardwood oak floors. Intriguing art work has been hung sparingly on the white walls.

Food is an important part of Victor's daily life no matter where he is. For breakfast one morning, Victor had served up one of his specials, a six-minute egg. When Victor is in the kitchen, it's best to stand back because he is a study in short-order efficiency. While Tatiana is the chief cook in the house, Victor knows what he is doing. There are few meals at home he doesn't help prepare. And with the six-minute egg there is no room for error. It is not a six-and-a-half minute egg, not a six-and-a-quarter minute egg.

A sauce pan of water is on the stove. When the water boils, Victor carefully inserts the egg(s) and starts the timer. Then he prepares a bowl of water and ice cubes. The second the timer goes off, he lifts the eggs from the boil and places them in the ice water. He waits two minutes, during which time he finishes running an orange, beet root, pineapple, lemon, berries, a kiwi, some ginger, and some apple through the juicer. Then he cracks the egg shell and peels it off before cutting the egg in half the long way with a sharp knife. The white is soft but firm. The yoke is liquid, but slightly cooked along the edges, and warm. Olive oil and soy are at the ready, along with Tatiana's homemade cottage cheese, delicious Belgian bread made by his friend, the baker down the street who used to be the head chef at an embassy in Washington, DC, and a glass of the fresh juice. One puts a few drops of oil and soy (to taste) on the yoke of each half, and consumes the delicacy in two bites, taking a bit of cheese and bread in between, pausing only to express with an appreciative moan how delicious it all is.

For lunch we went to a fish store that was astonishing for its immensity, the striking quality of its displays, and the extraordinary nature of the goods. Six kinds of shrimp. Eight varieties of oysters. Everything in profusion. One crab was as large as a football. In big wooden display bins slanted for maximum consumer impact, the colors of the creatures of the Tasman Sea glittering in perfect formation in a sea of ice under the bright lights, was stunning; an art gallery of seafood. Victor selected six Tasmanian oysters from St. Helens. Back at the apartment he warmed up potatoes, pork, and cabbage leftovers. First, we each had three of the smallish, plump oysters with a sip of wine, topped off with some fruit and Brillat-Savarin cheese.

With Victor it's all about moderation. "Test and taste," he'll often say. The first time we ate together in a restaurant we staggered out of the place feeling uncomfortable, complaining about the big portions. From then on, instituting Victor's plan, we shared an appetizer and a main course. We always left happy after that.

Over the preceding weekend he had arranged a meeting with as many of his sailing team's relatives as he could corral. His object was to persuade them not to go to Rio. "I did not say they should not go," Victor said. "You have to be careful. But my main message is, `are you sure you can bring positive input to your sailor's success in Rio ?' If not, make a choice. You have a chance to share the journey, or to share the the medals celebration. But in Rio, the chance something untoward will happen is high. You could be robbed, or get sick, whatever. The chance to see the "big Games" inside is very low because of security and tough management. The Olympic Games will be a big mess. Also you have to let the sailors focus on performance. If you are there, you will say, `can you come for dinner ?'

"It will be winter in Australia. Many in Sydney are sick. You give your sailor one kiss, and the next morning you call and say, 'Oh Johnny, I am sick.' These kids have been working for years, they have been prepared carefully, and then at the last stage a group of their friends show up and distract them by wanting tickets."

Victor told the assembled relatives that when he started with their sailors, he was a blacksmith, trying to bring about big changes in them. Now he works with a goldsmith's hammer, tap-tapping to make small corrections. "The parents were very understanding," he said over dinner. "They got the message."

Dinner. Tatiana presided, with Victor working as sous chef. She produced more incredible dishes from her Ukrainian larder, including a multi-layer cake so delicate it melted in one's mouth.

Victor spoke about his mother, who lives in Ukraine. She is in good health, but in the interest of advance planning, Victor had told her he would probably not be at her funeral because of his travel schedule with the team. "I told her instead I would come visit her once every year," he said, "that it would be better to see her alive." He said she was delighted with the plan.

The disturbing situation in Ukraine was discussed. Victor's homeland had been attacked and invaded over the past year, a situation that was very unsettling to a man with relatives and many friends there. "Historically," he said, "Ukraine and Russia were always close. World War II united us even more. We built the Soviet Union together, worked hard for the future and glory of our country. Then the Soviet Union collapsed. Ukraine and many other republics got their independence. The two countries were still close. But now the invasion of Crimea, and this blood bath in Donetsk, has destroyed all our feelings about 'one family.' Even here in Australia the Russian community is divided. One group watches the broadcast by Russian television. The other group watches normal Australian TV. Once Ukrainians and Russians were brothers. We are not brothers anymore. We are still friends, but we are not brothers.

"It is very difficult. My mother is Russian, Tatiana is Russian, my daughter-in-law is Russian. I have a lot of Russian friends, and we are still in very close contact. We always try to avoid this sensitive subject. But I am definitely not happy with what has happened, not happy when kids of my friends are killed, not happy to see wounded young boys in the hospitals of my city. Dnepropetrovsk is not far from Donetsk. Almost every day helicopters are bringing in more wounded young boys. Why? What for?"

Just a few weeks before we sat down to enjoy Tatiana's dinner, the Ukrainian city of Mariupol near the southwestern border of Russia on the Sea of Azov (a northern extension of the Black Sea), had been struck by "indiscriminate" rocket fire that had killed 30 people and wounded nearly 100 others.

The delicacies we were enjoying led naturally to discussion of other "top class" enjoyments. Victor's taste in music is wide and varied, ranging from jazz (John Coltrane) to popular (Diana Krall) to classical, deftly skimming the cream off each for his listening pleasure. He grabbed his laptop, and soon the opening, quietly dramatic bars of cellist YoYo Ma playing the main suite of Ennio Morricone's *Moses and Marco Polo* filled the room. Then he said he had a special treat if I had not heard it, and brought up cellist Sol Gabetta playing *Elgar's Concerto in E Minor*, definitely a treat for both watching and listening.

With the Elgar soaring, it was more testing and tasting as he brought out a variety of the best liquors: Johnny Walker 21 XR; Don Julio Reposado tequila; and the Macallan Fine Oak 18 year old. "James Bond liked this single malt," Victor said, "but he preferred the 50 year-old. You add three drops of water, from an eye-dropper. We don't drink. We taste small quantities."

In the end, it was back to sailing. "Have you ever seen the tape of 470 Race 2 in the London Olympics," he asked, "when Mathew barely missed the Italians after he rounded the mark." Soon we were watching as Belcher/ Page rounded the top mark in 18 knots of wind, set the spinnaker and started planning hard down wind. Suddenly there was the Italian boat converging with them from the leeward side, pedal to the metal, collision imminent, and Belcher somehow turned away without capsizing, avoiding what would have been two ruined boats and possible injuries. For Victor, it was 2012 all over again. He was mesmerized, kept playing the clip over and over and over again like he had never seen it, studying, looking for something that had escaped him the first hundred times he watched it; the detective returning once again to the scene of a cold case in hopes of finding a lost clue.

He stopped the video, turned away from the laptop, away from Yo Yo Ma, Sol Gabetta, and Belcher/Page missing the Italians. "It is 75 weeks to the Olympics," he said. "I had a meeting a few days ago with the whole team. I asked them what they thought the odds were for us to get a gold medal. Many of them said 100%. None of them have won a world championship. Only Mathew, who has won six world championships and a gold medal, and Will, said 80%. The rest don't know what it means to win gold. It is so difficult, even if you are ready." Victor paused. "They have no idea," he said quietly. Then he was bending over me, in my face, hands on the table, his voice rising, attaining a register somewhere between amazement and disbelief: "They have no idea!," he said as if his life depended on it. "They have no idea!"

The agenda

The annual series of five or six World Cup regattas sanctioned by World Sailing adheres to a flexible schedule. It always begins in January in Miami. In 2015, that regatta was followed by Hyères, France in April; Weymouth & Portland, England in June; Haifa, Israel (some years it is Qingdao, China) in October; and Melbourne, Australia (or it could be Abu Dhabi, United Arab Emirates) in December. Then there is Kiel Week (Germany), also in June, said to be the largest race week in the world, which is hard to resist. The World Cup regattas are an expensive, logistically challenging, and physically exhausting series that in 2015 included 14 different classes: Skud 18, Sonar, and 2.4 meter for Paralympic sailors; and 470 men and women, 49er and 49er FX, Nacra, Finn, IKA Formula kite, Laser and Laser Radial, and RS:X. The top teams in all classes try to participate in World Cup regattas because that's where the best competition is. And two of the regattas are the prestigious European and World Championships for many classes. All the World Cup regattas have a significant effect on world rankings, and a good result in any of these regattas also provides teams with selling points for landing sponsors. The Europeans and the Worlds have special value in that regard, as well as providing all-important bragging rights.

In a pre-Olympic year like 2015, it gets even more frantic with the need felt by many classes to accumulate time racing on Olympic waters in Rio de Janeiro. This was the 2015 travel schedule for the Australian 470 men:

1/24   Miami, USA

4/9   Marseille, FRA Spring Cup

4/20   Hyères, FRA

5/18   Rio (coaches regatta)

6/8   Weymouth & Portsmouth, GBR

6/27   Aarhus, DEN (European Championship)

8/13   Rio, BRA Test Acquece

10/10 Haifa, ISR (World Championship)

10/27 Abu Dhabi, UAE (world cup final)

12/15 Rio, BRA (Copa de Brasil)

Victor and the team are away from home at least six months every year. In between each event was a two week training camp for the team back in Australia.

The amount of air miles involved is daunting. From Australia it takes the team nearly 20 hours to fly almost anywhere – to the USA, Europe, South America, or the U.A. Emirates. The logistics of assembling and shipping the right packages of boat, masts, sails, centerboard and rudder to Europe, the USA, The Emirates, and South America, months in advance, requires strategic thinking as well as keen organizational skills. That has to be done by Victor and the team because no one else would know (should know!) what combinations are needed where, and why.

With such a long series of important regattas, the selection of equipment combinations becomes an important strategic element. As Will Ryan says, "The spread of events ranging from Dubai through Europe to Rio means more equipment, and it often boils down to who has better equipment at which events." Teams have to look at the big picture, determine what regattas are the most important to them, and make decisions accordingly. Regattas have to be evaluated for typical conditions – light or heavy air, flat water or choppy – and importance. Then teams get into the complexity of which mast with which sail, and which centerboard with which boat, and while we'd like this package for Europe, we definitely want this mast for Rio...

To start the year, Mathew and Will finished second in Miami, losing by one point to Great Britain's Luke Patience and Chris Grube, the team that won silver to Belcher's and Page's gold in London. That wasn't quite in line with Victor's game plan for 2015, which was to reduce the pressure to win all the time, and get Mat and Will to sail in a more relaxed manner while using the competitive regattas to study the conditions and test some "things," Victor called them – like rig settings, masts, sails, appendages – important tests that had been tabled during the emphasis on winning. Testing does not always provide positive results. But losing by one point wasn't exactly an indication of not trying to win.

"We're still working on how to do that," Mathew said with a laugh over breakfast just before the Miami regatta started. "We don't quite know how to approach it. We're competitive, keen on what we're doing. And we're not showing them everything, not sailing 100%. We're holding back on some things, and Victor is driving that. Sometimes we push that boundary because we want to win. But we also realize it's unhealthy to keep up the constant pressure on ourselves. There's a long way to go. But what happens when we don't win ? What happens when others do ? Does that build their confidence ? They don't know what we are doing. They win the event and think they have caught us. But every time we win we're motivating our competitors more and more. It's a no-win situation for us because when they win we're giving them confidence."

Victor took the second place seriously, and as always, focused on the positive side. "In all sports, once on top it is not easy to stay there," he said. "The top of the pyramid is very sharp. The higher you go the more narrow it becomes, the less space there is. It is not comfortable with all opponents trying to grab you. You have to be very strong. Once you get there, you can say wow, I am great, then get dizzy, lose your balance and fall down. But if you don't get dizzy, and get used to being there, you are harder to grab. We have some tricks. I talk with Mat and Will, explain psychological principles."

There's not a successful person Victor meets from whom he doesn't learn more about staying at the top. And the list of accomplished athletes, businessmen, teachers, other coaches, and professionals he encounters gets longer every day. Victor has an engaging way about him. He's a presence in a room, not from loud or rash behavior, but from the positive energy he radiates. Just as he can be a closed door when he feels it is necessary, in a crowd he is very available, a cornucopia of warm greetings and compliments delivered with a charming, Ukrainian semi-formality mixed with pithy comments that arrest people, make them listen – and talk. "Drop by drop," Victor says, "they bring their unique experience to me." That's a typically humble report from Victor, because as we have seen, more than one corporate CEO who races boats for sport has been engaged enough to bring Victor aboard to coach him and his crew.

"When you are at the top and you lose, that is a great learning experience," Victor says. "I am happy we lost in Miami because now we understand why it has happened. This understanding will give us more power next time, and that's very important. Why we lost? That's easy. The speed was right. It was psychological. It was a good time in the schedule to lose because there is plenty of time ahead."

One wondered what pulling off a tight, satisfying win did for Great Britain's Patience/Grube.

"Luke is a little more confident," Victor said. "He knows he can beat us sometimes, but he understands also we are much stronger and will beat him next time. Our boats were side by side on the hard. That was handy. From his behavior we could tell he was uneasy."

Risk

Management of risk, one of Victor's favorite topics, was creeping into his conversation more and more. There are hundreds of decisions during every sailboat race that involve risk, from jockeying pre-start (obtaining a favored position on the start line will involve taking more risk than going for a less favored position) to tacking on a wind shift and risking that it will sustain long enough for a gain. Victor's team has put all the factors to consider for taking risk, by situation, into a software program. He, Belcher and Ryan talk about risk on the water between races. "Risk is such an important part of the whole game," he says: "It's huge.

"Risk is everywhere, at your bank, in the stock market, everywhere is risk. Take too much risk, and boom, you are a loser. Don't take enough risk, boom, you are a loser. A broker I know told me he doesn't deal with money. He deals with people's emotions, their greediness to get more."

Victor said that Luke was both risky and lucky during the Miami regatta. "Some teams are risky and unlucky. Some are conservative – consistent – and they are winners. If you are sailing 11 races, and you are racing risky in all of them, and you are unlucky three times, bye bye. It's about learning. You have to take stock of your position in the regatta, and, as I have said, determine what risk area you find yourself in: must not take a risk, can take a risk, or must take a risk."

In the 2013 season (and into 2014) when he was dominant, Mathew Belcher was in the enviable position of "can take a risk." But he was in the habit of minimizing risk because he had a speed advantage. For that reason, minimizing risk gave him a more consistent result. At the same time, the rest of the fleet was forced into the "must take a risk" position if they wanted to beat Belcher. So while Belcher/Page-Ryan were enjoying a lower risk strategy, the rest of the fleet was developing a higher risk strategy. As the rest of the fleet began to make gains in the speed department, parity began to influence the proceedings.

"It got to the point that the two strategies – lower risk/higher risk – intersected," Belcher says. "We saw the higher risk strategy starting to pay off. We were still getting good results, always making the podium, but we were losing opportunity. We subtly tried to increase risk in specific areas. That's why I stress our detailed preparation, because we're not talking about general race risk, we're talking about breaking down elements of the race, and of the event, and looking at where we feel comfortable taking a risk. It takes a lot of time because I'm a lot more adverse to risk than Will. We still have a conservative strategy because we know that unless something goes wrong we'll be on the podium at the end, but we need to take enough risk to win the regatta. The start is the biggest risk, the most obvious area. We're getting more OCSs"…(on the course side, or over the starting line early)… "than normal. That's us trying to adjust and figure out where we are in the risk frame."

As Victor says, "The way you start reveals a lot about your character — bold, conservative, brave, wise… Coaches suggest different techniques and strategies, even philosophies. There are books about starting. Sometimes you are lucky, sometimes you have bad luck. If you are balanced and judicious you will perform the start well. But the start is not about what you know, it's about who you are."

There's nothing else in sports that compares with the start of a sailboat race. Most starts of sporting events begin with the competitors at a standstill, including ice hockey and lacrosse face offs, track and bicycle events, basketball jump balls, football plays and kickoffs. Car race starts are often in motion, but in those cases the cars have qualified for assigned positions. To those who have never started a sailboat race, the sight of a one-design fleet of 30 or more boats jockeying for position in a patch of water often smaller than half a football field, while the timer clicks off the seconds, looks like total chaos.

Pre-race, a team decides which side of the race course it prefers. That determines where the team would like to be on the line at the start.

Essentially, when the warning gun goes off, the team has five, sometimes ten minutes to maneuver, the idea being to cross the line in the proper direction at the right place and as soon after the starting gun as possible. That means a fraction of a second.

The start of a sailboat race is a Zen exercise. Putting your boat in a position to have the right of way over other boats is crucial, but of course to get where you want to be on the line requires deft maneuvering (superior boat handling) during which you are often without rights, and therefore at risk. As time runs out, 30 seconds, 20 seconds, the pace becomes more frantic. Heart rates increase throughout the fleet. An accomplished sailor once admitted that at age nine, when he started his first sailboat race, at 20 seconds to go he wet his pants. (He said the lesson he learned was never to wear blue jeans racing a boat). Because at 20 seconds, boats are diving into "holes" (spaces) that have suddenly appeared on the line. Teams that are early are trying to slow down, and vice versa. It's mad out there. But the start is where risk pays off big time. In a grand prix 470 race, which takes less than an hour, Victor says the start can account for between 30% and 50% of the outcome. Mathew Belcher says in certain conditions the start can be worth as much as 70% of the race.

France 04/09/15

The annual Spring Cup in Marseilles, in April, was considered a tune up for the annual World Cup regatta in Hyères 10 days later. The Marseilles regatta was not significant, and while that may not have been a fact on paper, it remained a competition among some of the best sailors in the world getting prepared for Hyères. Beer can races at local yacht clubs on Wednesday evenings may not be significant, but there is not a crew among the boats competing that is not doing its best to win. Multiply that by a factor of your choosing to arrive at the level of competition that exists on Marseille water every spring.

Belcher/Ryan finished 6th in Marseilles. One had to assume they were testing various combinations of mast, sails, rig tensions and positions that had been put aside in the interest of winning. Victor said no, no testing, they were just not ready. "They were just racing to get back into their style," Victor said.

One of Victor's analogies about not being ready is the story of the chess grand master who was spotted on a train by a young, accomplished player. The young man approached the master, introduced himself, said how much he admired him, and asked if he would play him. The master was at ease, reading, smoking a pipe, and graciously declined. But the young man wouldn't quit, using flattery and cajoling him until the master figured the best way to get rid of the fellow was to agree to play. They played, and the young man won, something he would brag about the rest of his life. But the point is that the master's heart, and his competitive fervor, was missing from the match. He was not totally engaged.

The other story Victor tells is how he once overcame an opponent who was all too ready and eager to play. During his badminton days, Victor found himself with a friend who was a champion at the game. Badminton was one of the few things the man had over Victor, and every time he laid eyes on Victor he wanted a game. Knowing this, Victor would decline, but this day he was unable to overcome the man's insistence. Finally he said okay, but demanded they have a warmup period. The champion player reluctantly agreed. Every time he said enough! let's play, Victor said he was not quite ready, and asked for a bit more warm up. By the time Victor said he was ready, the man was beside himself. The game was close, but Victor won. And of course he refused to play more than one game.

The moral is also about being ready yourself, by creating a situation of possibility followed by a gathering of all your strengths accompanied by intense focus. "You have to feel the liquid metal running in your veins," Victor says, "which gives you a feeling you cannot fail. That's how I felt that day."

Marseilles was the first time Belcher/Ryan had competed in three months. Liquid metal was on hold. Kinks were being ironed out as Victor suggested. But the competition had also improved. Many teams, including the top half dozen, were using the latest Ziegelmayer 470s, and the fleet showed very even speed in all conditions. "It changes how you race," Belcher said, "how much risk you take at the start, and your strategy on the race course. When you have the speed advantage, that's one thing. Without speed, you need to take more risk.

"It's good that our competitors have stepped up. It's been hard to find motivation the past couple years. We've had to source it from other areas to try to keep performing and winning. Now the fleet is motivating us to keep winning. I can see it in our physical activities and our discussions. It's an exciting time for us, this new level of motivation. The fleet is stepping it up. We know we have to make that next step as well."

Two weeks later Belcher/Ryan lost the Hyères regatta by ten points to the Croatians, a team that was coming on strong. Many teams would think placing second at a world cup regatta was nothing to complain about, let alone worry about. But for Victor, placing second was, well, it wasn't first.

"At the end of last season we were all completely drained," Victor said. "At the end we had to race in Abu Dhabi which was a tiring exercise, then we had to go to Brazil because we had to learn Brazil. Then we had to sail Miami. Mathew was especially drained because of the America's Cup, and Will too because when Mathew has fatigue Will is effected as well. When you sail with a fragile person in the boat it comes back on you. Every time we returned to Australia we were not really training. I was keeping them sailing, but not running a 100% program. Maybe a 55% program. We skipped Palma because Palma is a regatta to win and it would squeeze them again.

"In Hyères we often do well by going left. This time the weather man said the wind would go right. They ignored the forecast, and the forecast was correct. When you are winning all the time – Europeans, Worlds, gold medal – you become blind, focused only on yourself. When losing, this makes your eyes open. You see what others are doing, where they are going, how they are sailing, what techniques they are developing.

"Working with top ranked sailors makes my job difficult. I have to wait for opportunities to send a strong message, wait until they ask me, Victor, what is wrong? I sent one technical message about shroud settings that effect sail shape. They said yeah okay, and nothing was done. I remind them in Marseilles, yes yes, but nothing done. Then they say why are we losing, and I said because we have to develop in this direction."

Mathew admits that at times he is resistant to new ideas. "The hardest thing is to stay open," he says. "When you've had lots of success you tend to lock stuff in that you think works." Toward the end of the regatta their

Victor Kovalenko shares his remarkable story with biographer Roger Vaughan about his ascent to the highest levels of sailing. Victor's tenacity of pleading with those in authority to gain permission to race sailboats in the former Soviet Union is inspiring. Victor creates Olympic Champions by using relentless preparation, clever psychological methods, and innovative technology. There are lessons here for anyone interested in any sport. Readers learn what it takes to overcome adversity, and to win. Roger Vaughan is a master observer who writes in a readable style that takes you inside the head of a genius.

Gary Jobson

34 | Tatiana at home in Ukraine, 1997

35 | With parents and sister Natalia, 1997

37 | Victor with Soviet Legends
38 | Victor with Royalty of Spain
39 | Victor with Crown Prince Frederik of Denmark

40 | "Order of Australia" in 2012
41 | With the Oatley family

42 |
Celebrating with the
Blackmore family

43 |
With lovely wife Tatiana

44 |
2013 ISAF Rolex World
Sailor of the Year

45 |
Sport Australia Hall of Fame
2013

46 | Grandfather

34 | Tatiana at home in Ukraine, 1997

35 | With parents and sister Natalia, 1997 – On a visit to Ukraine.

36 | Birthday party – At Victor's 50th birthday party, Paralympic coach Irina Dvoskina arrived with an old poster from the 1980 Olympics in Tallinn.

37 | Victor with Soviet Legends – Victor with the late, legendary Soviet sailor, four-time Olympic medalist Valentin Mankin (left), and his former crew, Vadim Akimenko.

38 | Victor with Royalty of Spain – Victor with the future King and Queen, Crown Prince Felipe and Crown Princess Letizia, at the Olympic Games in Athens, 2004.

39 | Victor with Crown Prince Frederik of Denmark – Victor coaching the Crown Prince during a Regatta in Sydney in 2009.

40 | "Order of Australia" in 2012 – Celebration of awarded Medal "Order of Australia" in 2012.

41 | With the Oatley family – Val Oatley, Bob Oatley, Victor, Tatiana, Ian Oatley and his wife Tania.

42 | Celebrating with the Blackmore family – Victor with close friends Caroline and Marcus Blackmore, celebrating Mat Belcher's and Will Ryan's Olympic Silver Medal 2016 in Rio.

43 | With lovely wife Tatiana – Victor and Tatiana at the ceremony "Sport Australia Hall of Fame".

44 | 2013 ISAF Rolex World Sailor of the Year – Coach Kovalenko with Mathew Belcher.

45 | Sport Australia Hall of Fame 2013 – A proud Victor Kovalenko takes a bow at his induction into the Sport Australia Hall of Fame in 2013.

46 | Grandfather – With granddaughter Kseniya and grandson Misha, Sydney, 2016.

results were improving. The last four races they finished 3-3-7-1. "Croatia sailed well," Belcher said afterwards. "Sime Fantela fully deserved that win. It's good to know what he can do. We have to step up and match it. It was the first time in five years we weren't in a position to go for the win on the last day."

Brazil 05/18/15

It is in every team's interest to spend time sailing in Olympic waters as the Games get closer. But there is no gain in traveling all the way to Rio (in this case) and not having good competition. So teams cooperate for their mutual benefit, buy into attending a series of "coaches regattas" in Rio on dates they add to their official schedules. After Hyères, fifteen teams including the USA, New Zealand, Austria, Japan, Brazil, and Croatia were invited by Victor to attend two weeks of racing in Rio. It was a strong fleet. Coaches from the various teams alternated running races and setting courses. Belcher/Ryan finished first.

Victor said they were testing new philosophies in Rio. "It has to do with how a team approaches a race," he said. "There are racing philosophies, and also racing elements, techniques and tactics that have to be executed carefully and accurately. Elements like when you come to the top mark you have to protect your position before you hoist your spinnaker, otherwise you will be rolled by another boat while you are hoisting. If you ignore small details like that you will lose. If you do everything perfect, you will gain, gain. When we unite all these racing elements in one system, that is a racing philosophy."

Victor compares it with music. Notes are the elements (the constants) that must be mastered before students build their playing techniques. Using the same notes, every pianist plays a piano sonata differently. "As they study," he says, "they gain deeper understanding of the composer and how to join the music with their personalities, their life experiences, their vision. This is the same with racing philosophies. A different mood will give you a different approach to elements and principles, and the performance will also be different."

Victor said he was happy with his team. "But at the same time we have some issues, things to change, correct, because at some stage when you are at your peak, you know how good you are. Mathew became world sailor of the year. That was very good, but it brought negative things to our racing philosophies and our personal relationship because one's self-judgement – ego – is completely different. When athletes become super stars it is more difficult to deal with them. They become defensive, protecting their ideas and principles. Everything is changing around Mathew and Will. They are changing a lot. I have to use the positive changes to make them stronger, and eliminate changes that will have negative impact."

England 06/08/15

The team was looking forward to the Weymouth & Portsmouth regatta, the scene of Belcher's Olympic gold medal (with Malcolm Page as crew) in 2012. But four years is a long time to remember the nature of currents and wind patterns, and where the good restaurants are. Four years ago everyone had prepared long and diligently for the big exam. They would have four days to refresh their memories and cram for a replay.

They sailed well, but finished second to the USA by 21 points. Down seven points to the Americans (McNay/Hughes), Belcher/Ryan had a mathematical shot at winning going into the medal race – which counts double. But they finished 8th (16 points) to McNay/Hughes' 1st (2 points), and that was that. Once again, it was about risk. "McNay/Hughes had good starts in Weymouth," Belcher said. "The differences we gave up at the start were very difficult to make up by the top mark."

Victor saw the pattern emerging. "Mathew was second in Miami. Luke won. Why? He made risky starts. In Hyères, Croatia won because they were risky at the starts. Who was second? Mathew. Then Weymouth. The USA won. Why? They were very risky at the start. In Weymouth, Croatia, Great Britain, and France were all risky. Croatia was 4th, Luke was 8th, France did not make the top ten. And Mathew was 2nd again."

The problem was in the pattern. Everyone agrees that consistency is a sure-fire way to win regattas. Many grand prix regattas have been won by teams that registered single-digit finishes while never winning a single race. Nathan Wilmot and Malcolm Page won their Olympic gold medal that way in 2008. But when parity has been so evidently established in a fleet as competitive as the 470, a willingness to take risks becomes a huge factor in winning. If the Miami, Hyeres, and Weymouth regattas were each part of a triple-crown event, Belcher/Ryan would have been run away overall winners with their three, second-place finishes. But, like the Olympics, each of those regattas stands on its own. Like it or not, "must risk" now applies to every team in the fleet interested in winning.

"I'm older," Belcher says, "and therefore less willing to take risks. Now we try to remodel that attitude while making sure we stay stable within the campaign. That's where Victor is so great. He knows us well enough to analyze our performance from a high level. The starting philosophy is just one component. Right now we are too conservative for the fleet. We're looking for different ways, different dynamics in the boat so we are more consistently in higher risk areas. For five years we have medaled in every regatta in a variety of conditions and locations. That shows the experience factor is helping get us through this period, and will help us get through next year."

Denmark 06/27/15

Three weeks later, Belcher/Ryan finished third at the European Championship in Aarhus, Denmark, definitely a regatta to win. Five of the six days of racing were plagued by light, fickle winds. Belcher/Ryan finished 20th in the second race, and 24th (their throw out) in race six, all but negating any chance they had to win. "It would be unprofessional to say we had back luck, that we were caught by bad wind shifts," Victor said. "We can say it was bad luck, tough conditions, that some people are lucky and some are not. But it is our job to make luck in difficult conditions. Luck is a place where opportunity meets preparation. Their starts were very good. As soon as we had stable conditions, more wind, they won both races one day."

In sailing, the luck factor increases in lighter winds. In 15 knots of wind, a sudden gust to 18 knots isn't that big a change. But in five knots, a 2 knot change is a 40% difference. In very light wind, all sorts of odd things can and do happen to a racing fleet. There was the extraordinary light wind anomaly that took Wilmot and Page from a certain win to the back of the fleet in Thessaloniki, Greece. Another huge reversal that comes to mind occurred during the America's Cup defense trials in 1995. *Mighty Mary*, with the all-girl crew, was nearly a mile ahead of Dennis Conner's *Star&Stripes* in a deciding race when the wind fell out completely. In the next 20 minutes, Conner was blessed with an isolated strip of wind, sailed a great circle course around the stalled *Mighty Mary*, leaving 13 female sailors sobbing in frustration. But as Victor says, it's a team's job to "make" luck. Legendary American sailor Buddy Melges addresses the same point when he often speaks of the need to "set the boat up for Mother Nature."

Belcher's and Ryan's home waters are Sydney, and Gold Coast,

Australia, where the wind reliably blows 15 knots or more. "It's planing, wavy, technique-driven sailing," Belcher says. As a result, light air sailing is something this team has had to learn to love. It takes patience, and lots of discipline to stay focused on sensing miniscule elements that can indicate the impending arrival of the lightest zephyr. In light wind, for instance, the crew is obliged to sit uncomfortably for long periods in the middle of the boat, motionless. Both Weymouth and Aarhus were light wind regattas. Belcher wasn't happy with their performance in either of them.

"You simply have to raise your level of focus in those conditions," Belcher says. "There's a subtle difference between sailing well and not so well when it's light. Yes, it is luck in part, but if you break it down, it's a different kind of risk management, using different techniques. Many teams don't train in light wind because they don't enjoy it, and if you don't enjoy it, it's hard to register a good result. If you have big waves and a good wind it's fun sailing. Light air is a totally different feeling. We have work to do on our light air sailing."

When Victor talks about taking risk in light air it is all about sticking with the game plan. "If you have an idea where to go, you must go there. American Paul Foerster was very good at that. So was Braslavitz, and Nathan Wilmot. If you have a plan, then go, go, go. Stick to it."

After Aarhus, Victor arranged for the team to spend a week by themselves. They went to a hotel in a remote area of Northern Germany, near Kiel, just the three of them. They trained every day, ate three meals together, and relaxed.

"It was a fantastic place," Victor said, "with long beaches to walk on, a different world. It was German summer, and that is a very short season. The Germans were enjoying it enormously, riding bikes, having fun, laughing. If there are people moving around you, and the open sea with all the clouds and patterns on the water, it will never be boring. The emotions of people and the joy of German summer made a big difference."

"We'd been making silly mistakes," Mathew Belcher said. "Being together in an isolated place gave us a good opportunity to reset everything."

Resetting for this team means a lot because communication is such a vital part of their dynamic. When Victor, Mathew, and Will aren't talking face to face, they are talking on the phone, texting, or exchanging emails about various ideas and concepts that are on the table. Victor says he keeps a pad and pen on the nightstand of his bed, and never fails to force himself to wake up and make notes when solutions occur. "Do you know the story about the French businessman?" he asks. "He had so many ideas at night sometimes he had to take his secretary to bed with him."

"We'd all been so busy doing our thing," Belcher says, "racing, traveling, and Victor had a lot of pressure from the Australian team. We weren't quite all there. It's sometimes frustrating with Victor. I have my understanding of things, my ideas, and in some areas I have more depth of knowledge because I've spent more time doing it. In other areas, Victor has more depth with his decision making and ideas. And Will has a lot of knowledge in various areas. It's often a matter of tolerating each other. I've known Victor half my life. It's been an amazing relationship with him.

"If we're not on the right track on the race course, Victor knows us well enough to help us out. And vice versa. We can get him on the right track. Victor and I can help Will, and Will can help us. That's the strength of the partnership. We're there for one another and not just in sailing. That was a good week after Aarhus. It gave us a lot of confidence. I announced that Rike was pregnant again. We had a good string of wins after that."

Groove

The winning streak started in August, 2015, at the Rio Test Aquece, which means "heat," or "warm up" in the Portuguese language of Brazil; or perhaps "heating up," in more colloquial English, given that the Olympics were just a year away at that point. The uproar over the water quality in Guanabara Bay was in full cry at the time, and in fact several days during the Aquece regatta certain courses could not be used because of the quantity of garbage and trash floating upon them. Victor reported that his motorboat with its 70hp outboard was stopped dead when the propeller encountered a plastic bag big enough to wrap a couch. He emailed a photograph of his motorboat's bow line draped with a quantity of plastic and other garbage after being tied up for 12 hours. Victor said the smell in the harbor was vile. The mess moved with the wind and currents. The window for sailing in Rio tends to be three to four hours a day. The sea breeze generally arrives after lunch, and by 5:30 it is dark, meaning no race can start after 4:30pm. The garbage factor simply added to the complexities of the conditions prevalent in Rio.

Offshore there tends to be big waves with a stable breeze when it blows. Inside there is flat water with complex currents. When there is wind offshore, there will be no wind inshore, and vice versa. Sugar Loaf Mountain produces entertaining shifts. It's complicated. Rio requires experience, judgement, and a diversity of techniques.

Belcher/Ryan won the Rio Test by a slim margin (2 points) over the French. Croatia was third. In race 5, Belcher/Ryan were black flagged, meaning they crossed the starting line before the gun when that infraction meant automatic disqualification.

"They won that race easily," Victor says. "After they finished, their first question was, 'who was over?' When they asked that, I understood they were over, because they were worried about it. They were taking more risk, maybe more than required. They had discussed it because they discuss everything on the boat, risk and strategy, if they have the opportunity. If no opportunity, it is an instant decision by Mathew. But even if there is a small opportunity for Will to be involved, he is involved."

In Race 9, they finished 14th. "Too much risk," Victor said. "The advantage was the right side. With 22 seconds to go, they were middle right. Suddenly they are jibing, going toward the committee boat, but there was not enough time to obtain a new position. They tried to squeeze between the Greeks and another boat. There was no space. They were too close to the Greeks. The Greeks protested. The Greeks tacked, not because Mathew pushed them, but because it was the right thing to do, to go right. Mathew did a 720 penalty turn. The Greeks won the race.

"Mathew was being too conservative previously. But they have to understand when to take risk and when they shouldn't. Later he said he needed my support, and I said yes you need my support, but I am a professional, I know what I am doing. I can't pretend to be enthusiastic, pat your shoulder and say don't worry, you will do the job tomorrow. No. Sometimes I have to be tough for them to remember messages. If I am not tough I just betray them. They don't need my false enthusiasm. I show my fighting spirit, my real enthusiasm – not pretending to be happy.

"The great Michael Jordan said if you lose you have to be unhappy. Not disappointed – I don't like that word. Or upset. Those are the wrong words, not words for champions. Champions are never 'upset' or 'disappointed.' When they lose they are unhappy, much more eager to be winners again. There is no space for disappointment.

"When it is a bad time, bad luck, even when they are 14th I give them support. But instead of a pat on the shoulder it was better for me to make them a little bit angry, make them prove themselves the next day. That is the coaching business. Now they will remember this message."

The next day was the medal race. Belcher/Ryan placed second, and thereby won the regatta. The medal race has to have been the product of a diabolical mind. It first appeared in the Olympics of 2008, inserted as the last race of the regatta. It was designed at the behest of the International Olympic Committee, that was under pressure from network television's insistence on events that will provide instant gratification for viewers' brief attention spans. Only the top ten boats in the regatta qualify for this race, which is always much shorter than usual (roughly 50% of the distance of a standard race). On top of that, it counts double, meaning that placing 1st is worth two points, a 2nd is worth 4 points, and so on. The medal race is well-named, because if Team Alpha enters the race in 5th or 6th place, but relatively close on points, and Alpha wins the medal race while Team Beta, in 1st place going in, has a poor race, then Alpha will win a medal while Beta is off the podium. The shortened course plus the weight of double points makes getting a good start absolutely critical, because there is no time for a comeback. The medal race is an amazing opportunity for a team that has not sailed up to par to reverse its fortunes with one race. It also offers a team that has sailed itself into first place after ten races a heartbreaking opportunity to blow all that accomplishment in one race.

Diabolical or not, Victor likes the medal race. "It's a good concept," he says. "It's a big test for all sailors. It is the essence of all sport now. If you are good, you have accumulated enough points during the regatta to avoid the big battle in the medal race. If not, you have to be ready for that big battle. Because everything depends on it.

"If we had less wind in the medal race it might have been different," Victor said. "But we were definitely ready to win. In spite of being back a bit, with the black flag and the 14th, Mathew and Will were ready. I told them before that race they had to do their best race because there are six boats that could win the regatta. I said just do your best, I trust your skills and your ability to win." Pressure. But it worked for Belcher/Ryan.

The French played high risk, won the start, and were first at the weather mark. The Swiss were second, Belcher/Ryan were third. They needed to finish second to beat the French overall. The Swiss had good speed. Belcher/Ryan could not catch them downwind, or upwind. Toward the end of the second upwind leg, Belcher/Ryan came from the left on port tack. The Swiss were just a fraction beyond that imaginary lay line that would allow them to round the mark on starboard tack. Belcher/Ryan thought the Swiss had made a mistake by over-standing just a little bit, and tacked under them. Must risk! But it was the right call. They rounded the mark half a boat length ahead and were able to maintain their slim advantage to the finish line.

"I gave them the Australian flag and they raised it," Victor says. "It was a very special moment. To win in Rio gave us confidence. Next to the world championship, this regatta was the most important."

Streaking

The Rio Test Aquece turned out to be the first of six straight regattas won by Belcher/Ryan/ as they compiled a nine and one record going into mid-June, 2016. In Haifa, Israel, in October 2015, Belcher had won the 470 World Championship for the 6th straight time, a 470 class record. Before that, Belcher/Ryan had won the warm-up, the Israeli National Championship, by 31 points. When the Worlds began a week later, they were still hot, scoring 1-1-1-2 in the first four races. "Then we slept too well," Belcher says. "Will and I are the most competitive people you'll meet," Belcher says, "but we didn't maintain the fire we needed."

The Worlds were sailed in light wind after the first couple days, and after their initial romp, Belcher/Ryan slipped into double digit finishes four races in a row: 10-22-15-10. "Were they unhappy?" Victor asked. "Of course. They are normal people. But they just have to focus on the job they have to do. They have to remember how good they are. Even four bad races in a row can't make a difference. You can't change yourself in two days. They have to rely on the main philosophy, the solid formation we built for the team that is the foundation of their success."

They did, and finished strong with a 1-7-1 and a 4th in the medal race. Once again Croatia was their main competition, just 5 points behind them at the end. Victor stressed that work was needed in light wind, more of which would be available in the world cup regatta a week later in Abu Dhabi, where the scorching heat and high (80°F) water temperatures combine to forestall any chance of a sea breeze. Victor said the work he had in mind was simple: more time in the boat in light conditions. "Good trimming and good feelings make all the difference," he said with his easy smile, the signal that the subject was closed.

There was no chance for more time in the boat before Abu Dhabi. Perhaps just the thought of good trimming and good feelings made a difference. In any case, Belcher/Ryan nailed the light wind event with scores of 1-2-2-1-2-(6)-2 in seven races, beating second place Sweden by 11 points, and third-place USA by 18.

Mathew's wife Rike gave birth to a second child in late November, 2015. When the child, a daughter named Amelie, was two weeks old, she was diagnosed with Down Syndrome. Such news is a life-changing shock for any parents, but when the father is an Olympic sailor in year four of a four-year program, with all the commitment, travel, and singular focus that implies, it creates unique problems. Belcher got the news by telephone in a Sydney car park shortly before he was scheduled to preside at a press conference to announce his and Will's official selection to the Australian Olympic sailing team. "The press was gathered, and I was sitting in a car on the phone trying to process the news," Belcher said. "It was about family and sailing, should I leave immediately and fly home, or stick with the team and Will? It was the start of an interesting nine months for us. It was difficult balancing the priorities of family and racing."

Belcher did the press conference, then flew home. Within a month, Mathew and Rike had moved to Hamburg, Germany, where Mathew would be a lot closer to the various racing venues on the schedule. He would be flying back to Hamburg between races, whenever the schedule would allow. In Hamburg, Rike's family, the Ziegelmayers, would also be close by for support. Mathew's parents flew to Hamburg from Gold Coast, Queensland, to help. They stayed for two months.

Victor raved about how Mathew and Rike were dealing with the challenging situation. "They are great parents," he said. "The amount of love they give to Amelie is amazing. It makes a huge difference. Down Syndrome is different from person to person. If you treat a Down child as normal, they can be normal. They will get better and better. It depends how you approach them."

Two weeks later, the team was in Rio for the annual Copa de Brasil which they had won in 2014. It was a runaway. With scores of 1-3-(19 OCS) 1-1-1-5-3-1-4 in ten races, Belcher/Ryan were 36 points ahead going into the medal race. For good measure they won that too, ending up 45 points ahead of GBR, in second, and 46 points ahead of USA in third. Their OCS (premature start—On the Course Side) in race three was an indication they were taking more risk on the starting line.

Starts have been heavily analyzed for decades. Anything that important should receive a lion's share of attention. But Victor said he saw starting analysis evolving to another level. Like other mechanics of sailing — of all sports — starts are being broken down into very small elements based on time: what should be happening at 5 minutes, four minutes, one minute, 30 seconds... "I have three elements," Victor said. "Your vision of the line, your position on the line, and acceleration. You can see the line, you can have good position, but if you accelerate one second late you have no chance. You need all three. If you have only two, bye bye. The starts now are very sharp. Everyone is more aggressive. More risk is invested. There are more fouls at the start now."

With the Olympics then eight months away, Victor was appalled anew by the conditions on Guanabara Bay. "Rio is very dangerous," he said. "It is very important for us to avoid injuries and sickness. The Bay is dirty, and they are not doing enough to improve it. It's a terrible situation. They say everything is okay, people can swim. No one will swim! But sometimes sailors have to jump in the water to launch boats. It is absolute poison. We have some pills from Blackmores that we all take to strengthen our immune system. When you pee from the motorboat you usually wash your hands in the water afterwards. Not in Rio. I have a sanitary hand wash I use."

2016

There was a month before the next coach's regatta, so the team flew to Sydney for a few weeks of training and relaxing over Christmas before returning to Rio the first week in January. It rained every day in Rio, but that did nothing to distract the high-quality fleet of 19 boats that had gathered. The 470 fleet was split in three at this point. One group of 21 boats was in Miami for the annual World Cup regatta that was won by USA, with Greece second, Spain third. Another group united by their commitments with Zaoli Sails was practicing in Buenos Aires, site of the world championships in February. The teams in Rio had decided that spending more time evaluating conditions on 2016 Olympic waters was their priority.

The "coach's regatta" in Rio turned out to be three different regattas. Belcher/Ryan won the first two, and were 1-1-1-1-2 in the third regatta when they had to drop out to pack their container. "I don't like bragging," Victor said at the time, "but they are sailing very well. We are happy. The to-do list, searching for new possibilities with speed, starts, tactics, and strategies, is still very long. They are very focused, very motivated. I cannot say they have to invest more time in sailing. They do too much." Victor paused, contemplating the horns of his dilemma. "Maybe they should put in less time, but then to be a winner you have to put in the time."

Flower power

The 470 World Championship regatta a month later in San Isidro, north of Buenos Aires on the Rio de la Plata, was totally ludicrous. Conditions would have been unfit for a beer can regatta. To hold a world championship amid the thousands of floating islands of plant matter that descended upon the race course was unthinkable, but it happened. Race organizers and 470 fleet representatives – including Mathew Belcher, as a member of the 470 Management Committee – met and discussed the problem. All agreed the conditions would prevent fair racing for such an important event. But they found no solution other than to waive the fleet-imposed rule that prohibits the lifting of rudder blades during a race. With 46 international teams having made the expensive trek to Argentina with boats and gear, there was no way to cancel the event, and no way to move it without causing a monumental logistical problem and financial burden for all concerned. That tired saw about the conditions being the same for everyone was dragged out of the bag, and good luck was offered to the contestants.

They would need it. The culprits were Eichhornia crassipes, better known as water hyacinth, or (in Argentina) "Camelottes," aquatic plants native to South America. The date of the worlds was about a month after massive flooding had occurred in northern Argentina. The rising waters had ripped the roots of the hyacinths off the bottom and set them free. Camelottes are considered an invasive weed, a menace that can interfere with pumping and hydroelectric operations, that can kill fish, reduce water quality, and raise havoc with water traffic. It was the latter that applied to the 470s trying to race in their world championship regatta. The visuals coming from the Rio de la Plata looked like the boats had been photo-shopped onto a huge expanse of cut grass. It was possible to sail a boat through that pea soup, but crews had to be vigilant for the large clumps of the Camelottes that were connected by their tough, interlocking, underwater root structures. Several teams that miscalculated had to be towed out of the mess by their chase boats. Belcher/Ryan were one of many teams that hit one of the islands at speed. Their boat was stopped dead, flinging Will Ryan around the forestay on his trapeze wire. Boats had to either sail around twenty-foot circles of weed that got hung up on the anchor lines of marks, or become entangled. Even the coaches motor boats got stopped by some of the larger islands.

"We picked up and cleared our centerboard and rudder at least 25 times a race," Belcher said. Given the races, that's 250 times for the regatta.

Picking a preferred side of a race course is usually dependent on an analysis of wind patterns and current. At San Isidro, predicting the location of the plants became an additional, critical factor. "One race there was less current and a little more wind on the right side," Victor recalls, "so we go right. We had a good start, a leading position, and boom, the weeds came. On the left there was less wind, but no weeds, so the boats passed through. Mathew and Will were 18th at the top mark." The plants were moving with the current, which was 1.2 knots. Sometimes a big island of them would arrive after the five-minute signal, and the start would be delayed. Coaches would drive their boats through the weeds repeatedly, trying to shred them before the start. "We were complaining Rio was a dirty place to sail," Victor said, "and we cleaned our foils there maybe two or three times a race."

Victor considers the luck factor in a typical regatta to be in the 8% to 12% range. In San Isidro, he put it at nearly 30%. For instance, if a boat was sailing in close quarters between two other boats with little room to maneuver, and an island of Camalottes appeared in its path, there was nothing to do but hit it while the other two boats sailed on.

To make things worse, the wind was light on day one. In the initial race, Belcher/Ryan were UFD, or disqualified for being over the starting line early. Normally a boat over early (OCS) can re-start and continue to race. But when the race committee flies the "U" flag, any boat in the triangle formed by the starting line and the first mark of the course after one minute to the start is automatically disqualified. The U flag is a version of the black flag. The ISAF (now World Sailing) International Race Management Manual calls The Black Flag Rule "a rather drastic penalty," going on to say "this penalty should remain as a `last resort' for a Race Officer to communicate with the fleet, and its use is only recommended after every effort to use individual recalls has been unsuccessful." To have the U flag flying in Race One of a major regatta was unusual.

"In very light wind we got caught up with two back markers in the fleet and were dragged over the line by the current with 35 seconds to go," Belcher says. "We reversed the boat, backed out of the situation and got a fair start, but the damage had been done. We lost our focus to let ourselves be in that position. We should have collided with the other boat and done our penalty turn. But by trying not to hit anyone we went over the line."

The next race they finished 21st. "Because of being disqualified we lost a lot of confidence at the starting line," Belcher says. "We didn't have a good start. We were back in the fleet, but came back to 13th. At the last bottom mark we had a close situation with another boat. It was questionable if we were right or wrong, but as you can imagine when we already had a DSQ, teams were gunning for us. If we got another DSQ we'd be out of the regatta, so we chose to do a 720 penalty turn on the last reach and we dropped to 21st." Belcher/Ryan were 33rd after the first day's racing.

"They were expecting the debrief we do after every day's racing," Victor says. "That day I said guys, no debrief. Instead we discuss conditions. I said don't worry this is in the past, we have to be in the future."

"Normally when Victor is unhappy, he won't say anything," Belcher says. "That's probably a good thing as a coach. You don't want to say too much you can't undo. He thinks about it a lot, takes his time to make sure we have the right message."

"Why did they follow a DSQ with a 21st? Because they were sailing in an area where you cannot risk," Victor says. "Having gotten the DSQ they said no risk, no risk, and that's why they were in 21st. That's the wrong approach. You can risk, but not too much. After this bad start they were racing well. They built the right strategy for the last day, but luck was not on our side."

"It's a hard dance," Belcher says, "because you have to be risky enough to race the race. You can't be too conservative so you don't get a good start, or not be willing to extend to a side of the course to get an advantage, or maybe you don't push to cross another boat when you need to get that cross. There are lots of things that make you feel you mustn't make a mistake, but you have to be risky enough to catch up. We did pretty well, but there were situations here and there when we could have capitalized better. Being put in the same situation again, I'm pretty confident we could have won the event.

"We didn't know how to balance being conservative with keeping our leading status in the fleet, if that makes sense. Usually we would extend in a few situations and gain a couple boats. But we didn't do that because with the horrible start – the DSQ in race one – we were concerned about losing too many places. We went into each race trying to survive, make sure we weren't over early, make sure we didn't foul anyone, then tackle the race from there.

"We were too defensive. Each day we were on the defensive. That was good experience because we're not used to being defensive. We're used to going out and attacking. We talked about that before the regatta, about how a lot of the fleet was under pressure. We said let's be a bit conservative, not get any letters on day one, be patient, don't make silly mistakes. It wasn't about pressure, about being the six-time world champion coming in. It was a bad situation and bad judgement. Our top competition all did well on day one. They were enjoying our predicament, and I think they were interested in how we'd come back."

Did Victor have an answer for how to approach the first day of a world cup regatta? "Don't be OCS, or UFD," he said. "It is a long regatta. Don't try to win it on the first day."

Victor quickly found the positive slant to his team's unfortunate performance on day one by focusing on the opportunity it provided to engineer a sensational comeback. He reminded them of Nathan Wilmot's and Malcolm Page's comeback at Lake Garda when they were 64th after the first day, and went on to win the regatta. "Mathew knows about this of course," Victor said. "You can tell the stories of great comebacks like those Ben Ainslie accomplished in the Finn class – Ben was the master of the comeback, his latest was in the America's Cup – but you need your own experience to build your confidence that you can do it. If you find yourself in a bad situation, you will know you can come back. You need to have confidence in your boat, your sails, your team – and yourself…and if you have this experience it will double your chances of being able to come back."

Mathew Belcher already had a sensational comeback in his portfolio that would serve him well as a reminder of what he was capable of. That would be his comeback in the 2012 Olympic Games in London, when Belcher/Page won the gold medal after their calamitous first day. But that was four years ago, and Will Ryan had not shared that experience, so it was time to put another strong comeback in the bag.

Come back they did. Not all the way this time, but their scores for the next nine races were impressive: 1-6-3-7-4-6-8-2-8 (4th, medal race). The Croation team of Fantela/Marenic, was coming on strong, steadily replacing Great Britain as Belcher/Ryan's strongest competition, sailing very well, with good boat speed, and managing to stay out of trouble with the Camelottes. Croatia took the win by six points over New Zealand. Belcher/Ryan sailed back onto the podium by the skin of their teeth. They tied for third with France, winning in a three-place countback. Each team had a 1st, each had a 2nd, but Australia had a 3rd and France did not.

Belcher's consecutive 470 world championship winning streak was ended at six, a class record.

Palma

The European Championships were held in Palma, Majorca, in April, 2016. It made sense to arrive a couple weeks early, race in the Trofeo Princesa Sofia Regatta, then practice for the Europeans in an attractive environment that has reliably good wind. The Trofeo Princesa Sofia Regatta was initiated in 1968 for the Dragon class. It is named for Her Majesty, Queen Sofia of Spain, who was a competitive sailor, a reserve on the 1960 Spanish Olympic sailing team. Her husband, Prince Juan Carlos – who went on to be King and is now King Father of Spain – won the regatta three times in the 1970s when it was still being contested in Dragons.

Belcher/Ryan came off the starting line in Race 1 like they were shot out of a cannon. In the first six races, they had five firsts and a third. They won Princesa Sofia Regatta by 28 points over USA in second; by 36 points over Greece in third; and by 53 points over Great Britain in fourth.

Belcher said their strong performance simply had to do with being able to race again. "We were highly motivated after the worlds," he said. "Those conditions limited our ability to race. We weren't concentrating on sailing in Buenos Aires. We were focused on avoiding the weeds. They had a massive impact. We're tolerant, experienced, we deal with lots of adversity, but it comes to a point when you say you can't race, you have to focus on just trying to get around the track without losing too much speed, it's too much. We spent half our time cleaning the appendages – 25 times a race ! It was absurd. Yes it was the same for everyone, but the conditions weren't appropriate. Palma gave us the opportunity to get things back on track as a team."

Two weeks later Belcher/Ryan won the European Championships. It wasn't as easy, but then a lot was going on. First, Mathew flew home to Germany be with his wife and children between the two regattas.

Mathew returned the day before the regatta and participated in an eight-hour meeting of the 470 Class Management Committee, of which he is a member. His father-in-law arrived in Palma that day, so Mathew had a long dinner with him, with more talk about sailing. "I was extremely tired on day one of the Europeans," Belcher said. "When you get caught up in that management environment, it's hard to separate from it and get into racing. It took a couple days. It was a good reminder about minimizing distractions before an important regatta, but sometimes it can't be helped."

Belcher/Ryan began the Europeans with an 8-6-22, setting them up for still another comeback. They rallied with firsts in races four and five, had a bad race six (14th), before notching a third and a second in races eight and nine. It was race nine that Victor liked.

"They had a good start, went left where they were leading. Suddenly there was a big shift to the right. They were 16th at the top mark. The USA team started to fight with them. For many months the USA team was focused on beating Mathew and Will, trying to create uncomfortable conditions for them, create a bad atmosphere, destroy their confidence. In this race they were below Mathew, so they began to drive him up, up. Suddenly Mathew bore away and let them go, went low while they were sailing as high as possible. The wind went right again, and at the second mark, Mathew was four boats in front of the USA team. Mathew sailed a low loop to the bottom mark where he rounded in fifth place.

"Everyone expected the right shift again. But Mathew went left. He was third at the top mark. On the last run he was fighting with Argentina.

He had one last chance to get inside them at the bottom mark, and he did! He went from 16th to second. The USA ended up ninth in that race. I told Mathew and Will they sailed a phenomenal race. I was very proud to be their coach." They finished off with 7-2 and a third in the medal race, winning the Euros by 16 points over France, and 20 points ahead of the USA, in third.

Why did Belcher/Ryan go left on the final weather leg? Instinct, Belcher says, which is probably as close as one can ever come to the answer of when to take a risk. Developing finely-tuned instincts in his sailors is an ultimate objective of Victor's coaching philosophy. Instinct is a response to specific environmental stimuli, an impulse, an inborn pattern of behavior that can be polished like any other natural talent. Polishing one's instincts requires trust. For an athlete accomplished at his game, trust comes from his or her sum total of knowledge and experience, and implies a willingness – the confidence – to react to a stimulus rather than think it through. On the race course, sailors don't usually have much time to think it through. An instant reaction is often essential because timing is everything. On a race on New York's Long Island Sound many years ago, the late American sailor/designer Ray Hunt suggested to his skipper they should tack. Because Hunt was so esteemed, the skipper tacked immediately. Thirty minutes later, Hunt thought it was time to tack back. They did, and found themselves a mile ahead of the fleet. That night, in the red glow of the cockpit, a man on watch with Hunt asked him quietly what he had seen that caused him to suggest those very productive tacks. Here was Hunt's answer: "It seemed like a good idea."

So it was with Belcher/Ryan when they went left. "Going downwind we must have seen something," Belcher said. "We're conservative sailors, systematic and logical. We know if the right's been paying off all day, there has to be something out there on the left. We're open, we never stop going through the process of evaluating possibilities."

Fourth

Recall that Victor categorizes his team's losses as either tests, warnings, or punishments. When Belcher/Ryan failed to make the podium in the 2016, 470 World Cup Regatta at Weymouth – the first time in five and a half years Mat Belcher had not made the podium in a world cup regatta – Victor wasn't quite sure where to put that loss. "It was definitely not a test," he said. "A warning? Well, in some sense it was a test. A test of our relationships. When everything is okay, when you are winners, everything is good. When times are tough, it is not very easy."

They started slowly, with a 7 and a 14 in the first two races, then won the third race. The fourth race was more light wind in the 3-5 knot range. Once again, they got black flagged at the start. "It was a bit of a strange situation," Victor says. "Mathew and Will were close to the line. They were protected by France between them and the race committee. The black flag was flying, meaning if you were OCS you would be disqualified. There was a general recall, and the race committee called six boats over. Mathew was not on the list posted on the board, and I said good, we prepare for the next start. More than two minutes later, they added his number to the list. Usually with the black flag up the race committee doesn't have a general recall. They just identify the boats that were over and let the rest go. It was a little bit strange. We decided not to talk to the race committee. Just accept it as a test. But it was very odd.

"That was the only problem, their one mistake. Without that, they would have made the podium."

The Croatians won the regatta, despite their two, double digit finishes.

Spain tied the Croations with 32 points, with a black flag in one race ruining what would have been a certain victory for them.

With the Olympics a scant two months away, it was time for some final adjustments that would propel Mathew and Will toward a gold medal. Once again, the ethereal business of risk came to the forefront. Observers in Weymouth saw the Croatians taking a lot of risk at the start, fighting for the favored end along with the Americans and the young, aggressive French team. "Mathew prefers the middle of the line," Victor said. "But the middle is only good if you have speed. If there is not enough speed, you need to take more risk, and that is what lighter wind requires. Lighter wind tends to equalize boat speed. And this is modern sport. In modern sport, more risk is required, especially in sailing.

"It's good to get these lessons now," Victor said, "because it brings the team back to reality, makes them understand they have to work hard, because it is sport and anything can happen."

Malcolm Page, who won gold with Belcher in London, confirms that his former skipper is very much a conservative sailor. "Taking risks isn't natural for me either," Page says. "I could be more myself with Nathan Wilmot because he was a more natural risk-taker. My conservativism balanced our team. With Mat I had to teach myself to be more risky to achieve that balance. I would often be that little word in his ear

Page says the biggest thing he learned working with Victor each cycle was the psychological approach to the sport he was in. "Call it 'process,' " Page says. "That's where the gains come from."

Page tracks his own stellar Olympic career as an example. "It's about refinement, evolution, and Victor instills it very well because he coaches individuals. He could be a great success at any sport because of that. My first campaign was for the Sydney Olympics in 2000. The rallying cry was, 'win gold.' But frankly, we didn't know how. For Athens, 2004, at least we got selected. We thought we had the skill and the ability, but we weren't sure how to do it. On my third try, in China 2008, we changed the talk to 'let's go for a medal.' We had the skill and the ability, but we said let's just play the cards we are handed and if all goes right we'll succeed. And we got gold. In London it was definitely about winning gold, which we did, but we knew sport was sport. Someone might show up with a revolutionary development. And in addition to sickness and injuries, there's weird stuff thrown in by Mother Nature.

"Victor is the great master of ceremonies of all that. I was with him 12 years, and I'm still with him. Nathan too, and Mathew has been with him 16 years. We talk all the time. It's a family with all of us, a professional family.

"The process is about gaining understanding, getting wiser, being able to distinguish noise from reality. And receiving those messages from both Victor and life is key. A message can be a punch in the gut, and depending on what it is, and your mood at the time, it can effect your future. It's true that you learn more from failure. Success comes with the temptation to rely more on yourself because the ego gets overstimulated. As I got wiser, I got better at the whole game.

"You have to look backwards, never forwards, because you are always trying to develop yourself, sustain the process of improvement, develop that brain matter. Even if you have been winning easily, there are still many things you could have done better. My regatta reports were getting longer and more in depth the closer we got to London. Victor always used those reports as incentive, telling us we didn't have to write them if we won. But I kept writing them even when we won, and they got longer and more in depth because I was better able to understand our shortcomings."

Was Belcher/Ryan's decent from the podium in Weymouth a test, a warning, or a punishment? Certainly the delayed disqualification under the black flag had an element of punishment to it. The end of such a long streak of podium finishes in close proximity to the Olympic Games could be considered a warning. For sure, it was a test.

CHAPTER 16

XXXI Olympic Games in Rio

Half way through the Olympic regatta, Belcher/Ryan were right where they wanted to be, in second place, just two points behind the Croation team of Sime Fantela and Igor Marenic. Their 8th in race one, which Fantela/Marenic won, was followed by finishes of 1-3-3-2. Mathew and Will were feeling good about their performance. So was Victor. The team was sailing well. They had good speed, and were making good decisions on the race course. It looked like business as usual.

Even that eighth place in race one was acceptable, because Mother Nature had gone slightly berserk. They could have finished a lot further back. The wind varied in speed from eight to 16 knots that first day, not so unusual, but the nature of the shifts was far beyond anything even local sailors had ever experienced in Rio. By the third mark, the wind had shifted left 40 degrees. By mark four it had shifted another 73 degrees left. By mark five it had shifted 50 degrees back to the right. By mark six it had shifted another 60 degrees right. By mark seven it had shifted 16 degrees left. Just as remarkable, Fantela/Marenic were on the correct side of every shift. Belcher/Ryan were 16th at one point, then managed to pass eight boats.

Race two was just as crazy. The wind had shifted 62 degrees left by the fourth mark; another 70 degrees left at five; 44 degrees right at six; and 20 degrees left at seven. Belcher/Ryan were 10th at mark three, took full advantage of the left shift at the fourth mark, and won that race.

The first indication that something was amiss was when Victor was protested by the race committee after the second day of racing. After the start of race four, he was accused of being inside the exclusion zone with his motor boat. One of the judges in a small rubber boat told the race committee he had seen Victor between the starting line and the bottom gate of the course about four minutes after the start. This is an area restricted to competitors and course officials. Victor couldn't believe it. He said he was nowhere near that area.

The 470s were sailing the offshore course on that day, August 11th. It was blowing in the mid-20s, with waves of 10-to-12-feet. "At the start," Victor said, "Mathew and Will went left. I could not go left because of where I was. To go right was more dangerous because of the wave angles, so I took time to put on my life jacket." Victor also notes that the judge who reported seeing him was a good 300-meters from the starting line. With an eight second period between waves, visibility was not reliable. Plus, Victor had a witness, a member of the 470 race committee whose vantage point was the deck of the committee boat, 12 feet above the water. This witness told the jury that he had not seen Victor in the exclusion zone. "The jury took his testimony," Victor recalls with a smile, "but they said just because he did not see me didn't mean I was not there."

The protest hearing was held the morning of the second race day. The jury decided Victor would be disqualified for day two. Mathew and Will were stunned. "Looking back," Belcher said, "it was quite irresponsible. They could not prove Victor was in the exclusion zone. It was the jury wanting to make a stand, I guess, show their impact. What they don't realize is how much that effects the athletes psychologically."

Belcher/Ryan were without their coach for three hours that morning, the key time of preparation for the day's racing, while he was in and out of protest hearings. "He would talk with us between hearings," Belcher says, "and did a great job keeping us settled. Fifteen minutes before heading out on the water we didn't know who our coach would be. Victor ran from the protest hearing to the motor boat and off we went."

Victor's DSQ had been suspended because the case remained open. Victor brought in three more witnesses. He said the jury asked him why he had not brought them in before. Victor said he thought a member of the race committee would be a sufficient witness.

The morning of the third race day (race five), Victor's protest hearing continued. The jury reinstated the DSQ for that day at around 11 am. "At least we knew we would have another coach for that day," Belcher said. The team met with their substitute coach, going over the procedure they were used to. Victor joined the discussion, passing the new coach the keys to the motor boat.

Finally, Victor asked to speak with the jury – many of whom knew him – unofficially. "I told them, all of you are selected by life to be here at the Olympic Games. All of us trust you because you are judges, good judges, and we trust your judgement. But you have to trust us as well. We are also selected by life to be here. I said can you imagine I would come into this room and lie to your face? Being in front of the committee boat is a rude and arrogant infringement. It is not my style. Even to be in this room is a big penalty for me."

The jury finally decided to penalize Victor by withdrawing his Olympic credentials for one day – the lay day, when there would be no racing. "I told them I accept your penalty," Victor said, "and I said thank you very much for your judgement, most of all your wisdom. Because they demonstrated to me they understood the situation. They could not ignore the statement of a judge. They could not admit he was mistaken. But for me it will be a bitter memory forever."

Victor ran to his motor boat again, just in time. Belcher/Ryan got a second in race five.

Peter Conde, High Performance Director of Yachting Australia, was in Rio in his official capacity. Conde says the real issue about Victor's ordeal was that the jury had standard, written operating policies that stipulate giving a warning for the first violation of the exclusion zone, and they didn't follow their own policies. "They apparently wanted to take draconian measures right off the bat," Conde says.

The Russian coach had been accused of violating the exclusion zone the same day Victor had been called out. The Russian admitted he was both in the zone, and too close to the 470s racing. He took his penalty on a day when, as it happened, only one race could be held. "What was never in contention," Conde says, "is that Victor was nowhere near any race boats. He was never accused of that. The jury figured it didn't stack up, that a guy who admitted he was on the course and too close to the boats would get a one race penalty, and the next day Victor would have been penalized for three races. That's why they penalized him on the lay day. The alternative would have been patently unfair."

On the lay day, Victor's accreditation was taken from him and he left the site. The next morning, he picked up his credentials and went back to work.

On August 14th, race six was held in marginal conditions, three to five knots in large waves with the more usual 10- to 25-degree shifts. There was a bit more wind for race seven, but not enough for the use of trapezes. Will Ryan was sitting inside the boat all day. Belcher/Ryan did not fare well, finishing 8th and 10th while the Croatians stayed hot with a third and a fourth. "It was a black day for all our team, in all classes," Victor said. "All dropped down that day. I have no idea why."

August 15th there was no wind. Storms were forecast, but the race committee was eager to stay on schedule. In the late afternoon, they took the 470s offshore in hopes of getting a race in. Instead, the fleet was hit hard by a squall after a sudden, 180-degree wind shift. The initial gusts were in the mid-20s, and building quickly. As one, the fleet dropped its sails…all but AUS 11, the Belcher/Ryan boat. Their mainsail would not come down. It turned out the halyard was jammed inside the mast. They finally got the sail down, but not before it had taken a violent flogging in gusts as high as 45 knots. The sail suffered a 40-millimeter horizontal rip at the leach between the top two battens. There was also a small vertical rip. The seams had been stretched.

On the water, it was a dangerous situation. Many boats were upside-down. Teams without coach boats struggled to get reorganized. Some teams took two hours to make the usual 30-minute return to the dock. Mathew Belcher was angry the fleet had been sent out into those conditions, calling the organizing committee "irresponsible."

Ashore, the measurement tent was filled with sailors from the 470 class (both men's and women's fleets), and from the 49er class, that had also been racing on the outside course. Rules for the 470 class specify that sails (including spinnaker) selected for the first race must be used throughout the regatta. But the measurement committee had decided that every boat in both fleets would be allowed to use a new jib. "It's the first time I ever saw that," Belcher said. "That's how much damage there was. It was an unprecedented decision. Three of the top teams, including the USA, also changed their masts, saying they had damage. We've always focused on ourselves, and if those teams said their mast had been damaged and they needed to change it, we trust the equipment committee is doing the right thing. No one made an issue out of people changing gear."

Belcher/Ryan submitted their damaged mainsail to the measurement committee, requesting permission to use a spare mainsail. "For me, their mainsail was obviously not alive," Victor said. "When it is ripped, it is finished. Some looked at it and suggested Mathew rip it more so the official measurers would have to throw it out and allow him to use a new sail. Mathew said no thank you, sailing is a gentleman's sport, I cannot do that. He could not do that because it would hurt his internal honesty, his karma. He showed the sail as it was to the measurers." Among those who evaluated it was World Sailing technical expert, Jason Smithwick. He, and the others agreed it was damaged sufficiently to allow Belcher to use a new mainsail. Belcher had the new sail measured in and went to his hotel.

The leach, or trailing edge, is the most important part of any sail. Ideally the trailing edge has just the hint of a hook at the edge. Designers spend a lot of time adjusting the shape of the leach in minute increments to make sure the hook is not too pronounced, disturbing the air leaving the foil shape of the sail; or not pronounced enough, allowing the air to fall off the edge and lose its power upon exiting. A properly designed leach promotes maximum flow and power. "The amount of hook," Victor says, "is very critical for the mast settings, sailing technique…everything."

At 9pm, just before he went to bed, Belcher says he received an email from Dimitris Dimou, chief measurer for the Olympics and head of the 470 Measurement Committee, asking Belcher to come by in the morning because there was a lot of discussion about their decision to allow AUS 11 to use another mainsail. Belcher knows Dimou because Belcher is the sailor-representative on the Measurement Committee. "There were a couple other emails in the night I didn't see," Belcher says. "I got a call at 7.30am saying I had to come by right away — 'we've got some problems.'"

Unable to find a taxi, unwilling to wait for the bus because of the urgency of the call he'd received, Belcher ran the two miles from his hotel to the measurement tent. "I'd not had breakfast, and I didn't have my sailing gear," he says. By the time he got there, the Measurement Committee had reversed its decision to allow AUS 11 to use its spare mainsail. Belcher was told the decision had been changed because several countries had protested his use of a new sail. The measurers had now decided Mathew could use the new sail the following day, but the ripped sail would have to be repaired and be used for the medal race. "I had no opportunity to find out what was happening, or say anything," Belcher says.

The USA team, led by coach Morgan Reeser, had initiated the protest. Their sparring partners (Austria, Turkey) joined them, as did Great Britain and Croatia.

PROTEST NO. 90

Event: 470 - Men

Race: 8

Protestor: USA

Protestee: Request for Redress (EIC). Races 8, 9, 10.

Protest details: RRS 61.1(a); ER 3.2.b Heard togther with Case 91 and Case 94. USA represented by Morgan Reeser CRO (party requesting redress Case 91), represented by: Edo Fantela TUR (party requesting redress Case 94), represented by: Ricardo de Felice EIC represented by: Jason Smithwick

Description:

Facts found:

AUS damaged its sail when coming back from the race area on 15.08.2016. The damage consisted of a rip on the leech of a right angle 40 mm horizontal and 20 mm vertical in the middle of the panel in the area of the AUS Rio 2016 branding. On 15.08.2016, around 19.00 EIC inspected and deemed the AUS main sail not repairable and approved its substitution . After further inspections of several other teams' main sails the EIC decided to reinspect the main sail of AUS. AUS was requested to return its sail to be reviewed again in the morning of 16.08.2016. At 8:45 on 16.08.2016 the 470 Equipment inspector reviewed again the mainsail. At 09:30 EIC deemed that it was possible to repair the mainsail. The damage ocurred in a loaded part of the sail and needed to be done by professional sail maker. In accordance wirh EI policies and Procedures 8.2 the condition is that the repaired sail should be used as soon as possible.

Conclusion:

As a final authority for determining if equipment complies with the Eevnt Equipment Regulations and for interpreting class rules, EIC acted within their jurisdiction and is entitled to review its own decision. Therefore there is no omission or error by the EIC and no grounds for redress.

Rule(s) applicable:

RRS 62.1. (a); ER 1.2; ER 3.2.(b)

Decision:

Redress not given.

Short decision:

Redress not given.

Jury:

Andres PEREZ, Iskra YOVKOVA, Marianne MIDDELTHON, David DE VRIES, Nelson HORN ILHA

Under "Rule(s) applicable," (above), RRS (Racing Rules of Sailing) 62.1, reads as follows:

62.1 A request for redress or a protest committee's decision to consider redress shall be based on a claim or possibility that a boat's score in a race or series has been or may be, through no fault of her own, made significantly worse by (a) an improper action or omission of the race committee, protest committee, organizing authority, equipment inspection committee or measurement committee for the event, but not by a protest committee decision when the boat was a party to the hearing; (b) injury or physical damage because of the action of a boat that was breaking a rule of Part 2 or of a vessel not racing that was required to keep clear; (c) giving help (except to herself or her crew) in compliance with rule 1.1; or Part 5 PROTESTS, REDRESS, HEARINGS, MISCONDUCT AND APPEALS 33 (d) an action of a boat, or a member of her crew, that resulted in a penalty under rule 2 or a penalty or warning under rule 69.2(c).

Under "Rule(s) applicable," (above) ER 1.2 and 3.2(b) reads as follows:

RIO 2016 OLYMPIC SAILING COMPETITION EQUIPMENT REGULATIONS

1.2 The Equipment Inspection Committee (EIC) shall be the final authority fordetermining if equipment complies with the Event Equipment Rules and for interpreting the Class Rules during the Regatta.

3.2(b) (b) The equipment being replaced has either been lost or severely damaged and cannot be repaired in the time available before the next race. Equipment shall not be replaced if it has been mistreated, damaged or lost in a deliberate manner

"Of course the sail was repairable," Victor says. "But it would give us a huge disadvantage compared to a sail that was not repaired. I would say a 30% disadvantage. If we used a spare mainsail, we would have a 20-30% disadvantage because it is brand new. After we break it in, maybe it would give us a 7% advantage. But if we use a repaired sail we would have a huge disadvantage. They allowed every boat to replace its jib. It would have been fine with me if they allowed every boat to also replace its mainsail."

"The Americans were in fourth place at the time," Mathew Belcher says. "They thought the only way they could medal was to get boats disqualified, or bring about a change in other teams' rhythm. There was pressure on the Measurement Committee. They didn't want to accept responsibility for their decision to allow us to change sails. They didn't want the hassle. It was one boat. They didn't want pressure from everyone else. I think they were somewhat concerned it would look like they were giving us an advantage. I'm on the 470 Management Committee. I've been the leader of this fleet for more than five years. No one wants to show favoritism. So they made a decision they figured was going to produce the least impact.

"But there's a reason we chose the sail we were using. We thought it was the best sail we had. If the spare sail was so good, it would have been on the boat. Three of the top teams, including the Americans, said their masts were damaged and got permission to use a new one. No one made an issue out of that. If you apply the same mentality to the new mast, it should be better. But if I have to change mid-regatta to a new mast or sail, there's no advantage because it's not the first choice. And the new piece of equipment disrupts the tuning, the feeling of the boat. It's a new variable you wouldn't want in any event, especially at the Olympics. But the repaired sail was surely going to be a lot slower than the spare."

The morning the day of races 8-9-10, Mathew was told the Americans had filed another protest against them under Rule 2, Fair Sailing:

A boat and her owner shall compete in compliance with recognized principles of sportsmanship and fair play. A boat may be penalized under this rule only if it is clearly established that these principles have been violated. A disqualification under this rule shall not be excluded from the boat's series score.

PROTEST NO. 92

Event: 470 - Men

Race: 10

Protestor: USA

Protestee: AUS

Protest details: Race 8,9,10

Description:

Facts found:

Protest withdrawn.

Conclusion:

Rule(s) applicable:

Decision:

Withdrawal approved.

Short decision:

Withdrawal approved.

Jury:

Jan STAGE, Nelson HORN ILHA, Francisco JAUREGUI, Ana SANCHEZ DEL CAMPO, Peter SHRUBB

"Protesting under Rule 2 is what you do if you think drugs are involved, or cheating," Victor said, obviously incensed. "If they kept this protest we would have to send this case to an international court of arbitration because it is huge. We are gentlemen. Our reputations are above this sort of thing. This is more important than gold medals. Mathew is known in the fleet for his honesty."

Peter Conde says the USA coach, Morgan Reeser, was effectively accusing them of ripping the sail beyond the damage the flogging had actually caused in order to get it replaced. "He was accusing them of cheating," Conde said, "a very serious accusation. He did that on the basis that he had seen the original rip and said it was only 50mm long. The reality was that when first inspected by the measurement committee, the rip was 40mm long. We pointed that out to the USA team, told them the accusation was false, and based on that would they withdraw the protest."

Belcher said the jury had scheduled the protest hearing fifteen minutes before he was leaving the dock to go racing. He went to the jury room where the protest would be heard. The Americans did not show up. Belcher said he was steaming. "I told them if you schedule a hearing so close to racing, I am not going to be here. You can disqualify me, do whatever you want, but I am prepping for racing."

Belcher then saw a message on WhatsApp from the Americans to the entire 470 fleet. The message read as follows:

Dear 470M coaches, AUS men have been allowed to use a new mainsail today. I am and I suggest that you all put in a request for redress immediately under 62.1 (a) as all 470M teams will be prejudiced by an error of the EIC today. The facts are: The mainsail was inspected last night and a replacement was allowed. Complaints were made about that decision. The mainsail was reinspect ex about 9am this morning and it was decided that there was not enough R time now to repair the sail. Had the repair begin last night it would not have been a problem to complete.

"The implication," Belcher says, "is they were urging the fleet to turn on us."

Belcher said he lost it at that point. "I went to the car park and sat in the car with Rike and cried for twenty minutes," he said. "I never told Victor, or Will, but it was just too much to handle. I really struggled to be able to cope with it. I talked with Rike, got the emotions out, and went sailing."

"They went racing with the new main that had not been broken in, not stretched at all," Victor says. "The leach was completely hooked. They had no speed. The first race (race eight) they got a 7th. With the sail properly broken in, they won race nine." Belcher said he did not sense a change in the fleet's perception of him and Will. They didn't feel isolated, segregated, or harassed.

But Victor said that during race eight, Morgan Reeser drove his coach boat next to Victor's boat and shouted at him, accusing him of cheating.

"Psychologically," Belcher says, "some athletes need to hate their competitor. It takes a special person to separate the aggression, dedication, and commitment required to achieve a good result, from life off the water.

Some people can't separate it. It takes too much self-control. They just need to hate the person. When the pressure came on, it seems the Americans needed to take that approach."

After Belcher/Ryan finished race nine, a motor boat approached them. It was the Measurement Committee, bringing them the repaired mainsail and telling them they must use it for race ten. "I was surprised,", Belcher said. "We could have anticipated it, the way we had been treated, and we were prepared it could happen, but it was still a shock they would come out on the water with a mainsail they had repaired with no input from us, a mainsail that had been damaged to the point they said we could replace it, and demand we put it up just before we were about to start the last race of the Olympics, the third race of the day with time restraints over being able to get the race in before dark…"

When asked how he would describe the repaired sail, Will Ryan said, "It was white." He laughed. "I don't know," he says. "It was repaired by someone we don't know. We gave it to the committee, and two hours later they brought it out to us, so it was obviously a rushed job."

Outwardly, calm prevailed. "We were all calm," Victor said. "Mathew and Will are strong people, amazing athletes. They understand our job is to race. There is no room for emotions in big business. If we cannot change the situation, we have to accept the situation. We changed sails on the water. We raised the sail up and performed the best we could." But Victor took one look at the repaired sail as his team tested it for a couple minutes before the horn sounded the countdown for race ten, and shook his head. "It was two different sails," he says. "At the top, where it was repaired, the leach was open. At the bottom, the leach was normal. If they tightened the leach line to make the top look right, the bottom was hooked. They had no speed and finished seventh in race 10.

"Seventh in a fleet of 27 boats is not so bad, but it is definitely below our skill level and team standards. And 7th is not good enough to win the Olympic Games."

"The sail wasn't responding the way it should," Ryan says. "When a boat doesn't have that balance we are used to, it makes you feel uncomfortable, that you have to take bigger risks to do well."

Seventh was the same result they had gotten with the new sail in race eight. "It was different," Belcher says, "because we were falling back. We could not hold positions. It became apparent we were slower, and that impacted our strategy for the medal race."

Most notable for races 8-9-10 was the fact that the Greek team logged three second-place finishes, catapulting them into second place overall entering the medal race. "The USA coaches pushed the case for their protest," Victor says, "used it like a lever to create anxiety, used all their energy for this case. Those involved in this protest hurt their karma. The Greek coach sent me a message saying that he was not in a position to be involved in the protest because his job was to help his team race. The Greek's comeback was an amazing moment of the regatta. The USA team was penalized by the universe and eliminated from medal contention." USA finished 1-11-14 in races 8-9-10.

"It's too bad," Victor said. "The USA team of McNay and Hughes are amazing sailors. I respect them a lot. They were one of the best prepared teams. They should have a medal around their necks. But their coaches were too involved with the politics. They created their own karma, and the karma of the team."

Commenting on the rash of protests (109) that were filed during the Rio Games, Peter Conde suggests the jury brought that on themselves. "Regarding on the water protesting," Conde says, "the jury had made it clear that if you lied to them you would be brought to account for that. There were some early protests resulting in disqualifications that were reopened and dismissed when video of the situation became available, making it clear the protesting boat had lied. But the jury did nothing about it. In an Olympic Games when people tend to protest for incidents they wouldn't blink at in most regattas, because there is so much at stake, my view is by not coming down hard on that — by not enforcing their own policy — the jury opened the flood gates."

Medal Race

The medal race was held in 14 to 20 knots of relatively steady wind, ideal conditions for Belcher/Ryan. Mathematically, Belcher/Ryan could still have won a gold medal, but it was highly unlikely. They would have had to finish first in the medal race while the Croatians would have had to finish seventh or worse. It was possible — the Croations' worst race all week was an 8th (their throw out) — but a long shot even if Belcher/Ryan had been allowed to use a spare mainsail. Victor said before the race his team could not be talked out of going for the win. "I said to them, let's focus on the Greeks. Silver is much better than bronze, and 10 million times better than fourth. The odds aren't good. And with the destroyed main they would have no speed at all. I did not say their mainsail was crap before race 10 because they needed confidence. But the mainsail was dead."

After sailing for 30 minutes before the start of the medal race, they had to admit Victor was right. "Tuning up in our strongest conditions," Belcher says, "we simply couldn't get the boat moving. We have tunings we know are comfortable. But we struggled with the main. We had no leach control. It was breaking (losing its shape) very early. We tried to modify the tuning, but it didn't work. Will and I talked about it and said it's not gonna happen. We decided to control the Greeks as much as we could, but that was going to be close."

Watching the medal race streaming on NBC TV, it was evident AUS 11 was having a difficult time. The Australians ignored the rest of the fleet. It was simple: between them and the Greeks, whichever boat finished ahead of the other would win the silver medal. The rest of the fleet didn't matter. For them it was a two-boat race. Belcher/Ryan got the better start, and employed the right strategy, establishing a proper cover on the Greek boat — a boat length or two ahead and to windward as they sailed upwind. But the Greeks seemed to be slipping away, gaining slightly on every tack. Gary Jobson, a world class sailor who was calling the race on NBC, and who was unaware of the Australian's mainsail situation, commented several times that the Australians looked slow. "It was desperate sailing to protect our position," Belcher said.

Approaching the top mark for the final time in this short race, the unthinkable happened. During their last tack for the mark, Will Ryan fell off the rail into the water. He reacted with all his athletic ability, and somehow clambered back into the boat with an assist from his helmsman. In a flash, he was back on the rail, but in that same flash, the Greeks passed the Australians, gaining the silver medal position with only one downwind leg to go.

There is a small, multi-part tackle on a trapeze wire that allows a crew to adjust his body angle to the boat. The crew wants to be parallel to the water when suspended on the trapeze. When the boat is heeling in heavy wind, the crew eases the adjustment. In medium wind, with less heel, he tightens it. In the interest of speed, the small (5/16) line of the tackle runs past a v-shaped jam cleat that tends to engage easily when the line is moving past it. On the previous tack, Ryan says he made an adjustment to the trapeze. He thinks maybe his body weight didn't properly jam it. In any case, on the next tack the line ran out until it hit the knotted end, dumping Ryan into the water.

"When I let go of the top part of the handle on the trapeze," Ryan said, "holding just the bottom – I do that all the time, it's a faster way to tack – I sensed the line wasn't jammed, I could feel it running, but there was nothing I could do. I didn't have the physical strength to overcome my inertia. I knew I had to release the jib sheet and do my best to hold onto the boat. I remember having hold of the metal ring of the trapeze with three fingers, so I managed to hold on and stay in touch with the boat.

"Mat did a great job helping me back in. And the focus stayed on the Greeks as it had all race. My natural instincts are super competitive, so there was no hesitation, no give-up because we made a mistake. Credit Victor the way he's taught us to handle all situations."

Ryan says the only other time he can remember a similar situation was the day before the 470 world championships in 2014. He and Belcher were out practicing when it happened. "That's what allowed me to think about releasing the jib sheet," Ryan says. "Victor wasn't with us that day. We were practicing on our own. So I don't think Victor knew we had practiced that maneuver, me falling into the water."

Victor was full of admiration for his team. "Many people would have collapsed in those circumstances, just given up. Not Mathew and Will. They didn't take one second to worry about Will's slip. They concentrated on performance. They are strong athletes. I am so proud to work with them."

After rounding the mark, Belcher/Ryan had a quick spinnaker set and were at full speed about a boat length behind the Greeks. Downwind, boat speed relies a lot less on having a properly shaped leach on the mainsail, and they were flying in the freshening breeze. But so were the Greeks. Racing downwind, the trailing boat gets the puffs first, but the first third of the leg to the final turning mark the wind was steady. Then a strong little puff came along. AUS 11 was perfectly positioned to take full advantage of it. Belcher/Ryan trimmed precisely, angled the boat just right, had their weight well-positioned, and planed past the Greeks. Victor called it a "reward" puff. "It was for their passion, dedication, hard work," he said, "the way they quickly resumed fighting after Will slipped, and their resilience during the many protest situations. The whole regatta was a big test for all of us. Will's slip was the final test for them. Did they deserve a silver medal, or not? They proved to the world yes, they deserved it."

Oddly enough, while passing the final mark and heading up slightly onto a power reach for the finish line, the Greek crew slipped off the rail, and that sealed it. Out of ten boats, AUS 11 finished 9th to win silver. The Greeks finished 10th, winning bronze.

The USA decided to drop the protest against Australia under the fair sailing rule. But even that was tinged with drama. USA coach Morgan Reeser, who had filed the protest, had failed to sign the official document withdrawing the protest before he left for the Olympic Village. "I grabbed the USA team leader and some of the athletes who were around," Peter Conde says. "They said they didn't know what was going on, but they did tell the jury they wanted to drop the protest. The jury told them they couldn't because it was filed by their coach. That went on for hours. It was a ridiculous situation. The document was finally signed, but it was certainly poor form to make such a serious allegation with zero evidence, and then not manage the situation appropriately."

CHAPTER 17

Retrospective

Adversity aside, Victor's assessment of the Olympic regatta predictably had to do with the elusive element of risk management. "It was all about risk," he said. "The Croatians took a lot of risk at the beginning. They did not hesitate to take risk at the start, and they played the sides of the course a bit more. They had speed too, and were generally racing very well. They deserved the gold. Some other teams were trying to risk more and they were out of medal contention. Others like New Zealand and Spain were trying more risk and were out of the top ten."

Did Belcher/Ryan take enough risk?

"Probably a little bit not enough," Victor said. "Risk is everywhere," he said, warming to the subject, "at the bank, in the stock market, in your life every day, driving or walking, cooking or riding your bicycle. Everywhere is risk. You take too much risk, *boom!*, you are a loser. You don't take enough risk, *boom!*, you are a loser. An interesting statistic from the Olympic 470 regatta is that Belcher/Ryan rounded the first mark of the course in 10th position or worse in seven out of the 10 races. Will Ryan says they struggled with starts and initial windward legs. "It's hard to work back through a smaller fleet," Ryan says. "There are fewer passing opportunities."

"Risk could also be my responsibility," Victor says, "because they trust me. "I could say, after the start you should go right. Many teams work like this. But that is not our style. Mathew and Will were not conquered by the Croatians. They lost the regatta with some reasons. If any other team in the world had experienced half the adversity they had in this regatta, they would have been out of the top ten. Only Mathew and Will could have won silver under the circumstances.

"If we had not ripped the mainsail, everything would have been alright. The next three races in the harbor were in our conditions."

Tokyo ?

The big question was, would Victor, Belcher, and Ryan do it again, dedicate four more years of their lives to winning gold in Tokyo in 2020 ? A few weeks after the Olympics, Belcher was quite certain he and Will were ready to commit. "There are many details to discuss," he said, "but I think so. We're 85% there. Will is on board. We came away with silver in Rio, proving we can deal with a lot. We're proud of our performance. For Tokyo, we want to finish on a high note. It will be a different kind of campaign, more domestic based, with less intensive travel overseas. We'll focus on speed and equipment development, not try to dominate and be seen. We're getting older, but we firmly believe we can continue to develop and learn new things. That's how much we trust ourselves, how much we trust our relationship with Victor."

Sitting in the office of his home in Sydney, surrounded by the notes, books, memorabilia, and medals of his successful career, Victor expressed concerned about his age. He will be 70 in 2020, but he is still remarkably fit. "I have no choice," he said. "If Mathew and Will say one more campaign, it is logical for me to do it. If we had finished Rio with gold, I could have said that is my 8th Games as coach, my 10th medal. We have proved our team is number one, and we could stop. That would be enough. Stop at the top, leave the sport, unbeaten.

"If I had done this after London…" Victor pauses, shakes his head, his smile tinged with just a touch of regret. "If I had stopped my coaching career after London, I would have stopped when we were unbeatable. We had won the last 12 regattas, three world championships in a row, and the Olympic Games. I would have felt like a king. People would say *wow!*, nobody beats him. But then I kept going with Mathew and Will and it was the most interesting part of my life. We learned so much. We discovered unlimited horizons, This past four years of working with Mathew and Will and all our systems have been incredible. The things we have discovered are amazing. Of course we have taught a lot of other people how to sail the 470, how to race, and that's why they beat us. It would be very interesting to move forward. The silver in Rio makes us much stronger.

"Nothing happens without reason. If I had gold now, I would be finished with my coaching mission. But I am 100% certain that if I keep going and work with Mathew and Will, brilliant sailors and amazing people, I will be more than happy."

Surprise!

In Fairlight, NSW, the suburb of Manly where the Kovalenko's live, Tatiana had been planning a surprise party for her husband for more than a month. On a Sunday morning three weeks after the Olympic Games had concluded, when she persuaded Victor to take a walk into nearby Manley to buy croissants, he wasn't the slightest bit suspicious. When they arrived back ho me, Tatiana said she had forgotten to take her key, causing Victor to use his and walk into the apartment first. He paused when he heard music coming from the living room. Then all the doors of the apartment burst open to a startling cacophony of shouted good wishes from 28 of his good Ukrainian friends.

The food Tatiana and friends had prepared was a tasty sampling of Ukrainian and Russian dishes: stuffed capsicum, beetroot salad, pelmeni/Russian ravioli, home smoked trout, big mushrooms stuffed with caramelized onion and Italian porcini, herrings, two cakes, and home-made chocolate stuffed with ginger and honey were among the delicacies.

The decorations included a large poster montage of highlights of Victor's life, with a large photograph of himself in the middle, draped with his ten actual Olympic medals. On the dining table was a dart board decorated with gold tags imprinted with the venues of the Olympic medals Victor's teams had won. A dart was pierced through each. In the bullseye of the target was a gold tag without a dart. On it was written: "Tokyo." One dart was lying on the table in front of the dart board.

The music was provided by accomplished players of the accordion and violin, with a friend from the Sydney Opera Company leading the singing. Some of the songs had been written especially for Victor: *Captain, Captain smile, the smile is the flag of the ship, Captain captain draw up, this neck is needed for medals.*

"They expressed admiration for me," Victor said, "and I said to them, guys, you make me so happy, because I have great friends. This party is an indication to me that you would share with me a great time, but if something bad happens to my family you will always support me and give me a hand. What a fantastic feeling. That is what friendships are like. After this I feel absolutely great, ready for one more campaign."

ACCOMPLISHMENTS
OF VICTOR KOVALENKO'S ATHLETES

Games

XXX Olympic Games, London, Gold Medal M (2012) - **Belcher/Page**

XXIX Olympic Games, Beijing, Gold Medal M (2008) - **Wilmot/Page**

XXIX Olympic Games, Beijing, Gold Medal W (2008) - **Rechichi/Parkinson**

XXVII Olympic Games, Sydney, Gold Medal M (2000) - **King/Tarnbull**

XXVII Olympic Games, Sydney, Gold Medal W (2000) - **Armstrong/Stowall**

XXVI Olympic Games, Atlanta, Gold Medal M (1996) - **Braslavets/Matvienko**

XXXI Olympic Games, Rio de Janeiro, Silver Medal M (2016) - **Belcher/Ryan**

XXVI Olympic Games, Sydney, Bronze Medal W (2000) - **Taran/Pakholchik**

XXVI Olympic Games, Atlanta, Bronze Medal W (1996) - **Taran/ Pakholchik**

XXII Olympic Games, Seoul, Bronze Medal W (1988) - **Moskalenko/Chunikhovskaya**

XXV Olympic Games, Barcelona, 4th place W (1992) - **Moskalenko/ Pakholchik**

ISAF World Sailing Games, Austria, Gold Medal M (2006) - **Wilmot/Page**

ISAF World Sailing Games, France, Gold Medal W (2002) - **Armstrong/Stowell**

ISAF World Sailing Games, United Arab Emirates, Gold Medal W (1998) - **Taran/Pakholchik**

ISAF World Sailing Games, United Arab Emirates, Silver Medal M (1998) - **Braslavets/Matvienko**

ISAF World Sailing Games, Austria, Silver Medal W (2006) - **Rechichi/Parkinson**

First Goodwill Games, USSR, Bronze Medal W (1986) - **Moskalenko/Chunikhovskaya**

Second Goodwill Games, USA, Silver Medal W (1990) - **Moskalenko/Pakholchik**

XII Asian Games, Japan, Silver Medal M (1994) - **Show Her/Lim** (Singapore)

XIII Asian Games, Thailand, Bronze Medal M (1998) - **Tan Wearn How/Lim** (Singapore)

International Championships

470 World Championships, **Israel,** Gold Medal M (2015) - **Belcher/Ryan**

470 World Championships, **Spain,** Gold Medal M (2014) - **Belcher/Ryan**

470 World Championships, **France,** Gold Medal M (2013) - **Belcher/Ryan**

470 World Championships, **Spain,** Gold Medal M (2012) - **Belcher/Page**

470 World Championships, **Australia,** Gold Medal M (2011) - **Belcher/Page**

470 World Championships, **Holland,** Gold Medal M (2010) - **Belcher/Page**

470 World Championships, **Portugal,** Gold Medal M (2007) - **Wilmot/Page**

470 World Championships, **USA,** Gold Medal M (2005) - **Wilmot/Page**

470 World Championships, **Croatia,** Gold Medal M (2004) - **Wilmot/Page**

470 World Championships, **Hungary,** Gold Medal M (2000) - **King/Tarnbull**

470 World Championships, **Australia,** Gold Medal W (1999) - **Taran/Pakholchik**

470 World Championships, **Spain,** Gold Medal W (1998) - **Taran/Pakholchik**

470 World Championships, **Israel,** Gold Medal W (1997) - **Taran/Pakholchik**

470 World Championships, **Slovenia,** Gold Medal M (2001) - **Braslavets/Matvienko**

IYRU World Championships, **USA,** Gold Medal W (1991) - **Moskalenko/Pakholchik**

420 World Championships, **Australia,** Gold Medal M (2004) - **Wilmot/Page**

470 World Championships, **Argentina,** Silver Medal M (2016) - **Belcher/Ryan**

470 World Championships, **China,** Silver Medal M (2006) - **Wilmot/Page**

470 World Championships, **Spain,** Silver Medal M (2003) - **Wilmot/Page**

470 World Championships, **Slovenia,** Silver Medal W (2001) - **Armstrong/Stowell**

470 World Championships, **Hungary,** Silver Medal W (2000) - **Armstrong/Stowell**

ISAF World Championships, **Dubai,** Silver Medal M (1998) - **Braslavets/Matvienko**

470 World Championships, **Canada,** Silver Medal W (1995) - **Taran/Pakholchik**

IYRU World Championships, **France,** Silver Medal W (1994) - **Taran/Pakholchik**

470 World Championships, **Australia,** Silver Medal W (1991) - **Moskalenko/Pakholchik**

470 World Championships, **Australia,** Bronze Medal W (2008) - **Rechichi/Parkinson**

470 World Championships, **Slovenia,** Bronze Medal M (2001) - **Wilmot/Page**

470 European Championships, **Spain,** Gold Medal M (2016) - **Belcher/Ryan**

470 European Championships, Greece, Gold Medal M (2014) - **Belcher/Ryan**

470 European Championships, Italy, Gold Medal M (2013) - **Belcher/Ryan**

470 European Championships, Finland, Gold Medal M (2011) - **Belcher/Page**

470 European Championships, Italy, Gold Medal M (2008) - **Wilmot/Page**

470 European Championships, Estonia, Gold Medal M (2002) - **Wilmot/Page**

470 European Championships, Italy, Gold Medal W (2000) - **Armstrong/Stowell**

470 European Championships, Croatia, Gold Medal W (1999) - **Taran/Pakholchik**

470 European Championships, Turkey, Gold Medal W (1998) - **Taran/Pakholchik**

470 European Championships, Belgium, Gold Medal W (1997) - **Taran/Pakholchik**

470 European Championships, England, Gold Medal W (1996) - **Taran/Pakholchik**

470 European Championships, Sweden, Gold Medal W (1995) - **Taran/Pakholchik**

470 European Championships, Austria, Gold Medal W (1993) - **Taran/Oleksenko**

470 European Championships, Italy, Silver Medal W (2008) W - **Rechichi/Parkinson**

470 European Championships, Estonia, Silver Medal W (2002) - **Armstrong/Stowell**

470 European Championships, Ireland, Silver Medal W (2001) - **Armstrong/Stowell**

470 European Championships, Denmark, Bronze Medal M (2015) - **Belcher/Ryan**

470 European Championships, Belgium, Silver Medal M (1997) - **Braslavets/Matvienko**

470 European Championships, Norway, Silver Medal W (1991) - **Moskalenko/Pakholchik**

470 European Championships, Greece, Bronze Medal W (2007) - **Armstrong/Stowell**

470 South American Championships, Argentina, Gold Medal M (2016) - **Belcher/Ryan**

470 North American Championships, USA, Gold Medal M (2015) - **Belcher/Ryan**

470 North American Championships, USA, Silver Medal M (2015) - **Belcher/Ryan**

470 South American Championships, Brazil, Silver Medal M (2015) - **Belcher/Ryan**

470 North American Championships, USA, Bronze Medal M (2007) - **Wilmot/Page**

470 European Championships, Belgium, Bronze Medal W (1992) - **Moskalenko/Pakholchik**

470 Junior World Championships W, Austria, Silver Medal M (2003) - **Belcher/Belcher**

470 Junior European Championships, Switzerland, Bronze Medal (2003) - **Belcher/Ziegelmayer**

470 Master World Championships, New Zealand, Gold Medal W (1999) - **Lidgett/Bucek**

All athletes are from Australia or Ukraine unless otherwise indicated.

INDEX

Other Books by **Roger Vaughan**

Closing the Gap – World Sailing's Emerging Nations Program

The Strenuous Life of Harry Anderson

Sailing on the Edge (contributor)

Dropping the Gloves – Inside the fiercely competitive world of professional ice hockey

Golf, The Woman's Game

Mustique II

Listen to the Music – The Life of Hilary Koprowski

Tony Gwynn's The Art of Hitting

NASCAR, The Inside Track

Mustique

America's Cup XXVII, The Official Record

Herbert von Karajan

Fastnet, One Man's Voyage

Ted Turner, The Man Behind the Mouth

The Grand Gesture

Rhode Island, A Scenic Discovery